GLENN DRAPER

GLENN DRAPER

His Music
Changed Lives

An Autobiography

Compiled and Edited By

ROBERT H. SHIPP

Printed in the United States of America

07   06   05   04   03   1   2   3   4   5

Library of Congress Control Number: 2003107224

ISBN: 1-57736-305-1

Cover design by John Tracy and Kelly Bainbridge

All profits from the sale of this book will be shared with the Glenn W. Draper Endowment Fund in Vocal Music established by the University of Tennessee, Chattanooga, Foundation, the Glenn W. and Lounelle Draper Endowment for Music Ministry, Lake Junaluska Methodist Assembly, and the Glenn Draper Singers (a non-profit entity).

Providence House Publishers

PROVIDENCE PUBLISHING CORPORATION
238 Seaboard Lane • Franklin, Tennessee 37067
www.providencepubcorp.com
800-321-5692

Some men see things as they are and ask why.
Others dream things that never were and ask why not.

—George Bernard Shaw

CONTENTS

FOREWORD

Kim Cargile
Glenn's accompanist and assistant at Lake Junaluska,
University of Tennessee, Chattanooga, overseas tours, choral workshops,
and Glenn Draper Singers for fifteen years. Kim has been appointed as Glenn's successor
at First Presbyterian Church, Chattanooga, as of March 2003. *

I have the special privilege of introducing to you someone very dear to my heart. Dr. Glenn Draper is originally from Roanoke, Virginia, and he started organizing quartets when he was in the sixth grade. (I can just see him running around getting all his little friends to sing.) He directed Youth for Christ Choirs, and was the student director and president of the Young Roanoke Sings. He received his bachelor of music degree from Indiana University, where he attended on a trombone scholarship. After graduating, he went in the Air Force, where he organized and directed the world famous Keesler Air Force Base Male Chorus and Orchestra. They were heard on NBC radio and were on the *Ed Sullivan Show*. They won world championships for military choirs. They just went everywhere, including here. That is how Glenn got his start at Lake Junaluska.

He then went to Southern Methodist University (SMU) and received a master of music degree in conducting. On his first day at SMU he met the beautiful Lounelle Mayes, whom he married in 1956. He received an honorary doctorate from High Point University. He was the music director at Pfeiffer College from 1956 to 1960, and at the University of Miami from 1960 to 1968. It was during this time that he and his choir appeared on the *Ed Sullivan Show*. He has been at the University of Tennessee at Chattanooga (UTC) since 1968. He has taken many tours with them. He has also been the music director at First Presbyterian Church since 1968.

He has worked with Ben Haden on the "Changed Lives" ministry that has been seen all over the world. He has taken forty-seven overseas concert tours with all of these groups, including five concerts at the White House with Presidents Reagan, George H. W. Bush, Clinton, and George W. Bush; and two Billy Graham Crusades, including one in Moscow at the Olympic Stadium with fifty thousand spectators. This group has performed at three World Methodist Conferences. He has won countless awards and accolades for his teaching and his ministry, and as an ambassador in Chattanooga. He has two wonderful sons, Glenn and Dean, and eight beautiful grandchildren. Whew! That's a lot of stuff.

I have to tell you that if I were to stop at his accolades and his credentials and his accomplishments, I would do you and Glenn and the Lord a great injustice, because you also need to know that I have had the privilege of working with Glenn for fifteen years. We started together in 1988. I have never met anyone with so much zeal and so much passion, not just for music, but for presenting the gospel of the Lord Jesus Christ everywhere he goes and to everyone he meets. You all need to know. You see the professional side up here, summer after summer after summer, as he leads this group of singers.

What you don't see, and what I have the privilege of seeing, is how he works with young students. Their lives are changed because he preaches the same thing every day that you see in the songs they sing. When his university state-supported choir is singing Handel's *Messiah*, and they get to the part that says that he was "Despised and rejected by men, surely he hath borne our griefs and carried our sorrows, and with his stripes, we are healed," he is not just working on eighth notes, crescendos, and beautiful music. He tells them, "This is the truth. You are selling the greatest product in the world. You are not just singing, you are telling the truth, and you are telling the world about Jesus Christ." There have been kids from UTC who have been saved and have come to know the Lord from his ministry, and kids at the University of Miami where the same thing happened. I praise God that in a day where it is mandatory that you are politically correct, and that you can't present the gospel in your workplace for fear of losing your job, that there are people like Glenn who will stand up and tell people that it is true. "There is a living Savior, He did come for us, He did die for us, He does live, and He is taking us home."

* Recorded at Southeastern Jurisdiction Laity Conference 2001, *Witness Hour* by Dr. Glenn W. Draper and the Junaluska Singers, July 27, 2001.

Dr. Reginald Mallett
Physician; ordained Methodist minister of the
British Conference; frequent speaker at Lake Junaluska

It is a great privilege to know Glenn Draper and his wife Lounelle. For over thirty years his friendship and his musical genius have blessed and inspired our family. I celebrate Glenn's ministry for many reasons, but I think I would place at the top of the list my appreciation of his desire not just to share great music but also to share his faith. I have noticed again and again how, when presenting a hymn medley, he begins with some simple song of faith then quickly moves on to hymns that are profound theological statements of the gospel. An example is his frequent use of this great verse by Charles Wesley:

> O love divine, what hast thou done! The immortal God hath died for me!
> The Father's co-eternal Son Bore all my sins upon the tree.
> The immortal God for me hath died: My Lord, my Love, is crucified!

There are few lines in Christian hymnody more powerful than these. In such a choice of text Glenn goes to the very heart of the deity of Christ and finality of His sacrifice on the cross. In a day of shifting theological fashions and uncertainties, Glenn anchors himself in the changeless certainties of the gospel. Because of his faithfulness there are many, many thousands who have not only been enriched by his talent but renewed in their faith. We bless God for this devoted servant!

PREFACE AND ACKNOWLEDGMENTS

Robert H. Shipp
Kerrville, Texas

The genesis of this book was in St. Mark's Episcopal Church in Louisville, Kentucky, in 1935. William Pilcher, the son of the founder of Pilcher Organ Company in Louisville, was the adult choir director and organist, and his wife Camille directed the boy's choir in which I was a nine-year-old soprano.

As was common among better choirs then, the four adult section leaders and the members of the boy's choir were paid. I assume that they paid the adult section leaders more than the ten cents for each practice and twenty-five cents for the single Sunday service that we boys earned. We sang very traditional music, and our directors expected exemplary effort and attendance. I learned to appreciate high quality choral sound early in my life.

Until we came to Lake Junaluska in June 2001, the best choral sound I had ever heard was in Salt Lake City at the Christmas Concert in the Mormon Tabernacle in December 1975. That changed July 3, 2001, while we spent the summer in western North Carolina and first heard the Lake Junaluska Singers, directed by Glenn W. Draper. The unforgettable performance and sounds coming from sixteen singers astonished me. I fell under their spell, and was captivated by the exuberance of Dr. Draper.

Visits to the Cokesbury Book Store and the Lake Junaluska Methodist Assembly office revealed that no one had told the story of the Lake Junaluska Singers. I called Glenn Draper, talked to him at length over several days, and found that Lake Junakuska was only part of the remarkable lifetime success of Dr. Glenn Wright Draper. I felt strongly that his life story was too powerful and compelling to remain untold, even though I had previously written only three short medical articles for publication.

Fortunately, Glenn has almost total recall of his life, and friends and singers who were blessed by his excellent musical guidance and godly inspiration were eager to share their convictions and remembrances. Thus, I serve solely as an editor of both his spoken autobiography and the collection of observations and reflections of others. The story of the five decades of his unique choral brilliance deserved to be shared by more than his family, friends, and singers. The ripple effect of Glenn W. Draper and his music will continue for many years.

Although he had directed some small groups and choirs in college, his real career and fame began while on active duty in the United States Air Force. He organized and directed the famous Keesler Air Force Base Male Chorus for three and one-half years. That triumph was followed in succession by choral directing for four years at Pfeiffer College, eight years at the University of Miami and Coral Gables United Methodist Church, and thirty-four years at the University of Tennessee, Chattanooga, and First Presbyterian Church in Chattanooga. By arrangement with all of the above except the Air Force, for almost fifty years he has spent two and one-half months each summer at the Methodist Southeastern Jurisdiction Assembly at Lake Junaluska, North Carolina, directing the Lake Junaluska Singers. The best of all his singers have sung in his Glenn Draper Singers. He has recorded over fifty tapes, LP records, and CDs; taken choirs on forty-nine overseas tours; and his singing groups have sung for five United States presidents, including six performances at the White House and a Presidential Prayer Breakfast.

Glenn knows that he has had his hand in the hand of God and has been led throughout his life to tell the Christian message through words set to music. Also, he has felt strongly that excellence in performing almost any kind of choral work or arrangement, in any location, is a form of Christian witnessing. The variety of music in his performances has been one of his trademarks, since he wants everyone to find something in a performance that is meaningful or inspiring.

One of my real concerns was properly emphasizing the Christian dedication that has exemplified the life and accomplishments of Glenn Draper. I believe I solved that question by selecting Kim Cargile and Dr. Reginald Mallett to share their insightful views of the theology of Glenn in the forewords.

Whenever a contributor's name was first used, either in the text or in the epigrams beginning each chapter, a brief biography follows to let the reader know why the comments were considered useful in revealing some facet or aspect of Glenn's life. The biographies are not repeated thereafter.

A few people deserve to be thanked. Duane Beardsley spent many hours proofreading; Michelle Hozman was always there when I needed accurate transcribing done; John A. Murphy listed all of the Junaluska recordings from the vast amount of Junaluska Singers historical data he has compiled over the years. The Providence Publishing Corporation staff had a real challenge in bringing this book to fruition. Special thanks to Andrew B. Miller, president and publisher, and all of his team. Glenn Draper was remarkable to "interview." I did not interview him in the traditional sense, but simply turned on the tape recorder and said, for example, "Tell me about your Air Force years." His remarkable recall of dates, places, names, and events simplified this entire endeavor.

As Charles Middleton said, "Glenn has the uncanny way of surrounding himself with positive people—good people." The last seventeen months have been a challenge and an adventure for me while recording Glenn's amazing life and recalling memories from the people he has helped train and mold into fellow life-enhancers. Almost without exception, the people in his life reflect his remarkable effect on them, as best said in the hymnal verse, "I can hear the brush of angels' wings, I see glory on each face."

Glenn W. Draper

WE ARE CERTAINLY a part of all that we have met. Looking at life through my glasses at age twenty-one is very different after fifty some years conducting. There is no doubt in my mind that God called me to serve Him as a music director in many places around the world: four years with the Keesler Male Chorus, forty-seven years of university teaching, fifty years at Lake Junaluska Methodist Assembly, fifty-four years directing church choirs, thirty-five years with Ben Haden and Changed Lives, and eighteen years with the Glenn Draper Singers.

I want to say a deep word of appreciation to all of the people who have had a profound influence on my life. I owe so much to my parents; my wife of forty-seven years, Lounelle; our two fine sons and their families, Glenn Wright and Ashley, and their children, Sandy, Avery, Mary Glenn, Glenn Wright III, and Will; and Dean and Peggy, and their children, Dean, Riley, and Cal; and the thousands of loyal friends and singers who have prayed for me and supported my work.

I am grateful to my employers or leaders who had a great influence on my life: Maj. Gen. James F. Powell (Keesler AFB, Biloxi, Miss., 1952–1955), Maj. Gen. Charles Carpenter (Washington, D.C., chief of Air Force chaplains, 1952–1955), Dr. Travis Shelton (Southern Methodist University, professor of music, 1955–1956), Dr. James W. Fowler (Lake Junaluska Methodist Assembly director, 1954–1964), Dr. J. Lem Stokes (Pfeiffer College president, 1956–1960), John Bitter (University of Miami dean of music, 1960–1964),

Dr. John H. Hanger (First Methodist Church, Coral Gables, Fla., minister), Dr. Ben Haden (First Presbyterian Church, Chattanooga, Tenn., minister; Changed Lives television program), Dr. William Masterson (University of Tennessee at Chattanooga president/chancellor, 1968–1974), and Dr. William Stacy (University of Tennessee at Chattanooga chancellor, 1997–present).

The following people also had a great influence on my life: Ada P. English (sixth grade teacher), Nell Perry (high school choral director), Eula Ligon (church choir director), William Sanders (Young Roanoke Sings director), A. W. Hull (National Guard Band director), George Krueger (Indiana University choral director), Dr. J. Manning Potts (Lake Junaluska Assembly director), Dr. Edgar Nease (Lake Junaluska Assembly director), Dr. Mel Harbin (Lake Junaluska Assembly director), Barry Rogers (Lake Junaluska Assembly director), Dr. Reginald Ponder (Lake Junaluska Assembly director), Dr. Gordon Goodgame (Lake Junaluska Assembly director), Jimmy Carr (Lake Junaluska Assembly executive director), Joy Carr (Lake Junaluska Assembly ministries director), Dr. Peter Bolt (in England), Dr. Reginald Mallett (in England), Dr. Alan Hughes (in England), Dr. Phillip Lockett (in England), Dr. Sir Alan Walker (in Australia), Dr. Glouster Eudy (in Australia), Rev. Ken Anderson (in Australia), Maimunah Natasha (in Indonesia), Dr. Eddie Fox (in Estonia, Finland), Dr. Billy Graham (in Russia and the U.S.), Dr. Joe Hale (in Brazil), and Dr. Tom Curtis (in the Carribian Islands, Panama, and Costa Rica).

I'd like to acknowledge the following individuals associated with our White House appearances and the National Prayer Breakfast: George Saunders (F.B.I., White House), Zachery Wamp (Tennessee congressman), and Dr. Bill W. Stacy (University of Tennessee at Chattanooga, chancellor). Thanks also to Jack Turney with the National Religious Broadcasters Convention, who sponsored my singers in Washington, D.C., in 1988.

Friends and encouragers of my early career include: Frank Harris (college roommate), Marilyn Shows (Marion College), Julius Walthall (Roanoke, Va.), Reginald Hutcherson (Roanoke, Va.), Buddy Phillips (Roanoke, Va.), Pat Martindale (Roanoke, Va.), Bob Davis (Air Force), Roger Hinkley (Air Force), Harry Evers (Air Force), Bob Tibualt (Air Force), Esther Farris (aunt), Jack Draper (father), Carter Lois Draper (mother), Gene Draper (brother), Bill Draper (brother), and Douglas Draper (brother).

My accompanists: James Oxley (Air Force), Euel Belcher (Air Force), Maury Jones (Dallas, Tex.), Bobby Leanerd (Pfeiffer College), Glenda Dell (University of Miami, Fla.), Joseph Lowe (University of Miami, Fla.), Ray Ruckle (First Presbyterian Church, Chattanooga, Tenn.), Judy Glass (First Presbyterian Church, Chattanooga, Tenn.), Jim Wilson (First Presbyterian Church, Chattanooga, Tenn.), Joe Troxel (2 yrs., University of Tennessee, Chattanooga), Dr. Joseph Chapman (4 yrs., University of Tennessee, Chattanooga), Mike Lees (2 yrs., University of Tennessee, Chattanooga), Dr. Euel Belcher (2 yrs., Lake Junaluska), Glenda Dell (2 yrs., Lake

Junaluska), Michael Johnson (1 yr., Lake Junaluska), Marty Hamby (6 yrs., Lake Junaluska), William Christmas (10 yrs., Lake Junaluska), Brad Gee (2 yrs., Lake Junaluska), Tom Buchanan (Lake Junaluska), and Kim Cargile (15 yrs., Lake Junaluska). Without a good accompanist you are dead in the water. I have had the best!

I have to say a deep word of gratitude and appreciation to my wonderful secretaries and clerical assistants. Without their expertise and assistance, these tours and performances would never have taken place. Thanks to Gaye Sellers Slaten (10 yrs.), Lucy Henry (2 yrs.), Rosemary Hoenig (22 yrs.), and Kim Cargile (15 yrs.).

I rarely ever met anyone who did not like some kind of music. It is great therapy. Without Lounelle, my lifelong companion, and our two sons, I never would have, "Been there, done that!" They have followed me wherever the Lord has led us.

I am extremely grateful to Dr. Robert Shipp for writing this book after meeting and interviewing so many former singers and friends. We consider him and his sweet wife, Farra Mai, to be some of our dearest friends.

If you aspire to do God's will for your life and His will for you is to be a music director, hang on for it's some kind of ride! Make music for His glory.

1

DUETS *to* QUARTETS

1928–1947

All of us who were influenced by Glenn need to remember
that our paths crossed, in part, because God sent Glenn into our lives.

~DR. ALAN W. MILLER
UTC Choirs; Lake Junaluska Singer, 10 years; Ed Brothers;
Minister of Music; Glenn Draper Singers

FAMILY

My maternal grandfather, William Henry Wright, loved music. It was very evident in his children because all of his daughters played the piano—he made sure they had piano lessons. My mother used to say she could go in the parlor, play for an hour, and emerge feeling like a new person because music was such great therapy. My mother learned to play the violin, the accordion, and the organ. She started playing the organ for the Hickory Grove Methodist Church in Bedford, Virginia, when she was twelve years old. Years later, when I was in high school, I sang duets with my mother, and she would sometimes accompany me while I played the trombone. Many Sunday afternoons I played trombone solos in the Hickory Grove Methodist Church. My grandfather and his sons, Uncle Billy and Uncle Bryan, and friends Mr. John Taze and Mr. Ninneger, all played instruments; guitar, banjo, violin, and one of them had a bass. I do not think they made the bass, but they made the others out of wood. I do not know how they did all those things, but in those years, people learned to be self-sufficient—if you wanted it, you made it.

MY GRANDPARENTS had "party line" telephone service. Whenever it rang, you would hear people pick up their telephone. That was where you got information about what people did over in "this hollow" and what they did over in "that valley." People depended on each other for all kinds of things. If somebody was sick in your family and somebody else had the right kind of medicine, they would get on a horse and ride over to your house and give it to you.

That is the essence of living. Some people call it Christian living, but I have known people who claimed not to be Christians, who had as much brotherly love as you could find in anybody. I have met Christians who were "so heavenly minded they weren't any earthly good." So when someone says, "He is a good Christian," I always want to say, "What is that? What is a good Christian in your opinion? Is it a person who observes the law and doesn't get caught for anything?" I know people who aren't Christians who do that. That is not the only mark, to me, of a Christian. Other people have fine attributes, but suppose they grew up in a good family? I say, only God knows those things. I am not ready to decide that this is bad. What I am trying to say is that I cannot play God. I do love and trust Him, He is my Savior.

IN A STAFF MEETING at First Presbyterian Church a couple of years ago, Ben Haden was discussing suicide, and how you deal with suicidal people, or how you counsel family members after a suicide occurs in their family. Since ministers are confronted with those kinds of things, Ben asked each of us what we thought of suicide and what we thought would happen to the people who committed suicide. Some said they thought a person who commits suicide would not go to heaven. I said, "How can you say that? You do not know the frame of mind the person was in, and you cannot play God." So I refrain from saying anything, other than that. I am not ready to be a judge. We are too judgmental; all of us try to sit right beside God and judge in place of Him. I am not smart enough and only God knows those things. I will leave that to God.

I have enough trouble just keeping up with myself, much less keeping up with everybody else. On the other hand, it is amazing how you are influenced by people's lives, not what they say, but what they do and how they live their lives. In fact, at that Hickory Grove Methodist Church, where my mother used to play, I watched those people sing on Sunday morning and some of them had the most glorious expression on their faces. I used to think I would really like to have what they have. They never said a word to me about their faith and beliefs, but they sure sang their faith. They were involved in what they were doing and I knew I wanted what they had. It is amazing how much influence things like that have on you. At least it did on me.

We all have different memories of times past, some good and some bad, and we are today what we learned in those years, in spite of it or because of it. We are products of where we came from. We cannot hide our ancestors. They got here long before we did. I owe so much to my ancestors on both sides, especially my mother's side of the family. William Henry Wright, my grandfather, was well thought of in the community, and was a school principal for twenty-four years. He built a schoolhouse on his property so he could still have classes there for his nine children in case inclement weather conditions prevented them from going to school. I have been in that little building. It was just one big room that used to impress me as such a cozy place to learn on a rainy or snowy day.

I loved to hear him tell stories about the time he was a schoolteacher. He told a story about when he used to ride to school on horseback, and was a little late because of the extremely cold, harsh weather. Smoke was just pouring out of the chimney in the school. When he got to the door to go in, most of the students were already inside, and they had locked the door. He thought, *What am I going to do if they are playing a prank on me? They have locked the principal and teacher out.* So without making any big ruckus and slamming on the door with his hands, he said, "You know what I did?" I said, "Granddaddy, what did you do?" He said, "I went out to the woods and got some planks and climbed an old wooden ladder up on the roof and laid those planks over the top of the chimney." He said it was only about two minutes until the doors flew open and kids started flying out in the yard, coughing and hacking. "I didn't say a word to them, I went on in school and got my things together. They came back in after the smoke cleared out, they all sat down and not a word was ever mentioned about that problem." I said, "How did you think of that?" He said, "Well, when you are in a situation, you have to come up with something where you don't cause a scene, but you get your point across gently." He got his point across.

My grandfather used to say, "I really believe in education. It is the key to success." He came from a long line who originally immigrated from England. The property they lived on was given to them by the Native Americans, and has always been in the Wright name. Even today that property is in his name, because they have handed it down generation after generation. They went to a Methodist church, about three miles from the house. Many Sundays they would go to church in three or four buggies, because they had no cars. My mother played a pump organ there, starting at twelve years of age. After I got up in my teens, it was the greatest joy for me to go down to that little church and worship with my grandparents and my mother. I would sing duets for those people and they would brag on me as if I were one of the greatest things! They would say, "That is Lois's son." I loved music because my mother played all the time when we were home. I organized a quartet in the sixth grade when my voice changed. At home my parents had a major influence on my music life, and when I was down at my grandfather's house, any time they would play and sing, that was special for me. It had been in me from the day I was born, I suppose, that music was such a great element. I used to marvel at my grandfather, how he could play the violin while some others played the guitar and banjo. Then somebody else would play the violin and he would play the guitar.

The people helped each other for everything through the week. For instance, on Monday they might all go to Mr. John Taze's who needed a new tin roof on his barn and a dozen or so men would help put on the new roof. Then they would all eat their noon meal at that house. They would go catch six or seven chickens and wring their necks. I would help them pluck the chickens, then Mrs. Taze would cook them and have corn on the cob, green beans, tomatoes, and all the things they had grown on the farm. Often, we children didn't get to eat on the first load. We were the second or third table, because not everyone could fit at the table at the same time. We also had to do that for the men who worked on our farm, they ate first.

MY GRANDFATHER was a multi-talented person, and I always had the greatest admiration for him and his talents and his ability to work with people. He was an English gentleman. At the church, they had their own burial place, where he and my grandmother and four of their children are buried, right outside New Bedford, Virginia. The heritage of that growing up is very special. They prided themselves in being honest, helpful, and useful, being an educator, using good judgment, and helping neighbors whenever they possibly could.

MY DAD was a hard worker, very sincere, and wanted to do well. He was happy working for the lumber company drawing up plans for people's homes and he took great pride in that. He made friends very easily, and he had a good personality. I remember going to town with him many times, when it would take him forever to get someplace because of all the people who were stopping to say hello. My dad's name was John Wesley, but people affectionately called him Jack. He was a dear man, very caring about people. If you walked down the street with him and he was going too fast, he would slow down for you.

As boys, we played football a lot in the front yard. We had probably three or four acres of land and the huge lawn out front was about an acre. Many guys would come over after school and we would have football games. A boy named Melvin Matthews lived in the neighborhood. He was one of those guys that other guys picked on a lot. I always felt sorry for him. The kids would call him Melvews, which added to the problem. My dad was very good about these kinds of things, so I asked him, "What can I do to help Melvin?" He said, "Why don't you make your circle bigger and include him in it?" I asked, "What do you mean?" He said, "Include him in your football games." I replied, "He won't come!" "Well, go down there and get him." So I borrowed a bicycle, went down to his house, put him on the bicycle, turned around, and came back. We started playing football and his whole personality changed. I saw, for the first time, that you could make people happier by including them in what you are doing. Dad was sixty-six when he passed away with a heart condition.

Unlike my father, my mother would say, "Let's walk a little faster!" if you were going down the street with her. I have never seen anybody who could walk so fast. I would almost have to run when I was a boy to keep up with her. She was just a fast-paced, fast-thinking type of person. She made decisions rather fast; she was almost ahead of her time, if you know what I mean. She would have been a good corporate leader in a company, she had a good business sense. I can see myself in my mother, probably more than anyone else. Just the way she was, the way she reacted. If traffic was slow, she would get upset; if people couldn't make up their minds about doing something, she would be on their case. You couldn't walk down the street slouched, you had to hold your shoulders up and look like you knew where you were going. You had to have your act together. Many times she would correct our English. If we used the wrong pronoun, for example, she would say you shouldn't do that. Or if we had to make a speech, almost always she would correct us on something. But I am glad for that.

I was the oldest of four boys and I was extremely close to my family. My mother had four boys in five years. I don't say I would wish that on anybody, but we were a close-knit family growing up like that.

Gene graduated from Florida State and majored in business. A scholarship in Commerce Clearing House is given out annually in his name. The Gene Draper Memorial Award is an award for the best sales in the whole company. He and three or four other people owned an airplane, which he would use to pick me up and take me places. He would take his minister on trips or pick him up to get him back to Roanoke so he could speak on Sunday morning. He did a lot of favors for people like that. Gene had a lot of friends, he was a people person, loveable and driven, but not as driven as I am. Unfortunately, Gene died of a heart attack.

Bill is very intelligent, probably the smartest of all of us. He really wanted to be a doctor. He had the intelligence to be that, but when Gene and I left home, Bill was more or less left to himself. He attended Indiana Wesleyan for two years and then got married. I think that slowed him down permanently; to go to school with a family was just prohibitive in those times. He owned his own retail ladies shoe business, and he was very successful.

Doug was always tinkering with toys and lumber and building things like a treehouse, or putting together a stool to sit on. He has been in the house construction business all these years.

EARLY MUSIC

I WAS VERY CLOSE to my grandmother on my daddy's side. I was the oldest of the grandchildren and we went to her house often, especially on weekends. She loved the *Grand Ole Opry*. She had a rocking chair about three feet from her radio, which was on a table with a little lamp, and I would sit on her lap and listen to all those people from Nashville sing country music. She and I knew some of those people by name. Like Uncle Dave Macon and the Fruit Jar Drinkers. She would sit there for one and a half or two hours, so I got to stay up longer when I went to see her. I had to go to bed at 9:30 Saturday nights when I was at home, but with her we would get a chance to listen to the *Grand Ole Opry* for thirty more minutes.

My grandmother was a Christian and so was my grandfather, and I asked her once, "How did you know you were a Christian?" She said, "You just ask Jesus to come into your life and you are a Christian." I asked, "How do you know that?" She said, "When I was very young I asked that same question. I said, 'God, I will make a deal with you. So I know that I am a Christian, I pray that the whole church is singing "When I Can Read My Title Clear," when we get to church.' When we rounded the curve coming to the church in the buggy, you know what the church was singing? That old hymn, "When I Can Read My Title Clear." I knew from that minute that I belonged to Christ and that I knew him as my personal savior." I thought that was the most cozy story that I had ever heard.

"HOW TEDIOUS AND TASTELESS THE HOURS, When Jesus No Longer I See." My dad used to sing that hymn to me, over and over. It was probably one of his favorite hymns except for "Rock of Ages" and some older hymns. When I was away at school, he used to write me letters almost every day, and he would always include a verse of one of those old hymns. Sometimes it would be "When I Can Read My Title Clear" and he would always say, "Isn't God great? I do not know what the future holds, but I do know who holds the future!" That was ingrained in me from day one of my life.

BACK THEN they believed in having revivals—it seemed like one came along every two months. On a Thursday night of a revival, I was sitting on the second row from the front next to my mother, and the minister gave an altar call for people to come forward. Instead of going forward, I knelt where I was sitting and prayed that God would come into my life and that I would serve Him if He would forgive my sins. I promised to serve Him and do whatever He wanted me to do in life. I became a Christian, and I never have forgotten the peace and joy that came into my heart. From that day to this day, my life has belonged to the Lord. I have gone through some trials and tribulations, like all of us have from time to time, elevators don't go up forever, nor do they stay down forever. Life is like that, but Christ's love for us is not like an elevator. He doesn't love you today and not love you tomorrow. Sometimes our reactions to those things may vary, but it is not God changing, He does not change.

I always felt that God had something for me to do in life. When I was thirteen, we boys used to get all kinds of odd jobs, working on a farm for somebody, like picking tomatoes, apples, or peaches, and we would get maybe twenty-five cents a bushel. I remember that I would get five cents if I cut a bushel full of watercress salad. I made fifteen cents one Saturday afternoon by cutting three bushels of watercress. It took a lot of cutting to fill one bushel of watercress. My Aunt Christine, who was my mother's youngest sister, was very loving to us, and was staying at our house for two or three days. As I started to come in the house, she said, "Let's go back out in the barn, I want to talk to you." The barn was a combination of a garage and a barn, where we kept two or three cows and a smokehouse. She said, "I have noticed how you pray and read the Bible every night before you go to sleep." I said, "I make a point to read at least two chapters every night, and I am determined to read all of it." She said, "I want to tell you something that I hope you never forget. I feel that God has something very special for you to do in life," and she said, "Glenn Draper don't you ever, ever miss it, don't ever turn your back on that." I told her, "Aunt Christine, I promise I won't."

OUR FAMILY SANG a lot together, especially on Sunday afternoons, and we used to argue about who was going to sing the melody, because that was where we learned to sing many parts. We would gather around the piano while Mother played. She would often sing alto, because we didn't have anybody else to sing the alto part. One of my brothers would sing the melody, and I sang a baritone or bass part. Brother Gene sang the tenor part a lot of times, and Dad sang bass, of course. That is where I really learned a lot of hymns, not necessarily at church, but at home. We had a lot of those old hymnals, and it would seem like we would go through every page of those hymnals, many times. We listened to radio broadcasts like the *Old Fashioned Revival Hour* from California, with the minister Charles E. Fuller. He had a choir and a good quartet. We would go to church on Sunday night, but as soon as we got home we would turn on the radio and listen to the Charles Fuller broadcast. Our family loved that. After that was over, we would talk for a little while, then my dad would get out the Bible and we would have devotions, and then everybody else would go to bed, except me. I would slip in a corner under a lamp and read three, four, or five chapters in the Bible. I would not go to bed unless I had read the Bible. In those early years, it made me very much aware of Christianity, and how I might fit in the world through God's leadership.

DR. KILLEY, a neighbor, took care of my mother when she came down with diphtheria, when I was about sixteen. In those days, we did not have all the drugs that we have today, we didn't know about penicillin. Dr. Killey came to see my mother every day. One day in particular, I was out in the yard under a tree playing my harmonica, and he came over to me and said, "Glenn, I hate to tell you this, but it is nip and tuck with your mom. She may not make it." I told him she had to make it! He said, "We will certainly pray that she does. Let us have a prayer." So we both prayed that she would get better.

When he finished the prayer, he said, "I don't know why I didn't think about this earlier. You like to sing and you have a pleasant bass voice. Why don't you come to the Roanoke City Chorus rehearsal with me tonight?" I said I would love to do that! He said, "By the way, our concert is in about two or three weeks. You know my son died last year, and he was about your size. I know you don't have a tuxedo, so why don't you wear his tuxedo?" I remember running in the house and telling my mother, who was in bed gravely ill, that I was going to get a chance to go to the Roanoke City Chorus rehearsal.

When he had picked me up, we drove to the church and opened the door, and they were singing one of the most beautiful anthems I had ever heard in my life. I don't know that any anthem has ever had that affect on me. It was called "Fierce Was the Wild Billow." If anybody was going through fierce wild billows, I was, at sixteen. That anthem ends, "Peace be still, it is I."

I had the greatest assurance that my mother was going to recover. I could hardly wait to get home to tell her, "We sang this song tonight called 'Fierce Was the Wild Billow.' It ends with the most wonderful words and I had the greatest feeling of peace from God that you are going to get better. Mom, you are going to get out of that bed, you are going to get better." She lived to be eighty-one years old and died in 1984. She got hepatitis from eating fish or she would probably still be living today.

I ORGANIZED A QUARTET in high school, and all us fellows are still living, except Thomas Tobey, the baritone, who died just last year. I talked to Julius Walthall last week. The second tenor was a guy named Lowell Eller, who still lives in Roanoke, Virginia. We sang together for four years in high school. We all graduated and sang at the commencement services. Something was mentioned in that service that I have never forgotten. I do not remember anything else the minister said, but he said, "You have to make your friends before you need them."

If you think you don't need friends, you have never lived. I have come to find out that, without friends, you will never make it. It is the friends you make and your relationships with other people that determines what you do in life. What you major in is trivial. I also think that many people are in jobs today, not because they majored in it, but they found out what they like to do and what they do best. It may not have been their major, but that is what they end up doing. If money is the only criterion for you taking a job, then I question your reason for taking that job.

I tell people, I'm a doctor, but I am the kind of doctor who doesn't do you any good, not physically anyway, but mentally. I think music is essential for people. People don't sing just for the fun of it. They sing because they have to sing. I think almost everybody likes some kind of music. So I am in a field that gets everybody, and I just have to get on their wave length. I have long ceased trying to take *people* to make *music*, but to take *music* and make *people*. To me there is a vast difference. I used to read that poem, "I would like to live by the side of the road, and be a friend to man." That is me up and down, I would just love to do that.

WE LEARN SO MUCH from our parents, not only what they said but what they did and how they walked. Did they walk their talk? That is very important. I am indebted to so many people from my younger years. Mr. Christiansen was my band director when I was in the sixth grade and he taught me to play the trombone. Mr. Christiansen was originally from Denmark or Sweden, and he would say, "When I blow into this horn Swedish, it comes out English to you," proving that music is a universal language. For some reason, he took me under his wing and used to brag on the beautiful tone of my trombone. He would give me solos to learn and I would play them in assembly for the school. You talk about increasing your confidence, that was really something! I try to spend my life today encouraging young people. They need somebody to pat them on the back and say, "You have a great talent. I really want to see you succeed." I have had the greatest life teaching—not just teaching music, that has been a sideline—but teaching people to build confidence in themselves, to be honest, to be straightforward, to love people, to find out what they do best and do it well, and to set the highest goals for themselves.

Mrs. Eula Ligon directed the Green Memorial United Methodist Church choir, which was the best church choir anywhere in Roanoke. It was a top-notch group. My mother used to take me to many concerts—wherever there was a concert we were off and going. By age fifteen I had heard more concerts than some people will ever hear in a lifetime. I heard every kind of concert—band, symphony, or choral group. We went to Green Memorial Church when they would do concerts. When I was fourteen, I told my mother that I wanted to sing in that church choir. She drove me down to the church and I went in to see Mrs. Ligon. She asked me how old I was and I told her I was fourteen. She said, "I don't usually let anyone fourteen years old sing in the choir. This is a highly auditioned group and we only have forty-two seats with sometimes fifty people rehearsing. We can't let them all sing Sunday mornings. Do you know what happens to somebody if they call in and say they are sick and cannot sing? The secretary will call somebody and say, 'You can sing today because we have one extra seat.' However," Mrs. Ligon said, "since you have such a good voice and you want to sing so badly, I am going to let you in the choir, but do not tell a soul how old you are." I said, "It is a deal. I swear to God I will not tell anybody."

Mrs. Ligon said, "I am going to put you next to a gentleman called Governor." Robertson was his name, but they all called him Governor because he was a leader in the community and he loved people. I fell in love with that man and I sang bass right next to him. I learned so much from him and not once that I can remember did I miss a rehearsal or church service of that choir because I knew somebody else would come take my place. I wanted to be on her first row of people.

I had to walk three miles to catch the bus, and when rehearsals were over I had to catch the bus and then walk three miles back. That was six miles a night, I don't know many people who would do that. Now you see how badly I wanted to sing. Sometimes the bus would be a little late getting there and the front door of the church would be open because they rehearsed in the sanctuary, and I would hear that beautiful sound come out of the door. I would think, *I have to do that in my life!* Mrs. Ligon was a great encourager to me always, and so were members of the choir. They just became my friends.

After I went away to college and came home at Christmas, one of the first things I did was go to choir rehearsal. Mrs. Ligon said, "Glenn Draper, we are so proud of you! Will you come up here and direct the hymns that we are going to sing for Sunday?" It scared the living daylights out of me. I have never forgotten singing "Oh Come All Ye Faithful" and "Joy to the World"— it was the greatest joy to do that, I was thrilled to death. Little opportunities like that just kept pushing me on, but I was not really that good as a soloist, my forte in the music world was the trombone. I received two years of college credit to start at the junior level my first year of taking trombone. The dean did me a big favor at Indiana University (IU) when he did that.

WHEN I WENT to an all-state chorus, band, and orchestra concert in Indiana I was very impressed with the orchestra, it was tremendous. I could see myself directing the orchestra, cuing the violins and the trombones. Then the band played and I could see myself doing that—the band was spit-shine clean. I had an extra kick in my step.

It reminded me of when my dad used to take me to the parades down-town when I was just a kid and I would stand there with my hand moving and he would try to stop me. Sometimes they would have the "Military Classic of the South" a game between Virginia Military Institute (VMI) and Virginia Polytechnic Institute (VPI). Both schools had very fine bands, and often on Thanksgiving morning they would assemble downtown at 11:00 and have a parade in which they would march fifteen or twenty blocks to the stadium. I would march on the sidewalk and keep up with the band all the way to the stadium just to hear them play. What a joy and thrill it was to hear music like that.

MR. CHRISTIANSEN, my band director, would spend time practicing with me after school, on Saturday mornings, and on Sunday afternoons. He entered me in the state contest in Virginia. Twice I won top honors in the state playing trombone. I'll never forget the time my senior year when we had to play for judges for the whole state of Virginia. When I finished playing, I thought I had done a very good job, and I was really proud. Mr. Christiansen's wife rushed on the stage and said, "Glenn Draper, you can be as professional as you want to be in music." I said, "Do you really think so?" She said, "I absolutely think so. Anybody who can play with that kind of feeling on a trombone can make it." She has no idea to this day how much she ministered to me in those early years.

When her husband died, she called me on the telephone at 4:30 A.M. and said, "Chris is gone. He would have wanted me to call you because you were like a son to him." He was so proud when I got a trombone scholarship to Indiana University, and he would just brag on me to all his friends. Mr. Christiansen taught me how to play golf. The first time he took me on the golf course he said, "I want to prolong your life. The doctor said for me to live longer I have to get away from eighth notes, trombones, clarinets, etc. I have to do something else that I love to do, so, I want to teach you how to play golf." He went around with me two or three times playing golf and he would take me out on the golf course with some of his friends.

Think about a teacher doing that for a student. Sometimes I would go over to the Christiansens' house and they would feed me dinner, and we would just sit and talk. What an example that has been to me. Now we are so busy with two cars and twelve television sets and a huge home and into so many things. I am looking at myself as I say that. I do not have a chance to do that with all the jobs that I have, but I have often thought that life could be much better if it were simpler and we had time to talk to our fellow man.

SCHOOL

THERE WAS NO WAY I could afford to go to college. I knew that, everybody knew that—except my mother. She said, "We will not even discuss it. You will go to college." Two or three years before that, all of us boys had different jobs to do in the house and outside. You just did not have Saturday morning chores, you had something all week. At Christmas, it was my job to get the Christmas tree and to decorate it with the rest of the family since I was the oldest son. One day, around noon, when we were cleaning up the house in preparation for a large crowd of guests (Mother liked to entertain), she looked at me and said, "You know, I never had a chance to finish what I really wanted to do in life. I wanted to go into music and I really wanted to teach music in school. However, I didn't get the chance to finish because I had to take care of my parents on our big farm before I got married. I hope that you will continue where I had to leave off." I told her, "Mother, I promise you, *I will do that!*"

JULIUS WALTHALL was my closest friend in high school. We had known each other since sixth grade when a teacher said, "If you want to grow up to be strong and healthy and live a long time, never drink or smoke." Julius and I shook hands on it. I kept my word. I am grateful, since that was long before the surgeon general announced that smoking was bad for you. It seemed to me that anyone would know that smoking would be bad for you. Why did you have to have the government tell you that you should not smoke? Julius and I were friends to the nth degree. He played clarinet in the band and I played trombone and we were inseparable. He had an older brother, Frank Glenn, a senior who was a very good trombone player. Frank was a mentor to me when I was a freshman in high school. I sat next to him and played trombone, and I learned a whole lot of technique from him.

Julius Walthall
Glenn's friend since grade school;
sang in quartets with him through high school; a retired CPA

My family moved into the area when I was in the fifth grade. I met Glenn in class and it was around the sixth grade when he and I put together a mixed quartet. My family had always been musical. My mother taught piano, and with two older brothers and a younger sister, there was much piano playing and singing. I had always sung in church choirs and as a family we sang together. We had a mixed quartet since we added two girls we thought were very cute in the sixth grade.

OUR SENIOR CLASS had voted to go to New York City to see musicals and other sights. None of us had ever been to New York City, but we had heard about it and that was during the years of the musicals, such as "Finnian's Rainbow." I talked my parents into letting me go if Julius's parents would let him go. He did the same thing with his parents. They got on the phone and they both agreed, if we also agreed not to thumb at night. Julius and I had to hitch rides to New York City because we didn't have enough money to ride the train with our classmates. My daddy took us out to Highway 11, and we started thumbing. We got a ride immediately to Lexington and then from Lexington we got on the back of a truck. We were riding up a mountain and I took my jacket off and put my head on it. The bed of the truck didn't have any sides on it, and as I look back, we could have fallen off so easily. However, in youth, you don't ever think of that happening to you. While we were going up that mountain, I raised my head and the wind blew my jacket off the truck and onto the road. I tried to catch it, but, of course, I couldn't, so I turned around and was beating on the cab trying to get the driver to stop. However, the driver and his passenger were busy talking about something and they never heard me until we got to the top and he finally stopped. Just then a car drove up and a lady handed my jacket to me. She had seen it fly off, so they stopped and picked it up, knowing that eventually we would be stopping.

We thumbed all the way up through Washington, D.C., and on to Baltimore. We were in Baltimore around half past five and I suggested that we try to make it to Philadelphia. When we got to Philadelphia around ten, the fellow took us right into the middle of town and let us off. We were in the middle of town, and no place to stay, no hotel. What were we going to do now? We saw an all-night movie open, with the feature "Stairway to Heaven," so we went in and spent the night there. We watched one show after the other. Of course, we went to sleep while the show was going on, but for seventy-five cents, that was a cheap hotel room. The next morning we left the theater around five o'clock and caught a subway that took us out of town, putting us right on the highway going to New York City.

We arrived in New York by eleven that morning and went to the hotel, but the rest of the class hadn't come in yet. (Our other classmates had the money to take a train.) Part of the group finally came in and we were so excited to see them. They were all sleepy because they had been on the train all night. I mentioned to two of the girls in the group that I really wanted to see Radio City Music Hall, and they said they did too. So I said, "Why don't the two of you meet Julius and me there?" We did not know how we were going to get in or what it would cost.

Julius and I went to the YMCA, checked in, went swimming in the pool, and just had fun. That afternoon we got a hot dog somewhere on the street and went to Radio City Music Hall. While we were waiting there for the girls to show up, a man got out of his car and asked me, "Are you going to see this show?" I said, "We're planning on it if we can get tickets." He said, "Here are four tickets that we cannot use. I want you to have them." The girls came up and we were so excited—we had tickets. The funny thing was, our seats were on the front row of the balcony, and when an usher showed us where they were, people were sitting in the seats. She forced them to get out of the seats, so that four kids who had tickets that somebody gave them could sit down.

Julius Walthall

There are certain characteristics of Glenn Draper that I have not really seen in many other people. I was very close to Glenn, but he always had what I consider a good luck feature about him. It has been said that people who work the hardest have the best luck and there is something to that! Yet with Glenn, things would just occur so nicely (like getting the free tickets). Many times that sort of thing would happen. Just like the hitchhiking from Roanoke to New York—we did not have any trouble, we did not lose any time on the way, we just went right along.

AFTER THE SHOW was over, we got something to eat and went walking in Central Park. It never entered our mind at the time, of the dangers that might be there. Finally, we walked the girls back to their hotel, and we walked back to the YMCA on 34th Street. Since then, I have passed it several times because a musical organization that I frequently attend is located in an old place right across the street, in the same block as that YMCA. I have never forgotten the little towels and soap that they furnished. I think I paid about seventy-five cents a night, or maybe a dollar and a quarter at the most, to stay there.

After a while, we learned some tricks like how to get on the subway and what train to get, and we could get around very easily. I remember going to the Empire State Building and looking over the whole city—it was great. I also remember going to Carnegie Hall and saying, "Someday I am going to bring a choir here." I did in 1986, when my choir from the University of Tennessee, Chattanooga, sang in Carnegie Hall. I have often thought about that. You do not have to be any particular age to set goals. You can set goals whenever you want to, and sometimes the goals you set are your incentive to do it. You look for opportunities that will make things happen.

Julius and I thumbed all the way back home. We left Sunday morning, probably around ten o'clock, and went through the Holland Tunnel. A man from Richmond, Virginia, picked us up. Frank said that he was going to Washington so Julius got in the back seat and slept while I sat in the front seat the entire time. This man was very talkative and interesting, and I learned a whole lot by talking to him. When we got into Washington that evening, he asked me where we wanted to go. I said, "We promised our parents that we would not thumb at night, so if you could take us by the YMCA in Washington, we will spend the night there and the next day, we will go on to Roanoke." He let us out, we went inside, and I put my $1.50 on the counter. However, Julius couldn't find his billfold, and he said that he knew he had it in his pocket, but he couldn't find it. I said, "Julius, you left that billfold in that man's car. It must have slid out of your pocket." I did not know how to find him, all I knew was that he was going to Richmond. The desk clerk let us stay there, without Julius paying. I paid my part, and we knelt down beside a bed in the room and told God our situation, and that the billfold had to be in that man's car—may he find it. *Lord, you know how badly we need that billfold.* Julius had about four or five dollars in it, and that was part of our food money.

The next morning about 5:15 the telephone rang, and it was Frank. He said, "I suppose you have been looking for me. After I let you out, I got sleepy and decided to spend the night in the southern part of Washington. I checked in a motel, and when I came out this morning and looked in the back seat there was a billfold. I said to myself, *I bet these guys are looking for this billfold."* He drove all the way back to the YMCA and brought the billfold to us. Julius was beside himself with joy. Later I think we went up on top of the Washington Monument and did a couple of other things, then left about 11:00 that morning to thumb home to Roanoke.

Julius Walthall

Glenn and I had summer jobs together often. One difficult job I remember particularly was with the Northwestern Railroad in a scrap yard. It was one of those work gang jobs; our main job was in a gondola, which is a low side railroad car in which was stored short but heavy pieces of rail. Our job was to unload those gondolas and sort the materials that were coming out of it. We were in a gang with a big guy at the end of the car with a clock and the water bucket. We even had to ask him before we could get a drink of water. It was a really hard job, as I look back on it, but back in those days we were getting paid and that was very good, because neither Glenn's family nor mine had much money as we were growing up. We had to live very frugally.

REVEREND WINSLOW, now retired in Florida, loaned me five hundred dollars for my senior year which I paid back while in the Air Force. He was the minister of the Nazarene church close to my home and he asked me if I would direct their choir. I learned a whole lot about directing choirs by doing that. You need to stay one chapter ahead of everybody else! I also worked on the railroad, up to the time I left for college.

PROFESSOR HERMAN BAKER, who was a music director at Marion College in Indiana came to our church to speak, and talked a great deal about the school. He had heard me play the trombone for a service, and had offered me a trombone scholarship. Also, the chorus that I was in, called "Young Roanoke Sings" offered four scholarships for the first time. I auditioned, sang a solo, played the trombone, and was the first place winner. So I had that scholarship, and the trombone scholarship at Marion College.

2

TROMBONE *to* VOCAL CHORDS

1947–1951

I can sum him up; he does with amateurs what Fred Waring and Robert Shaw did with professionals.

~LEE S. ANDERSON
First Presbyterian Church friend;
Chattanooga Times Free Press *associate publisher and editor*

MARION COLLEGE

Before I first started to Marion College, I told my dad, "Don't send me any money because you don't really have it anyway. I will find a way to make it." The scholarship that I received from Young Roanoke Sings, and the trombone scholarship, and the jobs I had, plus singing in the college quartet helped me at least get from one day to the next. When I left for Marion, I remember catching the train that day by myself, but before that, when I passed through the kitchen in my house, my mother said, "This will probably be the last time you will ever live at home!" I said, "No, I promise you next summer when I get out of school I will be back home." I was the one who loved home the most. Of all my brothers, it is ironic that was the last time that I ever really lived at home, but sometimes it just works like that.

When I got to Marion College in Indiana, my parents had called to tell the school that I would be coming on a certain train, so I was picked up and taken to the school. The first thing I did was put my luggage down in the corner and go sign up for classes. As I was looking on the bulletin board for a place to stay, a fellow was standing next to me, looking for the same thing. I told him my name was Glenn, from Virginia, and he said, "My name is Frank. I'm from Georgia." I said, "Frank, we need to find a place where we can stay." Someone told us about Ms. Thompson's home, and we stayed the whole year there. It was very close to campus and Frank and I became very good friends. Job opportunities were put up on the bulletin board in the hallway of the administration building, and I went by there every day looking for jobs of every kind. One day there was an opening for two people to distribute or sell penny candy machines in filling stations, barbershops, grocery stores, restaurants, and places like that. You know what I did? I took both of them down, so I would have no competition. I worked that whole town over, so instead of two people doing that, I was the person that did both of them. I made more money like that.

My first Christmas in college, I took my first real long trip thumbing. I had thumbed short places, but I had never thumbed six hundred miles and through the night, but I was a daredevil. I knew I could make it. When I left school, about two or three in the afternoon, it was starting to snow just a little. I was so excited. I could not wait to get on the road. When I got to Muncie, Indiana, it was about five o'clock—it took me that long—it's only about thirty miles away! However, thirty miles in those years was a long way because we didn't have super highways. I remember walking through part of Muncie until I got right in the middle of town. My parents had always said, stand in the light so people can see you, and I wanted to see into the car when they pulled up. If they didn't look good, I wouldn't get in. I would take a quick look and walk away. Anyway, this family stopped and said, "Where are you going?" I told them I was going to Roanoke, Virginia. They said, "We aren't going that far, we are just going about thirty miles down the road." I said, "Do you mind if I ride with you? At least I would be closer than I am now." So I got in the car, and by now it was pitch dark, and I was in the back seat with their two boys. We drove on for a while, and the mother said, "We are not going to let you go on toward Roanoke tonight, it is too bad." I said, "But I have to go." They said, "Where do you think you are going to go?" I said, "I don't know, but I have to get started." They said, "We can't let you out on this road. You will freeze to death out there, son. It's going to be down below freezing and it's snowing." I said, "Well, what do you suggest?" They said, "You are going to spend the night with us." I told them I couldn't do that, but they told me I didn't have a choice. "We aren't going to stop the car, we are going to take you to our house."

We became great buddies, just that fast, as if I had known them forever. We got to their house and I said, "Let me help you. What can I do?" They were farmers, with some cattle. Mr. B. gave me one of his coveralls to put over my clothes and I went out to the barn and got hay for the cattle, while he was milking the cows. I helped feed the cattle and did other chores, and took food down to the pigs. When I came back to the house, his wife had the most delicious meal. Country fried steak with gravy and the best biscuits you ever tasted, with every type of vegetable that you could think of. I sat there with the family, and we talked and laughed. Later the mother played the piano and the boys played trombone and clarinet and we sang.

About 10:30 they were getting sleepy and they told me where my room was. I didn't give it a thought, I went on to my room, and said, "What time do I get up?" They said, "We are going to take you to Richmond, Indiana," which was about forty miles on the other side of where they lived. So I spent the night in a room with a nice bed. I didn't know that it was their master bedroom. You know when you are young, you don't think about those kinds of things. They spent the night on the couch in the living room. I felt so bad about that the next morning when I found out.

We had a delicious breakfast, and afterwards we all loaded in their car and they took me to Richmond. Snow was on the ground, the sun was shining, it was just beautiful. Since it was the Christmas holiday, the boys didn't have to go to school. I picked out a busy intersection, and we pulled over, hugged each other, and traded addresses. They corresponded with my mother and father for years after I was out of college, and I received a Christmas card from them every year for a long time.

I caught a ride to Chillicothe, Ohio, with a guy delivering a truck to Renear, West Virginia, a fairly long way from Roanoke. The truck had a governor on it and he couldn't go faster than fifty miles an hour. Of course, I was glad to get in that truck, it was heated and the guy was very friendly. I was so thankful I wasn't thumbing out there on the road. We got to Renear about two in the morning, and he let me out on the road under a light. I remember the Christmas decorations in the little town, with wind blowing the lights. I finally got a ride to another small town and the driver said that there was a little place about a block and a half down the street with a heater and shelter. I stood on that road for about twenty minutes and I was beginning to freeze to death. So I walked down and found a small cottage, and I could see a heater. As soon as I walked in, I heard somebody snoring and I immediately turned around and got out of there. It scared me and I thought *I'm not **that** cold*. So I went back under the stoplight and within 46 seconds, a car came flying through, picked me up, and took me all the way to Highway 11. Then I picked up a ride on a truck and it took me right on into Roanoke. That was the first time I had thumbed a great distance, and it was quite an experience. I didn't have a car so I spent a great deal of my life in those early years thumbing, and meeting everybody you can imagine. If you want to meet different people with all kinds of personalities, get on the highway and you meet them.

I SPENT THE SPRING singing in the Marion College Quartet. We had a lot of engagements and would get paid, ten dollars here and fifteen dollars there. I also had an arrangement with the lady who was the manager of the cafeteria. Anytime I was hungry or didn't have a meal, I could wash pots and pans for my dinner or lunch. One of the singers said he couldn't travel that summer, which was a blessing in disguise, because I thought he was one of the laziest guys I had ever seen. He was a senior that knew it all and didn't want to work anymore. I was a freshman, and couldn't wait to have our quartet sound better than any quartet they had ever had. I got Frank H. to sing bass; Gerald S., a senior, was first tenor; Ross V., a junior, was second tenor; and I was the baritone. We all had matching suits and ties. The college sponsored the tour and made up our schedule. Every day we went to a different city, and sang for various events that the college had scheduled. I got my tuition paid for the next year, and they paid me a salary for the summer for doing this; it was a lucky break.

When I first got to school, one of the things I wanted to do was get in the very good Marion College Choir. I auditioned for it and they put me in the second tenor section. I didn't tell them that I had sung bass and baritone in choirs. During the second rehearsal, the director was trying to get the basses to sing a low note, trying to teach them how to relax. I just sang it from over in the second tenor section. He said, "Who did that, where are you?" I thought he was going to kick me out of the choir. He said, "Was that you?" and I said, "Yes, sir." He said, "What are you doing in the second tenor section?" and I said, "This is where you put me." He then moved me to the bass section and said, "I don't have anybody who can sing this low." So I started singing bass. When they had tryouts for the college quartet, I made it, so I had to drop the choir to start singing in the quartet.

While on a quartet tour we had heard a preacher one night we really didn't like and we all agreed to leave the next morning. When we got in the car and drove out of that place, we had to cross some railroad tracks. We had to go up a little incline to get to the tracks and then go back down on the other side. When Jerry got to the top of the incline, right on those tracks, the car stalled. Off to my right I could hear a whistle and a freight train was bearing down on us. It was still a good distance away, and I said, "Jerry, do something." I had my hand on the door to get out of that car, I thought that train was going to get us. The whistle on the train was blowing like crazy. Jerry finally put it in gear and turned the starter on. We got it off the tracks, but it was close. That train flew by, and I said, "Man alive, next time keep your foot on the gas, don't let it stop and stall."

About a week went by, we were having fun, another week went by and we were having less fun. About the third week, of a twelve-week tour, I said, "Guys, we are seeing each other too much. You are getting on my nerves and I am getting on your nerves. We have to separate when we get to a town." When we drove into Toledo that morning, I said, "Let's don't even have lunch together. You go where you want to and I am going to go where I want to. Let's don't even tell each other where we are going!" We agreed that we were going to meet at five o'clock, before we were supposed to leave to sing in a church. I went to the YMCA, swam, and had fun playing handball and badminton with some other people. Frank went to the park and read, Jerry went over to watch a sandlot baseball game or something, and Ross, I don't remember where he went, but we all met at five. And we were glad to see each other. I said, "You see, we just can't be with each other all the time, because it is going to bother us." That taught me a lesson about the tours that I have directed. I will forcefully get people off of the bus and away from each other. I learned that at the end of my freshman year in college.

When we went to a town to sing in a program, everything in the world happened to us. Girls would bring us cherry pies and every kind of dessert as a gift. When we got to Upper Michigan, where the sand dunes are, we were very tired and almost asleep when the head of our bed fell down. Our feet were sticking up, but we just stayed there. Neither one of us got up, we just slept with our feet up in the air, we were so exhausted.

We did try to get out and exercise—play football, baseball, anything—because we rode in the car all the time, and the people all fed you like you were starving. Everywhere we went, the college had it all set up, with instructions on how to get there, where to go, and what to do. There might be a revival going on in this church, a youth convention here, a camp meeting over there, or the Rotary Club wanted us to sing for them.

We had a very busy schedule that we followed all the time for twelve weeks and it was a great experience. I learned to direct congregational singing, called a sing-a-long, which I have done at Junaluska. I also gained confidence in myself singing on the stage all the time. Later, when I directed the choirs in the Air Force, it was nothing new to me to stand on a stage, I had already been broken in, far more than most other guys who went to college. Most of the guys who went to college just saw the inside of books, with no practical experience. I learned, and as a people person I met everybody in the world you can imagine. It was a great experience and that was just in my freshman year.

In my second year in college, the quartet was beginning to be a very good group, since the same guys sang in it. That winter, the Indiana University Choir came through and gave a concert. Dr. Wilfred Bain, who was the dean of the Music Department and the director of the choir at Indiana University, talked about his first voice teacher being Herman Baker, with whom I was studying voice. He mentioned that they had scholarships for instrumentalists and vocalists. He said, "I solicit any of you when you get out of school here to apply." I thought, *I am really good on the trombone, I bet I could get a scholarship there, in a much bigger school with more prestige than Marion College.*

A guy in the choir was a good friend of a girl whom I had met the previous year. We talked this fellow into lending me his car, so we could drive down to Bloomington and audition for a trombone scholarship. I went to the school and you would not believe the instrumentalists from all over Indiana who were auditioning. I put it out of my head that I would even be considered. We all had to wait in a recital hall, and when Dr. Wilfred Bain came out, I remembered seeing him. I was called, and I went up on stage and introduced myself, and said, "You were just at my school about two or three months ago, and Herman Baker was your teacher." He said, "That's right, Glenn. I'm so glad to see you. Are you planning on coming to school here?" I told him I had just auditioned for a trombone scholarship, and I hoped I would make it. He said, "For your sake and ours, I hope you make it too."

I remember Dr. Wilfred Bain giving a speech in which he said, "In order to be successful in this world there are two traits you have to have, be good at what you do, and be able to sell it. If you only have one of those traits, you will only get part way up the ladder before people will find you out! You will be cast aside. If you are good and can't sell it, nobody will ever hear about you anyway! You might as well stay in your room and do your practicing because no one will ever hear you! You have to have both!" I thought, *I have those traits. I can play that trombone as good as anybody around here and I can sure sell it.*

While we were there, they read out the scholarship winners, and they read my name! I was so excited, I was like a jackrabbit—I couldn't believe it. I went back to school and told the orchestra director and Herman Baker that I had been accepted. They told me, "Glenn, we hate to lose you here, but for your good, that is probably best. We could never offer you the real opportunities that you will have at Indiana University."

I went back home that summer, and directed a church choir. I also went down to the University of Alabama because my girlfriend, Marilyn, was transferring there since she lived in Tuscaloosa, and she talked me into coming down there to audition with the band. It was called Alabama's Million Dollar Band, and Colonel B. was the director. He was straight-laced, not too tall, dark hair, and I was so impressed with him. He was a fine gentleman. He said, "We will give you a scholarship. Come to the University of Alabama, but you have to be here a week before school starts, because we have to get ready for all the games." I said, "I can probably do that." He wrote me a letter accepting me, then I got a letter from Indiana University that said I had to let them know by a certain date if I was going to accept their scholarship or not.

I was in a dither; here was a girlfriend who went to Tuscaloosa, who wanted me to move down there where they offered me a scholarship in the Million Dollar Band. But Indiana University has one of the best music departments in the country. I prayed really hard and the next morning I must have been awake at five, and I got up out of bed and went downstairs and I said, "Mother, I know where I am supposed to go." She asked, "Where?" and I replied, "Indiana University." Getting married was the last thing on my mind. I had so much to do before then. So I called Indiana University and asked, "Is my scholarship still available?" They said yes and that they expected me to report on a certain date.

INDIANA UNIVERSITY

DURING THE SUMMER of 1949, while selling Christmas cards, directing a church choir, and working at odd jobs, I had made my decision to go to Indiana University. I didn't know a soul there, but it's where God led me to go.

As I caught the train on the Monday morning, I prayed all the way to Indiana that God would go with me. When I arrived at the train station, I had planned to take a taxi to Indiana University and find a place to stay. As I got off of the train, a man came up to me and asked if I was from the South. I jokingly replied, "South of what?" He said, "My wife has a chicken dinner waiting for you at our house." He explained that he was the minister of the Church of the Nazarene. I asked how he knew me, and was told that, without me knowing it, Reverend C. E. Winslow from Roanoke, minister of the church I had been directing the choir for during the past two summers, had called to tell him that I was coming to Indiana.

His wife, Mrs. Moore, was a very gracious lady, and the dinner was delicious. Afterward, they took me on a tour of the campus. It was so big and I felt so small. The Moores invited me to spend the night with them, and then they would take me to school the next day to register for fall classes.

At breakfast the next morning, they asked me where I was planning to live. I said, "The dorms at IU." Mrs. Moore said that their son, whose room I had slept in, had recently gotten married and their daughter, Dixie, was away at school. Since it was going to be rather lonesome around their house, they wondered if I would just stay there. I could even bring my clothes down and have them washed with theirs. They would not charge me a cent for the room.

Reverend Moore then said that they needed me to be their choir director and that the pay was fifteen dollars per week. A lady in the choir even loaned me a bicycle to ride to school each day. I said, *Lord, I can't believe this! You are so wonderful, my life is yours!*

Directing the Christmas concert was very fun. I invited many students from IU to come and sing in my church choir, sometimes we had thirty-five to forty people. In the spring of the year, a couple in the church gave me a three-room apartment to live in for free. The church members also kept me supplied with hot rolls and cherry pies. Directing the church choir was indeed a great experience for me.

I WAS ALWAYS a better trombone player than I was a singer, but I had a very good ear. I learned a lot of that technique from singing in quartets as a baritone or a bass. That was fun and I loved choirs, but it was through playing trombone that I got scholarships. I was being groomed to play in a symphony, maybe like the Pittsburgh Symphony or Houston, or be an orchestral conductor. I used to dream of conducting Beethoven's Fifth

Symphony. I thought that would be one of the greatest things you could do. In fact, in my student teaching I got a chance to do that with an orchestra in Bloomington.

In the spring of my junior year, there was an all-state chorus, band, and orchestra concert held in Bloomington and we had to go to it because of the educational value. When the orchestra played, I could see myself directing the orchestra or cuing the violins. When the band played, it was just great. I could see myself doing that. But when the four-hundred-voice choir sang "Holy, Holy, Holy, Lord God of Hosts" written by Noble Cain, that was the most glorious sound I had ever heard in my life. I thought, *I must do that. I don't care whether I am a trombone major on a trombone scholarship.* I went to school the very next day and I said, "I have got to do choral music." They said, "You can't, Glenn, you are an instrumentalist." I said, "I don't care what I am. You are not hearing me, I have got to do that!" They said, "Your full scholarship is on the trombone. No, you can't do that." They sent me to a fellow named Ben V. who was the head of the voice department. He said, "Glenn, you have a nice voice, but you don't have the voice to make it in opera." I told him, "I don't want to do opera, I want to be a choral director." So I took voice and ended up doing a half recital with somebody else on voice. But my senior recital was on trombone—that was what I had to pass.

While I was playing in the band, I joined one of the choirs directed by George Krueger, a big 6'7" teacher for whom I had the greatest admiration. I didn't worship him, but I came close to it. He let me sing in his choir, and I cannot tell you the joy I had in that Indiana University Choir and what I learned from him. The dean used to say, "Glenn, if your grades go below a B, you are out of that choir. You are not here to sing in a choir, your scholarship is on the trombone, that's your forte."

IN JUNE 1950, I had just returned to my home in Roanoke to work for the summer by directing a church choir and selling Stanley home products. I certainly needed money to return to Indiana University for my senior year. Marilyn Shows, a girl that I had met while at Marion College, had invited my brother Bill and me to visit her and her family in Tuscaloosa, Alabama, before we started to work for the summer. The only way to get there was to hitchhike.

On Wednesday, we caught a ride to Bristol, Virginia. After walking a block or two, we stopped at a red light and stuck out our thumbs. Believe it or not, a Cadillac stopped to pick us up. A man by the name of Mac McRoberts of Charleston, West Virginia, said, "How far are you going?" We told him, "Tuscaloosa, Alabama." He and his friend said to get in since they were going to Knoxville, Tennessee, to attend a meeting that night.

As we rode along in the back seat of this Cadillac, I said to him, "I sure do like your car." He asked, "Have you ever driven a Cadillac before?"

"Sure," I said jokingly. "Then how about you driving? You see, we've been driving from Charlottesville, Virginia, and would love to rest." Bill and I then got into the front seat and started to drive, it was so nice. Mr. McRoberts told us, "You do okay." He then asked, "By the way, how much will you charge me to drive this car back to Charleston, West Virginia? We have to be there for a very important business meeting at nine o'clock tomorrow morning." I was greatly concerned by this time, and wondering what his motive was.

His friend said, "Oh, Mac, why don't you just let them have the car? We were young once." We said that we couldn't bring the car back until next Thursday, and he said that was okay. That sealed it for Bill and me . . . what a deal!

When we arrived in Knoxville, Mr. McRoberts took us to a restaurant and bought all of these sandwiches, drinks, and candy bars, and gave us seventy-five dollars to buy gas. He asked if that was enough. . . .What do you think? Oh, yes!

We then drove to an automobile agency where the two men rented a car to drive that night before they flew back to Charleston. They told us, "Have a good time. Go to the beach, the Grand Ole Opry . . . and we'll see you next week." That was a Thursday, so we had a Cadillac to drive for an entire week with our girlfriends!

When we arrived at Marilyn's family home in Tuscaloosa, they were very impressed—probably more with the car than with us. As they were oohing and aahing over the car, I took Marilyn's mother into the kitchen and confessed, "This ain't my car!" She asked where we got it, and I told her that a man gave it to us as we were thumbing our way to Alabama. Now that's a wild story. We kept it a secret the rest of the week.

We all had a ball. We went to the beach in Florida, went swimming, and met many of Marilyn's friends. We then drove them to church on Sunday. On Tuesday afternoon, we left Tuscaloosa and drove to Roanoke where we arrived about eight o'clock Wednesday morning. We wanted our dad to see this car because he wouldn't believe the story.

Our dad loved the car and was very glad to see us, but he said, "Without breaking the speed limit, get this car back to Mr. McRoberts as fast as you can. You can't prove that it's not a stolen car. Driving over a state line would be a federal offense!"

As we drove through the mountains of West Virginia, a news flash came on the radio . . . President Truman had just declared war on North Korea. This meant that we would probably be drafted into the armed services. One year later, we were both in the Air Force.

As we finally arrived in Charleston, we found Mr. McRoberts's place of business, McRoberts Automotive Parts Store. He owned these stores all over West Virginia and Ohio. We found him sitting behind a big desk, smoking a cigar, his feet on the desk, and talking on the telephone. He invited us in and then to have lunch with him. We told him that we had to get back to Roanoke, as we had to start work the next day. He asked how we were going to get home and we said, "Just like you first met us."

After lunch, we picked out several good places to stand and thumb. He said that he had a better place—that was the airport. He bought us tickets to fly home on Piedmont airlines. I said, "Mac, what can I do to repay you?" He said, "Come work for me when you get out of school." I replied that I was going into music, and he said, "Music? How in the world will you make a living in music?" "I don't know, but I'll have to try!"

We remained good friends for a long time. He often wrote to me after listening to the Keesler Male Chorus broadcast heard every Sunday on NBC radio.

I BEGAN DIRECTING the choir at the First Church of the Nazarene during my junior year. On Wednesdays before I would go to rehearsals, I would ask George Krueger, "What do I do with these country basses, cornfield tenors, and hog-calling altos? How do I get that out of them?" He would give me all kinds of exercises to use and I would try them out. Wow, they worked! So I would come back on Thursday and say, "You won't believe this, but you should have heard my altos last night." I was so excited at that first Christmas concert we did my junior year. That Christmas concert I directed was just the greatest joy of my whole life up to that point. I was going to thumb home that night and someone gave me ten dollars to buy food while I traveled. I owe so much to people like that who were so encouraging along the way. If I could pay everybody back for what they meant to me, I would be broke for the rest of my life.

At the First Church of the Nazarene in Bloomington, someone just happened to say one Sunday morning, "You have a good group of men, why don't you sing on Sunday nights?" That was my bag, even when I was in high school. I used to tell my director that I would love to organize a male chorus, and he used to say, "Glenn, if you do, you are going to have to do it in the military or do it outside of Roanoke, because I don't think Roanoke is big enough to get the kind of talent that you want." So, going back to the church, my men sang on Sunday nights and people were amazed that those guys sounded like that. All the guys were so excited about it. We had probably twenty-two or twenty-three men, including a lot of the guys from the choir at the university. I also had a quartet called the "Golden Tone Quartet." We traveled all over the countryside singing, and continued to rehearse on Sunday afternoons.

Little did I know that preparation was a forerunner for what I was going to do in the Air Force. I had no idea at the time how that would lead me. So, when I knew I was going into the military as soon as I graduated, I decided that I was going to organize a male chorus and direct the *Messiah*, because I had always wanted to do that.

AFTER SELLING Stanley products and Christmas cards and directing a church choir during the summer of 1950, I was ready to return to Indiana University for my senior year and to graduate the next spring. In early September, my brother and I caught the *Powertown Arrow* train to return to school at Bloomington, Indiana. Gene and I were very excited because we had made enough money in the summer to take a train back to school.

As the train pulled out of the station in Roanoke, Virginia, about 9:00 P.M., we settled into our seats. Being so excited about riding the train, it wasn't long before I was up and walking from car to car, meeting new people. I went through the dinner car where people were drinking coffee, visiting, and getting acquainted. I made myself right at home, meeting everyone that I could. At about eleven o'clock, I went back to my seat where my brother Gene was, and he had gone to sleep. I looked up ahead and noticed a small group of people talking. I didn't want to disturb Gene since he was sleeping, so I got up and joined them. They were all going to Cincinnati on business, and we all joined in chitchat until about 1:00 A.M. Finally, everyone decided to get some sleep since the train was due in Cincinnati about 11:40 A.M. the next morning. I went back to my seat and started to read the newspaper. I thought, *No need to wake up Gene with the light being on, I'll just go to the car behind this one.* I picked out a seat and read for awhile. About 3:00 A.M., I got sleepy, so I turned out my light and fell asleep.

I woke up about 7:45 and wondered how my brother was doing. I got up and went forward to the car he was in, but he wasn't there. In fact, all of the people I had talked to were not there. As I walked down the aisle of the train, the conductor was walking toward me with his train tickets. I tried not to look too alarmed as I asked him, "Hey, Mac, what time do we get into Cincinnati?" "Son, you will be in Columbus, Ohio, in about ten minutes." I said, "Oh, not me. You see, I got a ticket for Cincinnati and Bloomington, Indiana. I am going to school at Indiana University." "Not on this train!" he said. "What happened to the train I was on?" I told him that I had fallen asleep on the car behind this one and that I couldn't find anybody I knew. He started laughing and said that the car I slept on was switched to another train in Portsmouth, Ohio, which was going to Cleveland. "Your train has gone into Cincinnati."

I asked, "What can I do?" He said that there was a fast train coming from New York going to San Antonio, Texas. It was due to stop in Columbus about the same time we arrived. In ten minutes, I was off of that train and onto the other in no time.

It was one of the most beautiful trains I had ever seen, tan in color with beautiful cushioned seats where they showed movies to the passengers. What a train! And it was fast, too! We arrived in Cincinnati about an hour and a half before Gene's train was supposed to arrive. I wrote postcards, drank a Coke, and ate cake and an ice cream cone while I waited for Gene's train. I could hardly wait to see Gene and tell him what had happened. I walked down to the tracks and waited for the train. Finally, after forty-five minutes (it was late), I saw the engine of the *Powertown Arrow* pull around the bend. As the train approached the platform, I was so full of excitement, I waved at almost everyone who got off of the train. Finally, after I thought everyone had gotten off of the train, I saw the last car, and a trombone sticking out the stairway of the train followed by Gene carrying all of those suitcases, including mine. His first words were, "Where in the ——— have you been? What happened to you? Mother and Dad have the FBI out looking for you, and the police in every town are looking along the tracks just to recover your body." I then tried to explain to him just what had happened. We still can't believe it!

DURING MY SENIOR YEAR at Indiana University, I was appointed section leader of the trombone section of the "Marching Hundred." We were approaching our last football game with Purdue University. The game was to be played in Lafayette, Indiana, on the Saturday after Thanksgiving. During the Thanksgiving break from school, my brother Gene (who also played trumpet in the band) decided that we just had to go home for Thanksgiving to be with our family in Roanoke, Virginia, six hundred miles away.

We put on our band uniforms which had heavy overcoats so that we could keep warm while we were hitchhiking. We also thought we would have a better chance of catching a ride wearing the uniforms. We arrived home on Thanksgiving morning and returned on Friday so we would have time to catch the train on Saturday morning for the trip to Purdue. We arrived in Bloomington about 3:00 A.M., slept three hours, and caught the train at 7:00 A.M.

Soon after we boarded the train, we sat down to rest with the other band members. After a few minutes, I decided to visit the men's room and wash my face in order to wake up. When I saw myself in the mirror, I noticed that I did not have on my red crimson tie. I said, *I am not going to panic, I've been through crises before. I will find someone on this train who has a red crimson tie, and I will buy it or talk him out of it.* As a section leader, it was my place to inspect the band members for their instruments, ties, etc.

I immediately went to the dinner car and spotted the porter who had on a Kentucky red tie. I tried not to be overly anxious as I approached him. I asked him how much he would take for that red tie. He replied, "Heck, no! I have a whole box of ties in the kitchen!" When he gave me the tie, we unraveled it and tied it around my neck like a regular tie, and he pinned it so it would stay in place—I was home free!

When I went back to join Gene and the other band members, someone mentioned his instrument. I immediately thought of mine—*Where was my trombone? . . . No!* I had left my trombone in our room at the university. I could not believe it! *And I have to inspect the other band members before we go on the field at the game.*

I'm not going to panic! I have been through rough times before . . . hitchhiking, selling Christmas cards, working on rail carts . . . I will find someone with a trombone. I will not tell a soul, not even my brother.

As soon as we arrived at the dining room at Purdue, I ate my soup, excused myself, and set out to find the Purdue band room. After thirty minutes of searching, I found the band room about four blocks away. *The door just had to be open.* The door was unlocked, and I ran through, determined to find someone who had a trombone that I could borrow. It was then two and a half hours away from game time. *I would find him.*

As I walked through the door, I could hear someone playing on a baritone horn. I asked him, "Do you have any idea where I can find a trombone that I can play at the game? I know that we're on opposing teams, but that doesn't matter now." He said the most wonderful words I have ever heard. "My band director called me this morning and asked me if I could play baritone horn in the game this afternoon because one of the baritone horn players is sick. I usually play trombone—my trombone is yours, just bring it back after the game." I said, *Lord, thanks for Your great mercy.*

It really didn't matter that we lost the game, twelve to zero. No one in the band ever knew that story, including my brother Gene. Since then, I have been on forty-seven overseas tours and over one hundred stateside tours, and I have not left anything. Oh, the lessons we learn!

3

The
WORLD'S GREATEST MALE CHORUS

1951–1955

Everybody has said that Glenn has angels on each shoulder.

~DOT CARTER
First Presbyterian Church choir member;
Glenn Draper Singers; sang with Robert Shaw in Atlanta

I had a lonesome feeling as the train pulled out when I joined the Air Force on September 17, 1951. My parents were there and my girlfriend, Pat Martindale. In fact, it was her birthday. I told her I would be back for Christmas, without knowing how I would manage that. Once the excitement of leaving and joining the Air Force was over that night, as I lay down to sleep in the berth it dawned on me that I was going into an entirely different world. The coziness and familiarity with people and with my teachers in college were gone. Now I didn't know anyone, not one soul. I prayed, *Oh God, I am lonesome. I am actually scared, and surely you won't leave me now. You have stuck with me all through school, surely you are not going to leave me now! Oh God, you know how badly I want to organize and direct a male chorus, help me to organize one somewhere.*

During the first week at Samson Air Force Base, near the Finger Lakes in northern New York state, someone came around from the service club and said, "We are gathering all the talent we can find because we are going to have a talent show about two weeks from now. Anybody who can play an instrument, sing, or tap dance, or whatever, come to the service club on Friday night at 7:00." We had to get to bed at 9:30 that night because we had to get up at 4:45 the next morning. I went over to the club and they were auditioning twenty-four to twenty-five men to be in the glee club. I made it. During the first rehearsal after the first number, the director said, "Does anybody have any suggestions?" My hand went up. I had no idea why I reacted that quickly, but I did, and he said, "Have you ever done this before?" I said that I was a music major in college. He said, "Man, get up here. I have no idea what I am doing; I played in the band and I have never even been in a choir." So I started directing them, and my experience from the church and directing a male chorus gave me confidence. I knew what to do and what kind of sound I wanted. Two weeks later, we sang in that program. After the concert, one of the first people to come up to me was a colonel who asked, "Son, how long have you been doing this?" I told him we had just been rehearsing two weeks. He said, "Are you in basic training?" I said, "Yes sir, I am." He said, "I am retiring in two and one-half weeks and I want this group to sing for my retirement." That meant we would continue having those rehearsals in order to sing at his retirement. We not only did that, we sang for a number of other things on the base. As a result of that, the only time I did any K.P. was one morning when I handed out toast. I had no idea who that colonel was, but he did me a huge favor. It gave me confidence and attention immediately in the Air Force.

I was just getting out of basic training in the first part of December, and I had promised my girlfriend, Pat, and my parents that I would be home for Christmas. We were put in the local band at Samson Air Force Base, from where they would ship us out to other parts of the world to play in military bands. Through the chorus that I directed, a chaplain had come up and said, "You have done a really great job." I went to see this chaplain later because I had already been told that no one from the band was going home for Christmas. So I went to the chaplain and told him what had happened. I said, "I must get home, my brothers are all in the military and I have got to be home to see them." He said, "Draper, don't you tell a soul, but I guarantee I will get you a three-day pass." We were practicing on the twenty-third of December, and my three-day pass started the next day. Only the band director knew that the pass came from the chaplain, and that "Draper is being granted a three-day pass for reasons that you don't need to know." That is what he put down, a chaplain can get away with that! So I didn't say anything to anybody, and slipped out of the barracks without telling my roommates or anybody where I was going. I thumbed all the way through the night and arrived home the next after-noon. I was almost frozen. I was so glad to see my parents, I said, "I told you I would be home."

The day after Christmas, one of my brothers had to go to the airport to catch a Navy Neptune coming through to take him back to

Jacksonville, Florida. I rode with them in the car out to the airport, so I could get on the road and thumb back to Samson. While I was waiting with him for his flight, I noticed a private airplane pull up really close and three or four people got out of the airplane and walked right past me. I asked where they were going. "We are going to New York." I asked what part of New York, and they said, "New York City." I said, "Do you have room for another passenger? I am going to Samson AFB, way up above New York City, but that sure is a lot closer than this!" So they said, "Why don't you come aboard?" They fed me fried chicken and other food on the airplane. It carried about eight people and landed right in the middle of Brooklyn. I had to thumb across town, across the Hudson River, and by the time I got up as far as West Point, it was already a little after midnight. I had just a few hours to get to Samson AFB before my three-day pass ran out. I arrived an hour and fifteen minutes before I was supposed to check in, so I went into the barracks, got into bed, and then got up and went in to practice. I practiced all day and never said a word to anybody about where I had been.

Now you aren't going to believe this, but I was sitting in the rehearsal that afternoon, on December 28, and the band director who was there when I went on leave had gone on his vacation. The assistant band director (who was away when I left) was back, and now directing the band. That afternoon at 4:00, he stopped the rehearsal and said, "I have an announcement. I have twenty, three-day passes to give to the twenty people who can give me the best reason why they need to go home." Everybody perked up, and we all wound up in front of his office and one by one we went in. I didn't tell him that I had just returned from a three-day pass. I said, "Two of my brothers are home now, one of them had to leave, and I would give anything in the world to see them." He said, "Give me one hour or less to make a decision. In forty-five minutes he posted his list, and guess what? My name was on that list! I had just returned from a three-day pass. I never told anybody. I did my usual thing, got my little bag, ran out on the highway, and thumbed all the way back home to Roanoke. My family was thrilled to death.

I need to tell you this, and it is important. Before I took the first three-day pass, the male chorus that I was directing sang for a chapel service in the evening and there were chaplains from all over the eastern part of the United States who had come there for a meeting. I had no idea why they chose Samson. Maybe they just wanted to see how the rest of us suffered through the winter. After we finished, we were having cookies and punch, and were talking. I just happened to start talking to a man by the name of Colonel D. I asked him where he was from, and he told me Keesler Air Force Base in Biloxi, Mississippi. I said, "I bet you have a great male chorus there." He said, "Frankly, no, we don't! We have wasted so much money on buying music for a group, and in about two weeks the guys become disinterested and the group falls apart." I asked him how many men they had there. He said, "We have about thirty thousand men." I said, "Thirty thousand men, and you can't get a male chorus?" I thought, *What an unbelievable place to go!*

We wished each other a Merry Christmas and he went his way and I went back to the barracks. In two or three days I went to Roanoke on my first three-day pass. Now on my second trip, I thumbed down and all the way back, I didn't catch a flight! It was around four in the morning when I got back to the base. I went in and sacked out, then got up and that day, when we broke for lunch, the orderly room clerk came right up to me and said, "Draper, I have something for you." He said, "Look at these orders. You are being sent to Keesler Air Force Base to play in their band." I thought, *That Colonel, bless his soul, he heard my plea and he arranged for me to move down there.* I could hardly wait to see him. They paid me $104 to ride the train, but I put the money in my pocket, shipped my duffel bag, and thumbed with my trombone and a little tiny bag. I went through Roanoke again on the way to Keesler. *Here comes Glenn Draper again. This is his third trip within two and a half weeks. We can't believe it, how did he do this?*

My brother, Gene, was going back to Tyndall Air Force Base in Florida, where he was in pilot training. We thumbed together down to Birmingham, Alabama. He took the road out of Birmingham and went south, and I took the other road and went over toward Meridian, Mississippi, and then down to Biloxi. One of the last things I heard him say was, "Glenn, I will keep them flying, you keep them singing." I replied that I would do my best.

The next morning, I checked in a transit barracks. We had to go outside to clean the area, and when I looked across the way, there was a sign indicating that it was the chaplain's office. That was where I had to go. About eight o'clock, I told the sergeant, "I will be back in a few minutes, I have to run over to the chaplain section." If you ever said that, they thought you had a personal problem and it was none of their business. I ran over there, and guess who was in his office? Colonel D. I couldn't believe it! I said, "Colonel Daniels, when do we get started?" He said, "Son, how did you get down here?" I said, "You must have worked it out," and he said, "I had nothing to do with it—I didn't even remember your last name. I remembered your name was Glenn, but that was it." I told him that I had been assigned to the band here and asked when we could get started on that male chorus. He said, "Let's don't get too excited, let's take it slow. We have a lot of people to sell, since we have wasted a lot of money on music for previous choruses." He said, "Come to think of it, there is a choir rehearsal for a Lutheran and an Episcopal service tonight down at the chapel. Why don't you join the choir?"

After the band practice that afternoon, I went to the rehearsal that night. The director was doing a good job. At the break, I met a little blonde who was quite attractive and I started talking to her. All I could talk about was the male chorus and that I couldn't wait to get it started. I knew the Air Force was going to see a male chorus the likes of which they had never heard before. Why I believed that, I don't really know. I kept talking to her about this male chorus idea, and she said, "My daddy is Chaplain Hobgood, the Lutheran chaplain, and he is having all the chaplains over to the house tonight for homemade ice cream." I said, "Am I invited?" She said, "Sure," so I walked with her over to her quarters, and sure enough the chaplains were laughing and talking and eating homemade ice cream. She said, "Daddy, I have somebody who wants to see you." I said, "My name is Glenn Draper. You chaplains have the opportunity to have the world's greatest male chorus right here on this base." They said, "Who is going to direct it?" I said, "I am ready to get started," and they all laughed and thought, *Who is this young whipper-snapper who has come in and immediately says he is going to have a great chorus?* I said, "The reason that I mention this is because you gentlemen are the ones who are going to promote it. It needs to be in your department because we need to sing for religious events, as well as secular." Someone said, "Don't you think it should be sponsored by the service club?" I answered, "They are not interested in religious things, but you are. If you aren't, you should be!" Someone suggested, "Why don't we put him on a salary to recruit people for our choir?"

They paid me fifteen dollars a week to get people out of the sack on Sunday mornings to come and sing in their choir. That fifteen dollars a week was a big supplement to the ninety dollars I was getting monthly. The church choir started getting bigger, and in January or February, the lady who was directing and her husband shipped out, and they appointed me director of the chapel choir. The choir kept growing as I got people to sing in it. We sang an Easter program that everyone thought was really good. Easter Sunday night, Chaplain Hobgood and Colonel Daniels came to me and said, "We are now convinced that you are the person we need. We would like to take your band director out to lunch tomorrow and sell him on the idea." I prayed really hard that he would say yes. They told me to come by about one o'clock on Monday, which I did. They came back with long faces, and didn't have to say a word. The band director had scoffed at the idea, and he wouldn't hear of giving up a trombone player for a ridiculous thing like trying to start a male chorus. He said that we have a glee club here in our band. They told me that they couldn't buck him, since he was my commanding officer. I said, "Chaplains, look at me really well. I have just started to fight and you know I am not going to quit." They said, "We know you are sincere about that, but you don't have a chance."

Bob B. Davis
A roommate during Air Force years;
recorded Lake Junaluska Singers albums for several years

Glenn Draper never would take no for an answer. I remember more than once we would get to the chow hall five minutes late, and the sergeant would say, "I'm sorry, it is closed, you cannot come in." Glenn would say, "That's okay, we aren't whipped yet, come on." He would take me around to the back door of the chow hall and he would knock loudly on the door and plead hunger, and the corporal would say, "We have some bread left and maybe a piece of ham we could give you." We would get fed.

I LEFT THERE and walked right past the band quarters to the service club. I had to have some quiet time, so I went in there to get a Coke or something. I was sitting at the fountain drinking a Coke and a lady came up beside me to get a refill. She was all dressed up in a beautiful cotton dress and I said to her, "Wouldn't it be incredible to have a male chorus on this base that is second to none? I need your help." She said, "Who are you, sonny?" I told her that I was a member of the band, but I had to organize a male chorus of some kind. She pointed over toward twenty-five or thirty women, all dressed alike in cotton, summery dresses, since this was right after Easter, and said, "You see that lady over there with the white hair, the white dress, and black hat? That is Mrs. James F. Powell, the general's wife, and if anybody can help you, she can." I said, "Would you introduce me?" She asked what my name was again, and I told her it was Glenn Draper and that I was with the band. She said, "Mrs. Powell, I don't mean to interrupt you, but this gentleman wants to talk to you." I said, "I am so glad to meet you. You are the answer to my prayers. Will you help me organize the world's greatest male chorus on this base? Your husband is going to be the reaper of the benefit of it, and he will be very proud." She said, "What do you do?" I told her I was in the band. She asked, "How can I help you?" I said, "Please get your husband to have me transferred to the chaplain's office, for the sole purpose of organizing choirs." She said, "Let me write down your name and serial number." I said good-bye to her, knowing that something was going to come from it.

One week went by, two weeks went by, three weeks went by, and in the fourth week, I hadn't heard a thing from anyone. I was afraid to say anything to anyone, because if the band director had heard that I had gone over his head, I would have been court-martialed or who knows what. One evening about six, I had just come back to the barracks with Bob Davis, my roommate from North Carolina, and the Charge of Quarters (CQ) sent word for me to come in to see him. He said, "Draper, here is an order from

Major General James F. Powell stating that you will be transferred on the fifth of this month to the chaplain's office for the sole purpose of organizing choirs." I was so overjoyed that I could hardly wait to tell everybody in the morning. That morning, about eight, I got a call from the band director, to be in his office on the double. I have never seen anyone so mad as he was at me. He threw a book across the desk and it landed up on a shelf where some books were and half the books fell on the floor. He said, "How dare you go over my head like this? You don't do that in the military." I wanted to say that I just did. But I didn't dare say that! He said, "What do you think you are going to accomplish? You will be back here in three weeks. Who is going to come out and sing with you? You are nothing but a corporal." I wanted to say that Jesus wasn't anything but a carpenter either, but I didn't say that. I said, "Sir, I am supposed to report there day after tomorrow." He said, "I know when you are supposed to report, but I am going to get all I can out of you before you go. I want you to help me police up this area." He had me working under the barracks and cleaning everything as punishment.

I had a stack of music under my bunk, and every night I would go over to the chapel and practice that music when all the other guys had gone to sleep. I knew that I was going to direct the chorus, and I knew how I wanted it to sound. I couldn't wait to get started. The chaplains were so amazed that this had happened. They had an old bicycle with just bare wheels, and I rode that bicycle to every telephone pole and every theater on the base, putting up signs, "A Base-Wide Male Chorus to Tour the USA." You couldn't go to a theater without seeing the announcement. I set a cut-off date, with two weeks to audition.

I had about two hundred men audition from which I chose fifty. The first guy who came in to audition was Gerald S. from Georgia, and he had a beautiful tenor voice. He had been in the Berry College Choir, and had graduated from there. I thought, *If they are all like this, we are going to have one great chorus!* Seventy-five percent of those men were college graduates. After the Korean War started, many of them were deferred long enough to graduate, and then they went into the service. They were smart guys because they were all in electronics, since Keesler was the electronics training center for the Air Force. The chaplain's directive was that they would be excused from whatever they were doing to rehearse three days a week from 3:00 till 5:00. That was six hours of rehearsal on government time, and it was only natural that a guy would like to get out of his work, and come over and sing. What a deal.

Three or four of the chaplains came to the first rehearsal, and were very proud. They had debated all around the clock about what to call the group. I said, "What do you call vanilla flavoring?" They said, "Vanilla flavoring." I said, "Yes, you call it what it is. This is a male chorus—not a glee club, not the Keesler Chorale." I said, "You call your hand, a hand, why don't you call it by what it is? But don't call it a glee club, this is far beyond a glee club." So they named it the Keesler Air Force Base Male Chorus. The first rehearsal was September 17, 1952, so the fiftieth anniversary was last year.

General Powell sent word to me that since he had done his part, he would expect a concert in a month. I sent back word that we would be ready. He said that he was going to make it a command performance, which meant that all the personnel who worked under him must attend. The theater was packed with people. The male chorus did most of that concert by memory. You see, I didn't wait until I got to Junaluska to start memorizing music. I wanted to show that our group was far above the average group. After that concert people stood and cheered for the longest time. They couldn't believe that a group that had been together not quite four weeks, was singing with that kind of sound. I remember a captain came up to me and said, "Draper, I was amazed at that sound, but I have a suggestion for you. When you go to take a bow, take a bow! You almost apologized for the bow, trying to be so nonchalant—like you didn't want to take the credit. Don't fumble around, because if the audience tells you they appreciate it, let them know that you appreciate their applause." I have never forgotten that.

In the audience that night was a famous director from Minneapolis, who had traveled around the world conducting orchestras. He wrote a letter to the general when he got back, telling him what an unbelievable potential he had in the male chorus and in me. He said, "I hope you will find a way to keep that guy Draper, because that group is going places." They printed the letter in the local newspaper. Somebody from the television station WDSU, in New Orleans, was at the concert, and they wrote the general a letter and said, "We heard your male chorus, and we want to know if they would be a guest on our show with Connie Boswell." The general said, "Absolutely. What do we have to do?" We took a bus from the base, drove the group to New Orleans, and sang two numbers by ourselves and two numbers with Ms. Boswell. There was a guy who wrote a column every day for the New Orleans paper, and he wrote that this newly organized male chorus was really great. So we had a fantastic start.

About two weeks after we organized the male chorus, I had gone into the chaplain's office and talked to Col. Roy Reynolds, the wing chaplain, about singing the *Messiah*. He said, "Glenn, don't talk about the *Messiah*. People in the military don't like that kind of music." I said, "I am in the military and I like that kind of music." He said, "Yes, but you haven't been here long enough to know the difference between military people and civilian people." I replied, "If you take a civilian and a military person, undress them, and put them in the middle of a field, can you tell me which is which?" He said, "Get out of here and go do the *Messiah* if you have to." So I went out again to put posters on all of the telephone poles, "Keesler

Mixed Chorus to be Organized. The *Messiah* to be Presented on December 12." People wondered where I was going to get the women, but I said, "If you have that many men, wives, nurses, and WAFs will come out of the woodwork." I went to squadrons and made announcements, I went to the hospital and talked to nurses, I called Gulf Park College (which was on the other side of Gulfport) and asked them to bring a busload of their girls from their choir. You won't believe how that took off. People were amazed that so many would come out to rehearse the *Messiah*. We had about thirty or forty tenors, fifty to sixty basses, and after adding the women, we had a great sound.

The next problem was an orchestra. I recruited as many people as I could get from the band. Some of them had been my enemies, like a flute player, David, who had really ridiculed me to the nth degree, and a clarinet player who was down on my case. You know what happened? They ended up playing in the performance. It was on NBC, not the first year, but the next. We needed strings. Dave F., a man I bought music from, was a dear friend to me. Dave was in New Orleans, and he owned Wuerlein's Music Company. I asked if he could help get some string players. He said, "Why don't you start at the top, go to the New Orleans Philharmonic?" and I said, "Why don't you ask them?" He got the general manager on the telephone, and said, "Glenn Draper has organized an Air Force choir. He is buying a lot of music from me, and his choir is doing the *Messiah* for the first time. Since they are in the Air Force, is there any way you could help them out?" You know what the general manager said? "We won't charge you a thing. We have a fund for something like this, if you don't charge admission. All you have to do is feed and transport us." I asked the wing chaplain to get a bus to pick up the musicians and feed them while they were on the base, so the orchestra didn't cost us a cent.

Roger Hinkley and I had to figure out some way to build a stage for the orchestra. Base services told us that they didn't have any risers and to get lost. We were determined to find a way, so we went to a lumberyard in Biloxi, bought some two by fours, and convinced them to furnish some supports, then we made a stage. The chaplain, on the night of the first performance, stood on the stage and introduced the general, who said, "I am asking Airman Glenn Draper if he and the chorus and orchestra will kindly present another performance tomorrow night, since there are more people outside than were able to fit in our auditorium." There were an estimated twelve hundred people outside who never got in. He said, "I hope you will consider my request." Well, you always consider a general's request. We did two performances, and I was in hog heaven. I couldn't believe how all these things could happen to me. I thanked God over and over. I remembered being in the berth on the train that night when I said, *Don't leave me now. And now you have helped me with the chorus and the* Messiah.

John E. Fowler
In chaplain's office, Keesler;
his late wife sang in Keesler Mixed Chorus and UTC choirs

When I left basic training and shipped out to Keesler Air Force Base on Thanksgiving weekend 1951, I was assigned to the chaplain's section and I was there when Glenn arrived, and was assigned to duty in the band section. Since he was assigned to the band but worked in the chaplain's section, there was some jealousy between the wing chaplain and the squadron commander of the band. I remember in December when Glenn conducted the *Messiah* for the first time, it was a tremendous success. After the program was over a lot of people came up to shake hands with Glenn and tell him how great it was. Then everybody made way for the guy who had two stars on his shoulders. Major General James F. Powell came up and shook hands with him and congratulated him and told him how glad he was that they had something like this on the base. From then on, Glenn could do no wrong.

AFTER CHRISTMAS, some choir members talked together and then they said to me, "Glenn, we can't stop now, this chorus is great." One lady who was an alto soloist asked, "Why don't we do the *Elijah*?" So we set our sights on doing *Elijah* around Easter time. I remember a young couple who came up after the first rehearsal and said, "Glenn, we love singing with you and this group, but if you don't mind we will forego the *Elijah* and come back when you do the *Messiah* next year." I told them, "I will make a deal with you. If you will come to three more of my rehearsals, and you still want to back out, it is my fault. But if you stay, then it means you will be sold on the *Elijah*. I have never conducted the *Elijah*, but I am not about to back out. It is a tremendous work, and if you stick with me, I will be so grateful." I remember looking at them, especially the lady, during the singing of "His Mercy on Thousands Fall," and tears were just pouring down her face. She hugged my neck and said, "Glenn, I wouldn't have missed this for anything in the world. I have just been out of college a year, and here I am doing all these great musical works."

THE SPRING OF 1953 when I took leave, I told Bob Davis that we must get this program on a network radio broadcast out of New York City. We took some tapes from the wing chaplain's office, and Bob and I thumbed to his home in North Carolina, then to my home in Virginia, and then on to New York City.

We spent three days trying to find the right person at Mutual Broadcasting, CBS, or NBC. On the second day, we were on the second floor of the Radio City Music Hall, and I noticed a door sign that read "NBC Radio Productions," and I told Davis that this was where we were supposed to go. We went barging in the door right into a man's office. He said, "My secretary is down the hall, go see her." I said, "My name is Glenn Draper and this is Bob Davis, and we have a great recording of a male chorus we want you to hear." He said, "You need to go see my secretary." I said, "We only have one more day here." He asked, "Can you go down and see my secretary?" I said, "I will, if you promise to see me." He looked at me and he thought, *This man is really in earnest,* and he said, "The only time I have tomorrow is at 8:00 in the morning. My business appointments start at 8:30, just leave that tape with my secretary."

Bob Davis and I came in the next morning at a quarter of eight, and we heard the sounds of the male chorus coming out of the office. I said, "Bob, I didn't know our chorus sounded that good!" It was incredible. I had never heard it played on big speakers like that. Bob Wogan greeted us and asked, "Where has this group been?" I told him we were organized last fall. He said, "Do you think you can handle a radio broadcast, at 10:00 every Sunday morning? I have a slot open for fifteen minutes." I said, "I think we can arrange that." He asked, "What is your general's name?" I said, "Don't call him, he has no idea that we are up here with these tapes. Those recordings are military, and I didn't get permission to take those out of the offices." He asked, "Well, how am I going to reach him?" So he finally figured out to go through WDSU in New Orleans, and let them call the general. They would know of the Keesler Male Chorus since we had done some broadcasting earlier.

On my first morning back, the wing chaplain walked in my office and said, "Welcome back from your leave. I have an interesting message here, for you and me to report to the general's office at 11:00. Do you know anything about that?" I mean, my teeth were shaking, I was just scared to death. I knew the general had found out what we had done, and he was going to reprimand me, and he might take the chorus away from me. I didn't have any idea what it was about! We walked in his office, and there were colonels, majors, and sergeants milling around. He called us all to attention and said, "I want to congratulate the wing chaplain and Airman Draper. We don't know how this happened, but NBC wants to carry our male chorus every week." He said, "Of course, you know we are going to do it. Aren't we men? Aren't we, Glenn Draper?" "Yes sir, we are going to do that." To this day, believe me, they have never known that we had thumbed all the way up there and back. You can do a lot of things in the world, if you don't care who gets the credit. General Powell arranged military buses to take the male chorus to New Orleans, twice a month, and we would record two programs every Saturday. Bob Davis, my roommate, started writing the script for it, and James Oxley, a pianist who is now directing musicals in New York, was my accompanist and played the celesta.

Between numbers that Mr. Gay Batson, NBC radio announcer, would introduce, James played the celesta. Most of the broadcasts had four numbers between the beginning and the closing. We always closed with "Lord Guard and Guide the Men Who Fly."

I received a call from the Pentagon one day, soon after that, and they said, "Draper, are you the one who directs the Keesler Male Chorus?" I answered yes. "We were wondering where you came up with that piece, 'Lord Guard and Guide the Men Who Fly'?" I said, "It's in the old Army-Navy hymnal." I told them to look on page so and so, and they asked how I found it. I told them, "I was just looking through the hymnal and thinking how this would sound, and I started using it on our broadcast." They made that the official Air Force Hymn.

In the meantime, the general immediately promoted me to sergeant and the band director was all upset over that! But it doesn't matter whether he was upset or not.

John E. Fowler

Promotions were very hard to come by, and the captain of the band section wanted to save his promotions for his people. He wouldn't even consider Glenn for promotion because Glenn didn't work for him. Yes, technically, he was still under the band. He reported to the captain over in the band squadron, but his duty was assigned each day to the wing chaplain, who was a lieutenant colonel. Colonel Hanna would have promoted him in a moment, except for the fact that he didn't have any say so in it, so to speak. He could talk to the squadron commander in the band, but he couldn't tell him what to do. So Glenn was sitting there in no man's land, working for this guy, but the other guy is the one who has to promote him and he couldn't get promoted. This went on for the longest time. Finally, one day, the word came down from General Powell, "I think it would be a good idea if you put this guy in for another stripe, this is sort of an embarrassment to the Air Force." When the general thinks that you ought to do so and so, you don't think too much about it—you just do it.

THE GENERAL CALLED me in his office and said, "I am invited to go to a premier showing of an Air Force event at Samson AFB." I replied that I had been stationed there. He said, "Would you kindly go in my place?" I asked if I could take someone with me. Bob Davis couldn't go, so I took Roger Hinkley. He was the one who did the production work for me and was a good writer. So we got on a B-25 at Keesler and flew to Washington, D.C. Over South Carolina, the bomb bay doors flew open and cold air was rushing in, so we had to make an emergency landing. They tied the doors up with ropes.

You can imagine how cold it was back there. When we got into Washington, it was snowing. We were going to Samson, so we hitched a ride on another B-25 that took us up to Rochester, New York, and then we thumbed over to Samson. We checked in, and the next night attended the performance.

After that, we had two more days before we had to be back at Keesler, so we hopped a flight to New York City and went to Bob W.'s office where I asked, "Bob, how is it going?" He said, "Glenn, we have just had tremendous response to the broadcasts." I said, "I have a great project for you, the *Messiah*." He said, "Nearly everybody and his brother in San Francisco, or St. Louis, or Boston want me to carry the *Messiah*, and I can't." I said, "You ought to carry us, because those folks are just from those places, but we are from everywhere. We have blacks, whites, yellows, every race you can imagine, and we don't come from any one place, we are America." You know what he did? He carried the *Messiah* because of that argument. He sent Ben Grauer, with NBC, down to do the broadcast. Keesler Air Force Base couldn't believe that NBC was carrying their Keesler AFB performance of the *Messiah* that had only been done one time before in the history of the base.

John E. Fowler

Once Glenn's male chorus began to travel throughout the Air Force, it took quite a bit of preparation. We were sending out interoffice memos to do this and do that, and we had to get transportation arranged. Now, the guys who were outside of the chaplain's section really thought that they had a Korean War to fight, and they weren't worried about somebody going to sing. The mess hall got involved in it, with forty box lunches for the guys, and a lot of details to take care of. What it boiled down to was that this was such an unusual type of situation that it needed to be handled by somebody with some authority. I became the NCOIC [Non-Commissioned Officer In Charge] of the section at one point, but I couldn't call over to the mess hall and say, "I need forty box lunches, or I need a pickup truck to pick up band instruments." So, the tail was wagging the dog. Glenn had a lieutenant colonel being his errand boy, getting all these jobs done for him, because it took somebody with that kind of rank and pull to get things done.

AT THAT SECOND performance, Major General Charles I. Carpenter, who was chief of Air Force chaplains, flew down from Washington, D.C., to hear it. He was a Methodist minister and singer before he went into the service, and he loved the chorus. He was the one who came up to me and said, "Glenn, I am going to dedicate a little chapel up in North Carolina, and I want you to bring your singers and sing at the dedication. I will send a couple of planes to pick you up." He just snapped his fingers and we went flying on the third of July 1954, to Lake Junaluska to sing at the dedication of the chapel. Then on July 3, 1955, we went back and did another concert. That was when I was asked to come to Lake Junaluska and work during the summer. It had been so hot at Keesler, it was nice with those cool mountain breezes blowing when we passed through Canton and all the guys were singing on the bus, "Let There Be Music From the Fruited Plains."

I have never forgotten the sound of those guys on that bus singing— everybody had their windows down. We got there that evening, had a rehearsal, and ate dinner. After dinner, a guy named Charles Poole (who had one of the lowest bass voices I have ever had in a choir, and who just retired this past year as a Methodist minister) was the first one through the cafeteria line, and he asked the girl taking up tickets for a date. They started dating, and he ended up marrying her. I remember that concert, it was a beautiful, cool Sunday afternoon on the Fourth of July, and those forty-four men stood up and sang "The Army Hymn," "The Navy Hymn," "God Bless America," and everything patriotic you could think of. I know the sound in the chapel was unreal. That night, we did a whole concert in the auditorium for the people who had come, and that is how I got started at Lake Junaluska.

***

Sara Smith Youngblood
Lake Junaluska Singer for ten years;
noted soloist; church choir director for many years

I remember shortly after coming to the lake as a Junaluska Singer, Glenn was telling us about his past and that he was the originator and director of the Keesler Air Force Base Male Chorus, and they were on the *Ed Sullivan Show*, and I remember vividly seeing that chorus on TV. I don't know how old I was, but I remember seeing them in ranks across the stage, and it just thrilled me to no end to think that Glenn had been the director. I can't remember what they sang, but I remember seeing that moment, and I thought, *What a small world.* I had been so impressed by that, and then here he was.

***

THAT MALE CHORUS took me a lot of places. Jimmy Stewart and June Allison were in the motion picture *Strategic Air Command*, and we sang for the premier showing of that movie in many cities all across the United States. That is when I saw my name in lights! "Famed Keesler Chorus directed by Glenn Draper." I was twenty-five or twenty-six years old, and I could do no wrong. People loved us everywhere, and girls flocked to the rehearsals since all these guys were coming in. We flew into Chicago one time, and on a Sunday morning three people from the Air Force Academy that was just being built then, had breakfast with me. They said, "We have a project we want you to consider. Would you consider being the first director of the choir at the Air Force Academy in Colorado Springs?" I said, "What are the requirements? Would I have to stay in the Air Force?" They said, "Yes, that is one of the requirements." I told them, "As much as I appreciate your offer, I am thrilled to death, honored, flattered, but I want to get out of the service. I would rather be my own boss with what I do. I love orchestras, and if a symphony job came by or a college position, I would want to be able to do that too." They said that they certainly understood.

In the middle of all that we were doing, I was accepted at Columbia University in New York to get my master's degree. The Colombia Artists Series had talked to me about traveling under their name and doing concerts across America, like the Robert Shaw Chorale or Fred Waring. That is when I had a fateful dream in May, before I was to get out of the service in September. I had a dream in which I saw myself as an old man. I can still see this home, beautifully lit inside, a fireplace burning, and a mirror over the mantel. My wife had gone to the door to tell our guests goodnight. I had just finished saying to them, "It was good to see you, take care, and we will see you next time," and I turned around with a smile still on my face, and I saw my receding hairline and gray hair in the mirror, and I looked out through the window and there were two cars in our garage. I thought, *How in the world did I get two cars?* That was an unbelievable luxury in those years. *How did I get this home?* It came like a thunderbolt. God said, *You left me out of your life,* and it startled me. My expression of joy became one of unbelievable agony and sorrow and I prayed, *Oh God, that can't be!* My mind went back to when I was nine years old, when I had knelt in that church and promised God that I would serve him, and I hadn't done that. I said, *Oh God, will you ever forgive me? Most of all, you have to let me start over. I will never get in the driver's seat again. If you will open the doors I promise I will walk through. Please let me start over. I haven't prayed enough, and I haven't read the Bible enough.* It was almost like, *I've got it made now, Lord, I think I can handle it from here.* I didn't think about New York not being religious, or the Columbia Artists Series being in the secular world!

When I woke up, sitting in the middle of the bed, I went to the window and looked outside and saw the moon shining, and I promised God that I would never get in the driver's seat from that day forward and that I would live my life for Him, and I didn't care if my name was ever in lights. I said, *Lord, if you will open the doors, help me to have sense enough to walk through.* The following Wednesday night I was at choir rehearsal over in Gulfport, Mississippi. I used to take six or eight guys with me in my car and during the rehearsal that night, someone came in with a telephone message and gave it to me. I stuck it in my pocket and continued on rehearsing, and when we were in the car going back to Keesler, Leo Throbridge, a fine baritone from Kentucky, asked me about that message that someone gave me. I told him that I would call tomorrow. He said, "Pull over right by that filling station, and call that number. If they had wanted to talk to you tomorrow, they would have waited till tomorrow to call you." So I pulled my car over and called, and the person said, "Glenn, I am so glad you called. We just had a committee meeting and we want you to be one of the judges for the State of Mississippi Choral Festival, being held in about two and a half weeks." I said, "Sure I will." My mind went immediately to my promise of, *Lord, if you will open the doors, I will walk through.*

I went to the festival, and guess who walked in? A man named Dr. Travis Shelton. I said, "Dr. Shelton, where are you from?" He replied, "I am from Southern Methodist University (SMU) in Dallas, and I have had a lot of great reports on your work here." He asked me if I was married, and I said, "No, I am still happy." I used to give that answer, and people would laugh! He laughed, and said, "What are you going to do when you get out of the service?" Before I could answer that he said, "I understand that you performed *Elijah* and the *Messiah*, with your male chorus. If you can do that you can direct anything." I said, "I hope so, I want to give it a try." He asked again, "What are you going to do when you get out of the service?" I said, "I am going to New York to be with the Columbia Artists Series and to attend Columbia University to get my master's." He said, "Let me give you some advice. I went to Columbia University and I got lost in the shuffle. That is exactly what is going to happen to you. We will give you a full assistantship and pay you a salary. We need a graduate assistant next year because Charles W., who has been our graduate assistant, is graduating this year." I said, "Dr. Shelton, I have got to work in a church." You see, that dream was still fresh in my mind. He said, "Well, let me look around. You will not regret coming to SMU, we have the prettiest girls in the world. I guarantee you will meet somebody there, and that you will fall in love." I was then twenty-six years old.

4

Can You Spell
MISENHEIMER?

1955–1960

Every performance is a new day.

~Jean Hanlin
Mrs. Hanlin and her late husband have been friends and significant supporters since 1968

SOUTHERN METHODIST UNIVERSITY

After I arrived at Southern Methodist University, I was offered the job of organizing and directing the Dallas Male Chorus, many of whom were policemen. Maury J., who was the organist at the Munger Place Methodist Church, worked at the police department, and he was able to recruit there. Our rehearsals were held at the church where I was choir director. Also on the bulletin board at school was a listing, "Needed—Choir Director for the Telephone Bells," and that intrigued me. They rehearsed twice a week, Tuesday and Thursday afternoons, on company time, and paid fifty dollars per rehearsal. I applied for the job and got it. Then someone else I had known in school at Indiana University had moved to Texas and was the leading producer of commercials for radio and television in Dallas. He found out I was an Indiana graduate and remembered me, so he called SMU and left word for me to call him. When I called he said, "I would love to get your help sometime. If you have some singers and soloists, I can get you some jobs for commercials." So I would get four singers, or three singers and a piano player, and I would write arrangements for them. Singers would make fifty dollars on a Saturday morning, which was a lot of money in those days. I would probably make a hundred.

I was having lunch with Dr. Travis Shelton one day, and he said, "Glenn, I have no idea how you do all this. You have already made some guys so envious. You came in and started dating Count Mayes's daughter, you have been on the *Ed Sullivan Show,* and you have all these jobs; and other students come to me and they want to know how you do it. I tell them, 'Glenn is just a go-getter. He is a good example for you to follow. Why don't you be a go-getter?' Some people don't want to see you succeed unless they succeed themselves."

One of the incentives for me was that I sat right behind Lounelle in the SMU choir. I thought that this girl, among all the girls I had ever dated, had unbelievable possibilities for what I needed. At twenty-seven, you have a much better idea of what you want out of life than you ever did at twenty or twenty-one. It was the first time it ever dawned on me that I probably needed to meet somebody and get married. I had never really thought of that—ever. The first time that I felt really comfortable, I asked her out on a date, but she had other plans. Finally, I got her to agree to sing in my church as a soloist, but I couldn't pick her up in the old Dodge I had. So I traded it in on a Saturday night before I had a date with her the next morning. I bought a brand-new white Buick on credit, and I picked her up the next morning in that car. It was black and red inside. We went to church, and after church, we went out for lunch at a spaghetti place. It was the fall of the year, the air was cool and fresh, some of the leaves were turning on the trees, and we didn't get back till about four or five that evening. I had to get back to the church that night for the Sunday evening service.

The First Methodist Church choir was singing the Mozart *Requiem* at Baylor University in Waco, so I asked Lounelle if she would ask her director, Glen Johnson, if I could go along and sing in it. She came back and said, "Glen would love to have you." I didn't know whether I had a date with her or not; but when I got on the choir bus, she was sitting with a girl-friend and I ended up on the very back seat. Any time anybody would get up and go forward to get a sandwich or something, I would go jump in their seat and start talking to the person next to them, and I ended up right behind her before we got to Waco. When we got off the bus, I carried her robe and helped her put her robe on. We had a warm-up, it's a big choir, I'm talking about maybe 120–130 voices. The soprano section was in the front of the choir and I was in the bass section, up on the side. Just before the performance started, I looked over towards her and she turned and smiled at me. It was the most wonderful smile I had ever seen on anybody, anywhere. I melted. I managed to sit by her going back, and we talked the whole time. When we got back I told her I would be happy to take her home, but she said someone was coming to pick her up. I didn't know that someone was her daddy.

At school about a week later, she said, "I want to ask you a question. Our sorority has a big fall party at one of the hotels downtown, and my mother and father are supposed to be chaperones. Would you be my date and meet my parents?" I wanted to say, "Are you sure you have the right guy?" She had boyfriends like you wouldn't believe. I told her I would be thrilled to death to meet them. So I went to that party—I have the picture upstairs on my wall of Lounelle, her mother and father, and me at that party. Rather than stay inside and dance (where all the guys break in and you might only get to dance with the girl you came with one time) I said, "Why don't we go outside and get some fresh air?" We went outside to my new Buick, and I turned on the radio at just the right time while the Keesler Male Chorus was broadcasting on NBC. I told her that was my group. My stock went up 300 percent as she heard that group sing with such a sound. I sat there and cried and told her how much I missed those guys and that this was what I had done for four years in the service. We left when the broadcast was over and window shopped downtown, then went back to the dance later. Her parents were still there. She said, "Mother, you have never heard such a chorus in your life like Glenn's chorus that I just heard on NBC." That sure caught their fancy.

We continued to date, and at Christmastime I drove 1,200 miles to Virginia and told my mother that this would be the last Christmas that I would ever spend without Lounelle. I knew she was the one, absolutely. Returning to Dallas, I drove nonstop through the night, got back about half past seven in the morning, took a shower, called her on the phone, and went over to her house immediately. At noon, her dad was watching football games with a whole lot of other people, so Lounelle and I went driving through the countryside, and the further I drove the more I knew this girl was the one.

Spring came and she changed her major to speech and drama so she could go on the choir tours. If she hadn't done that, she couldn't have been in the SMU choir the second semester. So we went on a tour, all over North and South Carolina, Georgia, Tennessee, and Arkansas. I would direct certain numbers with the choir on that tour, since I was the graduate assistant director of the group. When we returned, the Dallas Federation of Music Clubs invited me to conduct their big spring musical choir. People from church choirs all over the city of Dallas came together and made up a huge choir. I was thrilled to do that. Lounelle helped me organize the choir, and helped me write letters about rehearsals. The night of the performance, the church was packed with people, and at the break time I had the men sing a couple of numbers during the offertory. When I finished directing the men, I had everybody stand to start the second part of the performance. Lounelle had been in the soprano section on the front row in the corner and she wasn't there. I thought maybe she had gone to the rest room or something; the second number, she wasn't there; the third number, she wasn't there. When it came to the final number, there was no Lounelle.

Of course, I was elated with the joy of doing that performance, and people said, "Glenn, that was a great job. We are so proud of you." I wanted so much for them to meet Lounelle, but I couldn't find her anywhere. I was mad as a hornet, and wondered, *What in the world has happened to that girl?* I went home, but didn't call her. She had walked out, so I wasn't going to call her. Early the next morning, the telephone rang. "Hey, Honey, how are you doing?" I said, "Where in the world did you go last night?" She said, "I had a date." "A date?! You had a date with me!" She said that I hadn't asked her for a date. She said some other guy asked her for a date and since she didn't have one, he made arrangements to pick her up at 9:00 P.M., so at 9:00 she just excused herself and left. I said, "You helped me with all this work, you typed letters and other things." She said, "Yes, that's right, but you never asked me for a date." I told her that we had to meet. We met at her sorority about noon and talked. I said, "I have never dated a girl steady in my life. We have two and a half weeks before school is out. If I promise, will you promise that we will go steady for that time?" We promised. I had never asked a girl to do that in my whole life. We went steady, and it seemed like we were closer then for some reason. Maybe it was because I had almost lost something, and it made me appreciate her more.

Lounelle knew I was leaving to go to Lake Junaluska, but she didn't know anything about the place. She just knew it was in the mountains of North Carolina somewhere. I made her promise that she would come to see me in the summer. I had finished all my graduate work at SMU in one year. They told me I would never do it, but I said, "It is not a matter of me doing it, I have to do it. I will do it, because I will be the director of music at the World Methodist Center next summer." One of the teachers laughed and said, "We haven't had a graduate student here in a long time, as our assistant, who passed theory." I told her, "I can pass theory and I grant you I will." At age twenty-seven I had a lot more motivation than I did when I was younger, and I knew a lot more questions to ask. That was one of the advantages of being out of school for a while and then coming back and getting a master's degree.

THE FULFILLMENT OF A DREAM COME TRUE: LAKE JUNALUSKA

IN 1954 AND 1955, the Air Force flew the Keesler Male Chorus to North Carolina to sing for the Fourth of July activities held at Lake Junaluska Methodist Assembly. We sang for the dedication of the Memorial Chapel on the Fourth of July 1954. We had never seen so many pretty girls in all our lives. They followed us around and came to a reception held for us.

After the worship service on Sunday morning, Dr. J. W. Fowler came up and said, "I feel led to offer you the job as music director here when you get out of the service." The memory of that dream that I had in May was very vivid in my mind. I said that I would pray about it. On Labor Day 1955, the Keesler Male Chorus was singing some concerts at Ridgecrest, the Baptist conference center near Asheville. My mother and father had come down to see me, and we drove over to Junaluska where I signed a contract for one hundred dollars per week, beginning June 1956—the rest is history.

EARLY LAKE JUNALUSKA

AFTER GRADUATION AT SMU, I drove down to Keesler Air Force Base to see some friends and to visit the male chorus and to see Roger Hinkley. I spent a day or two there, and then drove nonstop all the way to Lake Junaluska. I arrived about two in the morning and everything was closed, so I parked under a tree on the street, right beside the lake in front of the Terrace Hotel, and went to sleep. I woke up about seven, went over to the Gulf station which is not there now, washed my face, combed my hair, and went in the director's office and said, "I am ready to get started." The director showed me where my office would be, gave me some pads and pencils, and said, "Okay, I don't know what to tell you to do. We hired you to be the music director here, so get started." In the meantime, he had given me forty-five dollars a week per person to hire a quartet, so I had these four singers coming in that week and we began rehearsals.

That first Sunday there was a huge youth conference and I took out "The Hallelujah Chorus" and directed that with all those singers. We must have had seventy-five to one hundred singers in that choir. On Sunday mornings we [a volunteer choir] started to sing for the worship services, but there were no risers. I kept telling them that we had to have risers, but they didn't listen. One Sunday morning, I had people on tables, benches, everything you could think of, and one fell down during a prayer. The next week, we had risers.

That summer was very successful. The choir started growing on Sunday mornings. I would recruit people from all over to sing in it. Billy Graham was there that summer; Richard Nixon was there also. William Sangster, from England, whom Billy Graham called the world's greatest preacher, was there. It was just far beyond what I had expected.

LOUNELLE CAME UP TO SEE ME on August 17, 1956. Her plane landed at seven that night at the old airport in Asheville. She was the most beautiful lady I've ever seen when she got off of that airplane. She had on a cute little suit and hat, and she gave me a gift from her daddy, a shirt from his store. At eight I had to start the downbeat with a huge sing-a-long with the congregation. I had one hour to get back, change clothes, and the whole bit, with no super highways like there are now, but I made it. I have always been determined, if I set myself a goal, I will be there. You may have to drive a little fast, or you may have to pass someone on the right side or left side, but you will get there. So that was her first initiation to Lake Junaluska.

After being there two days, they needed somebody in the dining room to wait tables because one of the girls had to go back to school, so Lounelle took her place. The World Methodist Conference was in September, right after Labor Day, and I directed the music for that my first summer there. It was a huge choir, with people from everywhere you can imagine. I never heard "hallelujah" pronounced so many different ways in my life! We rehearsed on Sunday morning and, of course, the quartet was there to sing too.

Lounelle kept asking when she was going to get to go home. I told her, "I want to take you to meet my parents. I want you to know us, it is only fair. Before our relationship goes much further, it is very important to do that." So we drove all night long, and the next morning coming into Roanoke, I woke her up about five, and said you must see these mountains, they are the most beautiful mountains in the world.

My mother and father just fell in love with her, so I went down to a jewelry store and bought an engagement ring. I was going to give her the ring, but my brother Bill, said, "Let's go to Washington." So I thought, *I will give her that ring on the steps of the Capitol, or at the top of the Washington Monument, something special.* Just before we left, he said, "There is no need for us to take two suitcases, put all your things in my suitcase and we will take just one." I took everything out of the suitcase—except the ring! I left the ring in the pocket of the other suitcase, back in Roanoke, so I couldn't give her the ring. We were in Washington, and I couldn't tell her about the ring. So I thought, *I will give her the ring in church, then she can't say no until church is over.* The only problem was there were so many people on our bench that I couldn't get my hand in my pocket. I could feel the ring in my pocket, but there was no way for me to get it.

After lunch at home, my parents said, "Let's drive down to the old home place where Mother grew up." So we drove down there and we were looking in the parlor, and my dad said, "This is where your mother and I got married." We all went from room to room reminiscing, and then we walked to the barn. I told Lounelle, "Let's go back up to the house, I would love to see it a little more." So I took her in that same parlor and said, "I know your mother and dad have been asking you when you are coming back, but I have a very important question to ask you. Will you marry me?" She started screaming and yelling, and my parents came running in the room to see what was going on, and that was the announcement of our engagement. I gave her the ring on Sunday, and on Tuesday, the two of us left and drove to Pfeiffer College since I had to report for the job I had accepted there.

Barry Rogers
Program director, Lake Junaluska Assembly, 1965–1970;
executive director, 1985–1989

It has been my high privilege to know Glenn Draper and his family for forty of the fifty years he has headed up the music program at Lake Junaluska, and I treasure every moment of our friendship. He is indeed a dynamo— no, he's more than that—he's a spaceship blasting off the launching pad in every performance he directs! Glenn has always brought an incomparable energy level to his music, whether it be an oratorio or an old hymn, a love ballad or a patriotic tribute. And he, in turn, has touched the hearts of people all over the world. What a tremendous experience it is to see and hear and feel his amazing spirit and to rejoice even now that he still has plenty of rocket fuel to burn!

PFEIFFER COLLEGE, WEDDING

THAT FIRST SUMMER at Lake Junaluska, it was announced that I was looking for a job. I had forty-seven invitations from schools, churches, and community choruses. The World Methodist Conference took place that summer, and people from all over just came up and started talking to me. There were not a lot of people in the world of music who did what I did. If you went to school and majored in music, they didn't teach you how to direct congregational singing. I learned that in the quartet up at Marion College. There were a lot of people who majored in music, who learned the really highbrow stuff, but they didn't learn the down to earth "people" music. At Junaluska I had the chance to do that, and I did it in the Air Force for four years with a national radio broadcast every week. So the material that I followed and learned was just unbelievable. I had done the *Messiah* on NBC, so my credentials were very big, and that is why I had all these offers.

A man by the name of Dr. J. Lem Stokes came up to me one Sunday morning right after church, I can even show you where we were standing. He said, "I know where you are going next year—Pfeiffer College." I said, "Where in the world is Pfeiffer College?" He said, "It is not going to help you much, but it is in Misenheimer, North Carolina." I started laughing, and he said, "We have a saying at our school, if you can spell both of them we give you a full scholarship." I said, "I don't know if I can spell either 'Pfeiffer' or

'Misenheimer.'" Dr. Stokes said, "I want you to go over and see the school."
I said, "Well, I don't know if I will have time." He said, "I will take you over
there, it only takes about forty-five minutes. You see, I have an airplane!"
So he flew me in his airplane from the Asheville airport to Pfeiffer College.

It was summertime, and there weren't many students on that beautiful
campus. When Lounelle came up on August 17, he invited me to bring her
up to his house at Lake Junaluska, and he talked to her about Pfeiffer
College. He said to Lounelle, "By the way, I would love to have you teach
speech." She replied, "Dr. Stokes, we are not even engaged." He had
jumped the gun, thinking that we were engaged and that our marriage was
imminent. She had to explain to him that we were only dating, and he said,
"I'm sorry, I jumped too fast."

So the two of us left his house, and that particular night I didn't have
to be in the auditorium. Somebody else was leading the music, and they
were singing a hymn as we walked down by the swimming pool. I told
Lounelle that I had been praying about what job to take. I'd had offers from
Memphis, Nashville, Arkansas, Virginia—all over the place—but I couldn't
get Dr. Stokes out of my mind and I felt led to go to that college. I went
back up to see Dr. Stokes and I told him, and he said, "I will tell you what
we will do. I will give you a place to stay, your food won't cost you
anything, and I will pay you a salary. Can you be there to start on
September 20?" I told him that I had to be late because I was directing the
music at the World Methodist Conference. We left Roanoke right after our
engagement, drove to Pfeiffer, and spent the night in Dr. Stokes's home.
The next day I took Lounelle to Charlotte to catch the flight home and to
plan our wedding. I didn't see her until Thanksgiving, right before our
marriage.

════════════════════════════

Tommy Holmes and Jerry Thomas
Members of choirs, Pfeiffer College; organized Singing Men of America

Tommy and I were part of a quartet (Charlotteens) that started when we
were in the seventh grade. We sang all the way through junior high and
high school, and when we graduated from high school in 1956, we thought
about going to college, but I (Jerry) was undecided. The lead singer in our
quartet, Tony, said that he wasn't going to college, but the bass singer,
Jimmy, got a baseball scholarship to Pfeiffer College. I decided to follow
him and then Tom decided to go, so the three of us went off to Pfeiffer
College in the fall. We were there for one week during freshman orientation, and at the end of that week they were going to have a talent show.
We were just bound and determined that we were going to get Tony to
come to the college to sing in the talent show. We got in the talent show
and we got thirteen encores. When we went back to our dorms that night,

there were a lot of guys around our room talking about how we sang. They really liked what we did, and they were interested in singing too. I said, "Well, maybe we can get a male chorus started."

That night, before we went to bed, someone came to us and said, "Dr. Stokes, the president of the college, is in his office and he wants to see you." The four of us went to his office that night. (Tony was going to spend the night, and go back home the next day.) Dr Stokes said, "I understand that only three of you are enrolled in the school." We told him that was correct. He explained that Pfeiffer had just become a four-year college, and that they needed some kind of group to represent the college and sing around at different places. He wanted all four of us badly, in other words. The next day, my folks came down to see the campus for their first time and they gave Tony a ride home. When Tony got home, Dr. Stokes's Cadillac was sitting in his driveway and Tony's mother was packing his bag. He went after Tony, so they were really interested in our quartet. That Sunday night, Tony showed back up on campus, and we were thrilled to death and just elated that he was there.

The next day, I went to the head of the music department and asked about starting a male chorus since other guys were interested. He said there wasn't any money in the budget and that they weren't going to start a male chorus. So I said, "The president of the college is sure our friend, I will go to see him." I went to Dr. Stokes, and I told him about the men who were interested in singing in a male chorus and he said, "Just hold on, we have a new guy coming next month who started the Keesler Air Force Base Male Chorus, and he is very good." I don't even remember him telling me his name, but I had never heard of Glenn Draper anyway. Evidently, between that time and the time that Glenn arrived on campus, Dr. Stokes had talked to him about that incident, because when Glenn arrived at the campus he came straight to my room early one Saturday morning at maybe six o'clock. I came to the door and he said, "Are you the guy who is wanting to get a male chorus started?" I said, "Yeah." He asked, "Do you have some people interested?" I said, "Yeah," and he said, "Okay, we are going to have our first rehearsal tonight!"

I STARTED SCHOOL the next morning. I got up real early, about six, and got a yellow pad. First day on the job, I didn't have a choir to rehearse. There was a choir director of the Pfeiffer College Mixed Chorus, but I don't think he knew I was coming. I didn't even know who he was, but anyway, I set sail. Dr. Stokes asked, "What do you want?" I told him I wanted a male chorus and probably the choral union, and a big mixed chorus to do the *Messiah*. At half past six that morning, I was in the men's dormitory, waking up guys, listening to them in the shower. I didn't ask if they could sing, I just said, "We are going to have a meeting tonight of all the men, to be called the

Pfeiffer College Male Chorus." Some men showed up and the camaraderie in that group was great, you know how a group of guys are. They started laughing and having fun, and got that sound. I made sure I didn't rehearse too long, because I wanted to whet their appetite so they would come back the next time. That male chorus took off, and Dr. Stokes told them that by the end of that year he would put them up against any other college glee club. Those guys believed him. I didn't believe him, but they did.

That fall the *Voice of America*, whom my Keesler Male Chorus sang for when I was in the Air Force, chased me down at Pfeiffer College, and asked if I had a group that they could use on their Christmas broadcast. I told them that I had the Pfeiffer College Male Chorus and that they were tops. They asked if we could get up there to record. I asked Dr. Stokes, and I don't know where he found the money, but he rented a bus and our group of guys got on that bus and we went to Washington, D.C., and recorded a Christmas program for *Voice of America*.

We spent the night in a motel, and the guys had a ball. They were now a team. We then took a tour in January up to New York, and everywhere they went people said, "I have never heard a group like that." The pride those guys had in themselves and the camaraderie they had for each other was incredible. I have never seen anything quite like that. Then it was time to start the *Messiah* rehearsals, and I went to Baden, Albemarle, Salsbury, and all those little communities all around the area, and recruited people to come and sing in the *Messiah*. Some people had never heard of the *Messiah*, but they did recognize the "Hallelujah Chorus."

I have to tell you something about Pfeiffer College (now University). It is out in the middle of nowhere, and I used to say if you sneezed going through, you would miss it. It is about forty miles northeast of Charlotte on the way to Raleigh, and between Albemarle and Salsbury. The little town of Misenheimer is just a little community of a few houses, a railroad track, and a filling station. That is about it. So the men would rehearse from 6:30 till 8:00 at night because they had little else to do. It was an outing for them. Then on Monday nights when we had the Choral Union, where else could they go, besides staying home and watching TV? They sure didn't have many outside distractions, so people came. They didn't have to belong to a social fraternity or sorority, they belonged to the chorus and they were making contributions, and I was always taking them some place to sing. I never believed that a choir should stay home. If you served food in the kitchen, and nobody ever came to eat it, would you keep fixing food? The ironic thing is that most people still rehearse choirs like that in college. The thought of singing for anybody out in public never dawns on them, but what are they preparing for? Why don't they get out in the community?

I was so anxious to show off the male chorus that I scheduled a concert on the campus for the fall of the year, but I wanted to take them somewhere else to try them out. So I called the First Methodist Church in Baden and asked if we could sneak in there on a Sunday night and sing a program while nobody was around. These guys had never sung in public before, and before we sang on the Pfeiffer campus or went to Albemarle to do a concert, I wanted to prove to them that they could do it. So we went over to their small church, and when we got there, cars were lined up everywhere. I said, "What are all these people doing here?" The Baptist Church in town had heard that the male chorus was coming and they had canceled their Sunday night service. That is a big deal for the Baptists to do that. I didn't know that Methodist churches all around and the Pfeiffer College Board of Trustees were having a big meeting on the campus. When we came out, the church was packed with people and there sat every member of the Board of Trustees on the back row. I asked, "How did I ever do this?" I thought I was sneaking over here, where nobody knew we were coming. We did the concert while I was scared out of my wits, but I was also very excited and I tried to down-pedal it to the men because I didn't want to make a big deal out of it, or they might freeze! Somehow they got through it, and the trustees were amazed that the group was singing that well after just starting. I found out one thing, if you want to do something, don't tell anybody, just show up there and sing and get out. They had that place packed. That was the biggest happening in that area in a long time, I suppose.

Anyway, I started teaching, and I had the band that played for basketball games. I taught voice, music history, music theory, plus directed the male chorus and the choral union. The head of the music department was directing the mixed choir, so there developed a big rivalry between the Pfeiffer College Mixed Chorus that he had, and the male chorus that I had just started. The male chorus began to say immediately, "We sing better than you do." That's bad, because it started animosities between the groups and most of the guys in the mixed choir left and came to the male chorus. Of course, that made the girls unhappy who were in his choir, but that was only temporary.

THE TIME CAME for our wedding on November 24. On Tuesday night of that week, I directed the band at a basketball game. When I went out to my car, there was rice all over it and "Just Married" was everywhere on my car. I had to erase all that because I was driving to my parents' home that night.

I arrived in Roanoke about two in the morning, slept till five, packed up my mother and dad, my dear buddy and brother, Gene (who was going to be my best man at our wedding), and his wife, and headed out to Dallas. We ate breakfast in Bristol, then I drove all day long, came right through Chattanooga, and at nine we stopped somewhere in Arkansas to spend the night. The next morning I had them up at three, and we were in Dallas before noon. I was a guy wound up! The Mayeses were expecting us to get there on Thursday, but we actually arrived on Wednesday. We celebrated Thanksgiving Day, then had a rehearsal dinner and a wedding rehearsal, and then the wedding on Saturday night.

I had never seen 1,000 to 1,200 people come to a wedding. It was a huge affair because Mr. Mayes knew everybody in the world, and Count Mayes's only daughter was getting married. Lounelle and her father were extremely close. Bob Davis, my roommate in the Air Force, was in the wedding. Some of my other friends flew out and, of course, Gene and my parents were there, so it was quite an affair. I was just honored to be a part of that and to be in that wedding. The next morning we went back by the house and unloaded some of the things that we had put in the car because we couldn't take everything back to Pfeiffer. We met my parents at the airport the next morning, and they all flew back to Virginia, and Lounelle and I set sail on our honeymoon.

We went through New Orleans, Atlanta, Kings Mountain, Charlotte, and then back to Pfeiffer College. We stayed in the president's home for a couple of weeks until an apartment became available. Dr. Stokes was one of the dearest friends you ever saw in your life, and he couldn't do enough for us. He didn't charge us any rent for the apartment that he found. The whole time I was at Pfeiffer, I never paid any rent, and never paid for a meal on the campus. He paid for all of that and a salary. I don't know many teachers that he treated like that. I didn't say to him that I needed meals or anything. It was just his incentive to get us to move there.

Lounelle started teaching speech, and I have to tell you a funny thing. After we had been there maybe a week, President Stokes had a big party at his home, inviting people from the community and the faculty to come over and meet the new couple who had just moved onto the campus. We were in the receiving line, and people said, "Glenn Draper, we are glad to welcome you here, we hear you're going to be the new choral director." They asked, "Mrs. Draper, what do you do?" She replied, "I teach spaeeech," with her best Texan drawn-out pronunciation of "speech." She has never gotten away from that. I have laughed at that through all these years. The people there laughed also, but we fit in that community and became friends with a number of wonderful people and teachers.

The next year I took over the mixed chorus, the male chorus, and the choral union, and taught choral conducting, voice, band, and one class of music history. As time went on, we just fell more in love with those people, and the students were just incredible. They had so much pride.

We took two tours a year. One in January that was usually the male chorus, and one in March with the mixed chorus. If we went to New York with one, we went to Florida with the other. It became a great recruiting tool, and Dr. Stokes used that. He flew his airplane to many of the places where we would sing. He would go ahead, sometimes with a couple of students in the airplane with him, or sometimes Lounelle would fly with him, and he would say a welcome to the people who would come to the concerts. Both the male chorus and the mixed chorus had much pride in themselves, and it was a great place to start. We made a lot of friends there, and we have never forgotten them.

Dr. John Stokes
Sang in Pfeiffer College choirs;
father was president of Pfeiffer College; Ph.D. in humanities

I had been introduced to Glenn by my dad, but my first real introduction came when all of my family was at Junaluska, and I was told I was going to rehearse with the then all-volunteer "singers." I did not like my dad very much for being made to go, but what can I say, I was hooked on choral singing for life. I will always be grateful to Glenn Draper for that and for much more. Afterwards, I sang with Glenn in male and mixed choruses at Pfeiffer College and absolutely loved the quality of music we, as mostly untrained voices, were able to achieve. I'll never forget that when we went as a male chorus to perform in various churches, the first thing Glenn would do when entering a sanctuary would be to snap his fingers, checking the acoustics, which were usually poor. "The sound gets soaked up by the carpets," and sure enough, the risers would get placed farther down front. We could do some pianissimo sounds when the lyrics called for it, and Glenn did pay attention to the words and to our ability to sing the words so they could be understood. He's absolutely right. What's the point of having words if the audience can't understand them.

IN THE FALL of my third year there, I was in the president's office one day talking about something, and I had a telephone call from a Herman T. from the First United Methodist Church in Miami. He said, "I met you last summer at Lake Junaluska about 10:30 at night in a prayer service in the chapel after one of the big services. I was so impressed with you and your music, and we have an opening at our church for choir director. Are you interested?" I said, "I can't really talk to you right now, let me call you back, or call me back in fifteen minutes at my number." So he called back and he said, "We have an opening, are you interested?" I told him I wanted to stay in education, if possible. He said, "I understand the University of Miami is looking for a choral director. Do you mind if I put your name in the pot?" I said, "I'm not seeking it, but you do whatever you want to do."

About six months later, Dr. John Bitter, the dean of the music department at the University of Miami called me at Pfeiffer and said he had received a strong recommendation from Herman T., that he happened to know in the city, and wanted to know if Lounelle and I would consider coming down for an interview. I thought, *Wow, here is a way to get a free trip to Florida. We could have a great time, like an extended honeymoon,* and I said, "Sure, we would do it, but we can't come until school is out." He said, "That is okay. We probably won't make a decision until in the summer." So we flew down there and Herman T. met us at the airport. I went by to look at the church, but I wasn't at all pleased with it. I wasn't going to give up Pfeiffer College and Lake Junaluska for that. Then we went over to the university. It soon became apparent that John Bitter was an articulate, charming, educated, lovable, and very caring man. Lounelle and I went into his office, and he showed me a stack of applicants for the job. I said, "Well, you probably won't even consider us, but we want to have a good time." He took us to dinner at a great Italian restaurant and we had excellent food.

The next day Dr. Bitter introduced me to certain faculty members, and one of the people he introduced me to was the president of the university. He had told him, "This guy is a specialist with male choruses. His male chorus won first place in the military when he was in the Air Force, and they were on NBC for several years, and his performance of the *Messiah* was broadcast on NBC." The president said, "I do not plan to retire from this university until I see a male chorus on this campus." I said, "If I come, I guarantee you will have one, since I have done that a lot in my life." We went out to dinner again that night, and had a ball. John B. was very amicable. We had a good time at the dinner and we went back to the hotel, and he said, "By the way, drop by in the morning before you go on your flight, I would like to say good-bye to you."

Lounelle waited outside the next morning while I went in and told him, "I want to thank you, John, for your wonderful hospitality and the dinner last night. It was great meeting you, and I know you will make the right decision in getting your director. Good luck with that." I promise you, it never ever dawned on me that he would be offering me the job. He said, "Sit down for a minute. On behalf of the Board of Trustees, the president, and the music department, we are happy to offer you the position of director of choral activities at the university." I couldn't believe it and I sat there in utter amazement. I said, "Are you sure? I am startled that I am offered the job with that big stack you have right there. What about all those people?" John said, "I don't know what you did to him, but the president thinks you are our man!" Anyway, I said, "I can't tell you right now, you have to give me a couple of weeks."

We were going to Lake Junaluska that summer, and after we had been there about a week, the kids from Pfeiffer College woke us up one morning about six. Get up Drapers, we have driven all night long, we are starving, and you are sleeping half the day! They came in and we all ate breakfast, went hiking all over the mountainsides everywhere, and played tennis. They left about five, saying, "We will see you at school. We can't wait." I want you to know that it was that kind of friendship with those kids. Lounelle was not a lot older than those kids, and I wasn't really all that old either, I was twenty-eight or twenty-nine, something like that. So when they left, I looked at Lounelle and said, "Honey, we can't move to the University of Miami." She said, "I know it. Next year is their senior year, and we are going to New York on a tour. We can't do it."

She got out the typewriter and wrote, "Dear John Bitter, we are so grateful and honored with your kind invitation, but we cannot come this year because the freshman we started with will be seniors next year, and we don't feel that we can run off and leave them. Keep us in mind in the future years, and if we can ever be of help to you, let us know. But I know you will make the right decision on getting the right person. Sincerely, Glenn W. Draper."

Less than a week went by and we got this letter from Dr. Bitter who said, "I knew I wanted you at the beginning, and now I know I want you to come. If you can't come this year, I will get a substitute for you, if you will come the following year. We are going to build a new choral suite and a new symphony hall. The choral suite will be right beside the symphony hall, next to the band, and I would love to get your input to help us design the facilities." I had never had anybody say, "If you can't come this year, how about the following year?" He got a guy named Bill L. from a high school to direct the choir for that whole year until I came the following year. I told Lounelle, this must be the work of the Lord, because I never had anybody do that. We didn't say anything at all at Pfeiffer College about it until the next spring. One of the hardest things I had to do was talk to Dr. Stokes and tell him that we were going to move to Miami. He had been such a good friend and had done everything in the world for us. He said, "Glenn, I knew the day would come when this would happen, I just hoped it wouldn't be this soon. Is there any way I can talk you out of it?" I said, "No, I don't think so, considering that I felt the day would come when we would need to move to sprout our wings and grow, and the University of Miami with thirty thousand people will afford us a broader base." He said that he knew that! So it was sad for us to leave Pfeiffer College, and the choirs, and the students, but we had four wonderful years of memories. We went to Lake Junaluska that summer and the Pfeiffer College Choir sang there the first part of the summer for a big event, and we had a great time.

Dr. John Stokes

Another thing I really appreciated about Glenn's interpretation of the music: He said, "Most choirs have two volumes, loud and louder." He's right. Even some very prominent choirs have only two volumes. Would you sing a love song to your best girl loudly? Or for that matter a lullaby to the Christ child? No wonder the "poor babe awakes." I believe those are part of the lyrics from a Bach chorale I happen to like very much, but no church directors I have ever sung under have ever gotten it soft enough. Glenn would.

5

They
PAY US *to Go on*
OVERSEAS TOURS?
1960–1968

*Glenn Draper is the embodiment of singleness of purpose
and boundless energy, a powerful combination.*

~LINDA POWERS BILANCHONE
University of Miami singer, early 1960s

UNIVERSITY OF MIAMI SINGING GROUPS

In the fall of 1960, we moved to Miami, pulling a trailer down through
Georgia. We stopped and spent the night with Frank Harris, who was my
former roommate and a part of our quartet when we were at Marion
College. We then drove to Florida and spent the night with Carol Phillips,
a former Keesler Male Chorus guy who came by Lake Junaluska that past
summer, and is now a Methodist minister. When we got to Miami, we
really had no place to stay, but John B. had arranged for us to stay at the
Wesley Foundation because I knew the manager from Lake Junaluska. So
we stayed at the foundation for a few nights, but then a hurricane was
coming through, so we went over to someone's home and spent the night
there. We finally found a house to rent until we could find a house to buy
close to the campus.

Whenever I went to a new place, it seemed like I always started something. I met a fellow named Chink Whitten who was manager of the
student union at the University of Miami, who became a very dear friend.
He helped me print posters, and I put them all over the campus. He said,

"I want you to be a judge for the talent show that we are going to have on Friday night." School started the next Monday and I said, "I would love to do it. That would give me a chance to meet some prospective singers."

On Friday and Saturday people signed up for classes, so I put up a table with a sign, "Choir or Singers," and started recruiting people. I didn't just sit there, I got up and literally stood in front of people as they were coming: "Good morning, my name is Glenn, I am going to be directing some choirs." Some said, "I don't sing, I can't carry a tune in a bucket," they all had typical answers. There were some, however, who said that they were interested. "Let me get your name. What part do you sing? I want you to come for a general meeting next Monday afternoon at three in the choir rehearsal hall."

Down the way just a little bit was a guy named Bob C. in his ROTC uniform recruiting people for the ROTC. He came down to see what in the world I was doing, and I told him, "I bet you are a good singer." He said, "Yeah, I sing tenor." "Good, you ought to sign up." He brought his table and sat it beside mine, and now I had a committee of two people. He talked to people he knew on campus, whom I didn't know. Judy I. came along and said, "Hey Bob, what are you doing?" He said, "I am helping this fellow recruit people for the choir." Judy said, "I want to be in the choir," so Bob became a right-hand buddy to me. When I eventually went on my first overseas tour, Bob was my roommate. For two days he was a tremendous help with my recruiting.

At the talent show there was a guy named Jerry De Gennaro from Boston. Jerry was in that talent show and won first place as a comedian of the highest order. I went up to him as soon as the talent show was over and I said, "You must be in my choir, I don't care whether you can sing or not." He said, "I sang a little tenor in high school," and I said, "Come and meet me next week."

Jerry De Gennaro
University of Miami choirs, 1960–1968; architect; TV commercial actor

It was September 1960, when I arrived at the University of Miami, after the devastation of Hurricane Donna. Not a great impression of Florida for a New England boy. The university was not my first choice. My high school buddy and former combo band member talked me into it, convincing me that I could study architecture and maybe become an alternate percussion player with the university band. After my arrival, without me knowing, he signed me up for the Freshman Orientation Talent Show. I told him that I was here to be a serious architectural student and was not going to do any high school comedy antics. Well, I won first place.

One of the talent show judges was also new to the university. He was a choral music director named Glenn Draper starting a new program. After the talent show, Glenn Draper approached me about joining the new men's choir;

not knowing if I could sing a note, but, that was Glenn Draper. Weeks passed, and the band did not need me; so I wandered over to the choral room. After a while, I loosened up, doing some comedy antics with my new choral friends. All of a sudden, Glenn recognized me. He got excited and stood me in front of the class, and proceeded to tell us all about our future plans.

That following semester break, we were off touring all the way to New Orleans, singing in churches. After the religious program, we would all gather at the fellowship hall for some refreshments, and Glenn would have individual choral members entertain the congregation with guitar playing, comedy skits, and barbershop. "The Singing Hurricanes from the University of Miami" was born.

Glenn Draper was a great influence (on me). I decided not to transfer, spending the next eight years studying architecture and continuing to entertain around the world with the 'Canes. It is ironic that Glenn and I started and finished our stay at the University of Miami at the same time. Glenn, going off to Chattanooga, and me, in Miami, becoming an architect and a TV commercial actor.

Through the years Glenn and I kept in touch. Now living on the west coast of Florida with my wife and son, retired from acting, but continuing my architectural projects, I often reminisce about the past and how I got to this point in my life. Glenn Draper of course comes to mind, with all the travel experiences and the surround of music. Frank Lloyd Wright once said, "Architecture is frozen music."

THAT NEXT MONDAY, I had all these students come in and I told them, "I am going to have a group that I'm calling the choral union starting next Monday night, and we will do bigger things like the Verdi *Requiem*, or the *Messiah, Elijah*, etc. I am then going to start another choir called the Concert Choir. It will meet on Mondays, Wednesdays, and Fridays about three in the afternoon. We'll then have a Male Chorus meeting on Tuesday and Thursday afternoons at three."

From a 1965 University of Miami article

Glenn eventually had five musical groups at the University: the choral union, composed of two hundred fifty voices, who usually performed two or three oratorios a year, accompanied by symphony orchestras, and was open to faculty members and off-campus singers; the Concert Choir, a sixty-five-voice group that performed on the *Ed Sullivan* television show and made numerous appearances over the Armed Forces Radio Network; the male chorus, composed of forty voices, who sang at numerous conventions, on local television, and at halftime during football games; the

Madrigal Singers, a select group of fifteen singing Medieval and Renaissance period music; the internationally famous Singing Hurricanes who made six Defense Department overseas tours and appeared on the *Mike Douglas, Ed Sullivan, Perry Como,* and *Liberace* television shows.

I WENT RECRUITING at fraternity and sorority houses, since they are big at the University of Miami. I was in a whole new world then, compared to Pfeiffer College. When I went to Sigma Chi, I met Vic Bilanchone and he said, "I used to sing bass in a choir." I told him he had to come over and join me and that I needed his help by bringing maybe a half dozen guys or more. He showed up with about seven or eight guys, and when I auditioned them, they were good, except one of the tenors. I told him, "You are not really good enough to get in yet." He replied, "Do you mind if I just sit over there and listen?" I said that I didn't mind. Then he said, "Do you mind if I just hold some music and sit over here?" He came to all the rehearsals. Then he said, "Do you mind if I move up to where the tenors are so I can get a better feel?" I told him I didn't mind that. I had told him he had to start taking voice, which he did, and he improved a lot. The next semester I let him in the choir.

That spring we got an invitation from the government to tour the Northeast Defense Command, which included Greenland, Iceland, St. John's, and Newfoundland. Bill Brett came in one day and said, "I understand you are looking for a banjo player." I asked, "Do you play the banjo?" He said, "No, but I'm going to learn. If I learn, will that increase my chances to go?" I said, "I don't know, Bill, it might." Every morning when I came in at eight, he would be sitting in the corner playing that banjo. That guy became one of the best banjo players I have ever heard, and he also played the organ. He was a multi-talented guy. Bill became a very good buddy, and later became president of the choir.

Bill Brett
University of Miami singer, in the early 1960s;
choir director and church organist for many years

For a new Defense Department tour, Glenn needed a banjo to be played during the "State Salute" medley, as well as for a folk group for the then popular folk music sung in the '60s. I wanted to go on that tour. I didn't have a banjo, much less know how to play one. You may have heard Glenn's motto, "whatever it takes," leads to dreams coming true. My Aunt Ethel had a banjo mandolin she gave me since it wasn't being used. I took it to Allen Reskin of Allegro Music in Coral Gables. He agreed to install a five-string neck on the banjo for twenty-five dollars, which was one week's living allowance for me at college at the time. As I was going out the door with my remade instrument, Allen gave me a book, *How to Play a 5-String Banjo,* by Pete Seeger. I thought my practicing could serve a double purpose, so I practiced outside Glenn's office door every day! To this day, I don't know how he took that abuse! Ten days later, I was playing in front of two thousand troops in Thule, Greenland!

BILL MET BETTY in the choir. In fact, the two of them invited Lounelle and me to go to Germany about five or six years ago, for their thirtieth wedding anniversary. They said, "This is where we met and started dating when you were with us, and we want to know if you and Lounelle would meet us in Munich, Germany. We will rent a car and go back to some of the places where we stayed before." We did and we had a ball.

IN THOSE YEARS, Lounelle wasn't a whole lot older than the singers, and we had a lot of parties at our house. Many of the kids who attended the University of Miami didn't have a home to go to. The mother lived in California, the dad lived in Maine, or their child was a member of their staff whom they paid a salary from the daddy's business just to go to school. They would come to our house, and we had lots of cookouts for them or Christmas parties and Christmas caroling, so they eventually became a team. The only way I have a choir is to make it like a family, a team. The University of Miami was far different from any place I had ever been. I learned a lot about people at the University of Miami because only a third were Protestant, about another third were Jewish, and the others were Catholic or agnostic. I learned to love all those people. We accepted each other in spite of our differences. Our differences were not our major problem. They could sing, and that was great.

BEFORE I WENT TO SEE the provost about getting money to take our first tour, the university had never had a choir travel anywhere. I arranged to go back through Keesler Air Force Base and New Orleans, because I knew many people there. I got the American Guild of Organists to sponsor a concert in New Orleans. I got a music club in Pass Christian, a group in Gulfport, Mississippi, and some people in Mobile, Alabama, to take care of the choir. Then I went to the provost but he didn't think tours would be a great thing at all. He said, "Where do you think you are going to get the money?" I replied, "I don't know, but we are going to get it. We are going, and it will be a great recruiting tool." He said we didn't have a problem getting students, we had thirty thousand of them. I told him, "But, they will stay with the university longer if they are in my choir." He wasn't sure that was true! I said, "I think it will be true and we have to have this money. I have accepted this tour and we are leaving in January." You know when I got permission to take that tour? One and a half weeks before we left. I already had it booked and everything was all ready. That was in January 1961. I went there the fall of 1960. That tour was the making of that choir. When they came back from that tour, they were one team.

WE HAD A GUY who was the chairman of the devotion committee, John Buell. I had to have somebody who could read scripture each night and who would give the devotion or prayer. John was in charge of that. I interviewed a lot of kids to get to know them, and John was the president of his Baptist Training Union (BTU), which met on Sunday nights. He was an art major in his junior year. I said, "John, I have a job for you. I want you to be my chaplain." John answered, "I can't do that." I said, "Sure you can. You get up every Sunday night and talk to all your people at the BTU, this is the same principle except the clientele is quite different." Anyway, I talked him in to becoming the chaplain, so each night he would have somebody lined up to do the devotion. On a Saturday night and Sunday we were in Mobile, Alabama, at the Dolphin Way United Methodist Church. We gave a big concert there on Saturday night, and were supposed to give another one on Sunday night. Sunday morning we were singing for the worship service, and just before it started, Linda Powers came to me and said, "You know we have about seven Catholics in the group, and we are not supposed to listen to a Protestant preacher." I counted to ten and counted to ten again. I wanted to tell Linda that when you are in this choir you do what everybody else does, that is just part of the requirement. But I didn't say that. I said, "If that is offensive and bothersome, I will talk to the minister and tell him that you need to be excused after we finish the singing, just before he starts to speak. You can slip out the side door and wait until it is over and we will meet you after the service." That is what they did.

That Sunday night, John had asked Linda to lead the devotion before our concert. She talked about Christ and what Christ meant to her, from the standpoint of the Catholic Church. The choir gave the concert, it was supposed to be strictly a concert, but the minister, Dr. Peacock, was so inspired that he got up and gave an altar call. An altar call for the University of Miami choir, can you imagine something like that happening, with the agnostics and every denomination you can imagine in the group?! While they were singing the hymn for people to come forward, a big rawboned guy named Skip H., on the back row from upstate New York, left the choir and knelt at the altar. You could hear people saying, "What's wrong with Skip, what's wrong with Skip?" because some of them had never seen anything like that. When they closed the service and had people come forward to pray with him, the first person to kneel beside him was Linda Powers, the girl who said she couldn't stay in a Protestant service. The decision to allow Linda and the other Catholics to leave before the sermon on Sunday morning was probably one of the wisest decisions I ever made in my life. I would have blown it not only with her, but all the other Catholic kids and I would have made some of the others mad. That was a close one. The very next day that choir was like a family, and was the closest that we had ever been as a group.

On the bus going back to Florida, a Jewish girl named Stephanie Stryker said, "I never had so much fun in my whole life. Where are we going next?" I said, "We are going to Europe." I had no idea how to get to Europe, I hadn't even thought of it, it was just something I said. Lydia said, "That would be great!" I said I didn't know how we were going to get there, I didn't have any contacts, but we would work on it.

We returned from the tour, and in about two weeks the Boston College Choir came to sing at the South Miami United Methodist Church where I was the choir director. We signed up to host two of the students, and I went to pick them up and they called out names, and my name was not called. I asked, "Where are my two students?" They said, "We are going to let you keep the director!" Lounelle was really upset about that, because she thought all we would do is sit around and talk about business, and she was anxious to meet some of the younger people.

Anyway, after their concert that night we were having refreshments at the house and the director said, "Glenn, what are you planning for your choir? I know this is your first year." I said, "I must go to Europe, I promised some of the kids that it was on our agenda, but I have no idea how to get there, and I need your help." He said, "I was in Europe just two years ago. Colonel R. A. Lemay in Washington, D.C., is chairman of a music committee of five people, called the Intercollegiate Music Council. They select five groups a year and send them overseas as goodwill ambassadors to sing for our Armed Forces Personnel, with the Defense Department putting up the money." He gave me the address and I found out his phone number, and the next morning I had Colonel L. on the telephone before nine. I told him what I was looking for, and he said, "Let me give you some advice. We are tied up for three years, it won't do any good for me to send you an application." I said, "Sir, I was in the military too, and you are obligated to send me an application, you have to do that." He saw I was in earnest, and he said, "I will put it in the mail, but just remember that I told you it wouldn't do any good!" I said, "Let me suffer the consequences of that." So I filled out the long questionnaire to send with a recording of our choir. I put down as my three sponsors, Billy Graham; my former Keesler Air Force Base commander, General Powell; and the chief of Air Force chaplains, General Carpenter.

Weeks went by, it was then late March and there were only two people in the choir who knew that I had even applied for the trip. I confided in Bob C., who helped me recruit, and his girlfriend Linda D., who was the accompanist. I said, "What I tell you is not to go to anybody else. If somebody comes around and tells me about it, I will know where it came from." They sang in my church choir, and would ask often, "Have you heard anything?" I said, "No," but Easter Sunday I said, "I have a feeling we are going to be hearing soon."

Sure enough, about nine on Monday morning the telephone rang. "Draper, this is Colonel R. A. Lemay in Washington. Do you think you can get your gang together to leave on July 31 and come back on September 18?" I said, "Sir, I have been packed for a couple of months and I'm ready to go!" He said, "We will furnish your housing, send you airplane tickets, pay you ten dollars a day to live on, and furnish places for you to sing." He said, "I can't stand that name you gave us, 'Concert Choir.' You have to come up with a better name than that!" Our school was known as the Fighting Hurricanes, so I said, "How about the 'Singing Hurricanes?'" I can still hear him laughing on the telephone. However, he was completely flabbergasted that a choir director and University of Miami teacher would have the references I had given him. The two generals went to see him in person at the Pentagon. He said, "I never saw such a display of support for any individual in my life. You sent two generals over to pressure me, and then Billy Graham wrote me a letter about you. What in the world have you done to merit that kind of devotion?" I said, "Sir, I have no idea, but I am just extremely grateful."

I thought, *What kind of music am I going to do? The Singing Hurricanes can't do "Now Is the Month of May" with that kind of a name.* I thought, *If a musical or operas can move around on a stage, why can't choirs? Why do we have to be so staid in robes, with long faces, and people saying, "Isn't that beautiful?" They can't understand the words, it is impersonal, and nobody ever changes their expression!*

I had asked Don Muller, in my group, what he wanted to do in life. He was the secretary of the male chorus. He said, "I want to write and to arrange." I said, "Have you ever done it? When are you going to get started?" He said, "Give me something to arrange." A few days later, I went to Don and said, "I want you to arrange some things for me, and I will put it in a medley." At Lake Junaluska I had made up medleys for sing-a-longs. When Billy Graham had been there that summer, I had to sing for thirty minutes, one hymn right after another. I didn't say, "Now turn to page so and so," I just did it, with related keys and all that. I told Don, "Let's put together a group of military songs, Broadway songs, and maybe folk songs," and he said, "You pick them out." I picked them out, got them in the right keys, and he arranged them. *Now, how about movement?* I didn't know anything about movement. I was never a dancer. One of my girls named Joy M. was late coming in to school because she had been in Nassau with a dance troupe. She was also a good soprano. I got together with her and said, "Joy, I have something I want you to do. I have accepted an invitation for the singers to go overseas. Will you help me stage some kind of movement to the way we sing?" John Bitter used to bring people down to see the choir. He would tell people, "Draper is experimenting with movement."

Linda Powers Bilanchone

My husband, Vic, and I met Glenn at the University of Miami in 1960, while singing in the Concert Choir; Glenn was the new director that year. In addition to carrying out the regular duties of the choral director, Glenn had it in mind that he would create a new and different kind of group to tour Europe under the auspices of the United Service Organizations (USO). Prior to that time, college groups touring for the USO dutifully wore their choir robes and sang serious repertoires. Glenn's idea was that we'd call ourselves the Singing Hurricanes, wear snazzy stage costumes, and sing popular music, with choreography and comedy as well. My clearest memory of this effort is that Glenn called me into his office and asked in his usual, no-nonsense, high-energy way, "Can you put on a blonde wig and impersonate Marilyn Monroe?" I had never given such a thing a thought, but I swallowed hard and said, "Yes." I would do anything to be included in that group of singers who were going to Europe.

That tour did take place, July 31, 1961, and Glenn's groups continued to do Defense Department tours for many years. That first group rehearsed for the European tour not at the University of Miami, but at Lake Junaluska, North Carolina, where Glenn was employed in the summer to direct the Junaluska Singers. We spent ten days there rehearsing before we left for Europe. Those ten days were Glenn at his best—purposefulness and high energy achieving two tasks at once—daily performances for Methodists with the Junaluska Singers and daily rehearsals with the Singing Hurricanes getting ready to go to Europe!

ACCEPTING THAT INVITATION opened up a whole new world. Here is where I learned a lesson about people. I thought in order to be liked, you had to be successful and then people would immediately like you. At the University of Miami, I could hardly wait for the rest of the music faculty to know about the tour. It didn't work that way at all. Instead, they wondered who this guy was who had slipped in among them. *Who does he think he is, going overseas on this trip?* It worked just the opposite, except with the "big brass." The chancellor was beside himself with joy, and John B. felt I could do no wrong. They promoted the Singing Hurricanes to go everywhere.

Bill Brett

There was the time we were flying to Saundestrom, Greenland, in a C-47 with all of our gear strapped down in the center aisle and the fifteen of us strapped to parachute jump seats along each side of the aircraft. As we were approaching our destination by flying through a fjord with mountains on both sides higher than we were, our pilot emerged from the cockpit. He was reading a book with the title *How to fly a C-47 Airplane* in bold print. He then informed us if we were given the signal "three rings," we would have to jump! We turned onto our final approach, experienced a short, but sudden down draft, and heard the aforementioned "three rings." I can still hear the screams!

THAT FIRST YEAR, before the Singing Hurricanes were organized, my choir sang at a football game. I had met Ernie S., who was the manager of the Orange Bowl Committee, and he had said if we ever needed anything to call him. I went to him and said, "I am going to take the singers to Lake Junaluska to rehearse at the World Methodist Center because we have been awarded a trip by the government and we need some money to pay their way there and buy outfits." You know what he did? He gave us $5,000 like I asked.

We first started choreography with a group during those rehearsals. Since I could only take about twenty-five singers out of the group of forty, I needed to decide who was going. I picked out a committee and asked them to vote on it. I wanted to see how accurate my list was. I missed it by maybe two people. They picked those people out themselves.

I asked all of the singers to get a doctor's certification of good health, and one of the fellows said his doctor wanted to talk to me. I called the doctor, and he said that Scott had a kidney problem, "but I believe if he doesn't go, it will kill him." He said, "If I were you, I would take him, but make sure that he gets as much rest as possible." In Nuremberg, I said, "Scott, I notice that you have been slowing down a little bit." He replied, "Oh, I'm all right!" I said, "I will make a deal with you. If you start running out of energy and you don't feel up to par, just tell me and sit out a performance. Don't even worry about singing with us. Nobody else has to know. If somebody asks what is wrong with you, I will just say it is a thing between you and me!" So he said he would, but he was a trooper. When we got to Venice, the two of us spent most of that day riding gondolas, drinking coffee, and things like that. He loved anything about the Second World War. We had both read *The Rise and Fall of the Third Reich,* so we talked about the war, where things took place, and when we were in Würzburg what it was like under the Nazi regime.

One night we had a performance in Verona, and after that concert we caught the train to Livorno, which is just north of Rome. While we were eating breakfast in Livorno, I looked over and Scott was sitting at the table shaking. He had only about three or four glasses of liquid, and he didn't have any food. I went up to him and I said, "Scott, what is wrong?" He said, "I don't feel very well." I said, "Maybe we need to get you to a doctor." While the singers were still there at breakfast, I got the fellow who was in charge with me, Major Hanson, to take us to a military hospital. After we had been there for ten or fifteen minutes, a doctor came out and said he needed to talk to me. He asked about any medical problems Scott had, and I told him he had kidney problems. The doctor said, "You have a very sick boy on your hands." I asked, "How sick?" He said, "In my opinion, I don't think he will ever walk out of the hospital alive." You could have swept me off the floor. How do I explain this to his parents? I called his dad and he immediately flew over. We had to leave by train that day to Florence and do a performance there, then went back to the Munich area and continued on the trip.

About a week and a half later, I took a military taxi from where I was to a military hospital in Germany where Scott had been sent not far from the French border. I had to wear a mask to get in to see him. I had never seen so many tubes. It was bad. I told him we were praying for him, and I had a prayer with him. The doctor said that they would be flying him home, and that one of the doctors was going to fly on the airplane with him. We got back to the States about the same time. About two weeks later, the doctor said they were letting him out of the hospital and that he wanted to come over to a rehearsal. He came over on Friday and gave one of the most touching speeches I had ever heard. He said, "When we have something, we never think about losing it. The happiest year in my whole life has been this past year singing in this choir. I didn't know you this time last year at all, and now you are my brothers and sisters, and almost closer than my own family. I don't know whether I will ever get to sing again or not, I hope I will, but I just want you to know how much I love each one of you." Everyone started crying, hugging, and saying, "Scott we love you."

Would you believe that the next Monday we sang for his funeral? He was there on Friday, and on Saturday he had to go back into the hospital and his condition just went downhill. I didn't know that he had only one kidney, and that it was diseased and had shut down on him. We sang at his funeral, and they had a choir robe on his casket, with flowers on one side. All the kids loved Scott. He was so witty. He was the only one that was a unanimous choice when everyone voted on the choir trip. I have never forgotten him, but I told his parents many times, "I hope you don't hold me responsible," and they replied, "Glenn, we were thrilled that he got to go, at least he died happy and being accepted, and if you hadn't taken him, it would have killed him." That is what the doctor said, "If you don't take him with you, he is going to die, just out of disappointment." Do you think that hurt the morale of that choir? Oh no! Out of that group, eight of them married each other. I used to say, I will take the credit, but I'm not going to take the blame if it doesn't work out.

THE NEXT YEAR, the popularity of the group started growing like crazy. Let me tell you this wild experience. You know when you do something that is successful, not everyone likes what you have done. We sang a program for the Chamber of Commerce, a huge welcome home event. We then started going to high schools with our kick-up-your-heels group. There was no group that could even come close to that, anywhere around.

The supervisor of music for the whole city of Miami, Dr. Howard Doolin, called me one morning and said, "Draper, I need to come out and talk to you." He came out and said, "What in the heck are you doing that is causing all this stir among these kids?" I said, "Isn't it exciting?" He said, "Exciting?! It is terrible, and you are ruining music." I said, "I sure am getting a lot of people, what's the bottom line?" He said, "The bottom line is that these teachers don't know how to do what you are doing and they are mad at you." I said, "Don't hold that against me, have you ever heard of the word progress? What's happening today, in my opinion, is that there are going to be groups doing this everywhere, because I have seen the reaction in Europe to this group." There are show choirs all over America now, and as far as I know, we were the first show choir.

The chairman of the Military Intercollegiate Music Committee started using the Singing Hurricanes as an example of what was really appropriate for the military audience on overseas tours. He wrote it up in a journal that he sent out everywhere. Little did I know that a trombone player would ever be influential in arranging for show choirs to come about—that was not my bag. I didn't grow up in that kind of environment, but I grew up learning that if you want to sell something, make sure that it was freshly made. Nobody buys pancakes that were made yesterday. I don't want to be the last one to try anything. I like to be the first one.

So the Singing Hurricanes became very popular. That was my first choir at the school, now I had to get one other and that was a group of Madrigal Singers. I wondered how I was going to organize the Madrigal Singers. I finally decided that I would select twelve people from our choir that I thought would be good in a madrigal singers group, and invite them to come to our house for dinner. I sent out cards saying, "You are invited for dinner at the Draper home at six on Tuesday night." I asked Lounelle to fix the table with wine glasses, candles, and Madrigal books all around. I told them this was going to be a dressy affair. When we sat down, I said, "We are going to pretend that we are in old England in the seventeenth or eighteenth century, and we will start by singing a certain Madrigal that is in this book, because this was the tradition." I said, "Welcome to the Madrigal Singers of the University of Miami. You are now officially a member."

Then we started giving concerts on campus, with just the Madrigal Singers, doing a Madrigal Dinner, just like we had at my house, and no one around Miami had ever seen that before. When you run out of ideas, you need to try something new. That doesn't mean that everything that you try will work. Ask Thomas Edison, or ask anyone who tries new things. Did Columbus have everyone agreeing with him, and urging him on? It didn't work that way, did it? That is where I am different, I guess, from most people I know, because I am a daredevil of the highest order. I'm an extreme optimist. If I can see it in focus, it doesn't matter whether people agree with me or not. It really doesn't make that much difference. I must try. I don't know whether I'm hardheaded or hard-nosed. I got that from my mother, I'm sure. She was an extreme believer in whatever she was after. When I said, "I know I can't go to college because we don't have the money," she said, "Don't ever say that. You are going. I don't know how you are going, but you are going! You will not miss college. You have to go." That was the determination of the family I came from. You just go over it, around it, or work a little harder, but what you are after is worth far more than just your effort to get there.

I HAVE TO TELL YOU this story, because it's funny how things later down the road come back to either bless you or haunt you. In my senior year at Indiana University, the Indianapolis Symphony was giving a concert, and I wanted to go so badly. I did not have the money to go. I pleaded with the lady at the box-office to let me usher, and she finally agreed. The conductor was Fabian Sevitsky, whose uncle was Kosevitsky, the former conductor of the Boston Symphony. After he immigrated here, Kosevitsky would not allow another Kosevitsky in America because of the competition with his name, so Fabian Sevitsky had to take off the "Ko" and he became known just as Sevitsky. It is crazy, isn't it? The symphony was doing the Rachmaninoff Piano Concerto no. 2. I have always thought that was one of the most beautiful things ever written. On this particular night, the temperature was twenty-five degrees below zero, and the moon looked like it was right in your yard, with snow everywhere. It was a winter scene of the highest order. I put some water on my hair to comb it before I went to usher, and when I got there, I got icicles out of my hair—it was that cold. At intermission, when we didn't have to take tickets anymore, I thought I would go back to watch the conductor. I slipped backstage and hid in the curtains on the side so I could see him clearly. He conducted, cued the pianos, and I thought, *Wouldn't it be unbelievable to work with a person like that?* I searched him out at the end and told him I had really enjoyed that performance, and that I hoped to be a conductor someday. In those years, the orchestra was my bag!

Little did I know that when I went to the University of Miami, the conductor of the orchestra would be Fabian Sevitsky. He had the university Orchestra plus the City Orchestra, but they rehearsed on the campus and his office was right beside mine. I would go out the door and turn left and there was Fabian Sevitsky's office, the man I saw conduct the concert that night! We became incredible friends, and I learned so much from him. He loved Lounelle. His wife was a gracious lady. In fact she sent me his picture after he died, he had written an inscription on it. Sometimes he would want me to pick him up and take him to Rotary Club. I had joined the

Rotary Club, and he had been a Rotarian for a long time. People would say to him, "We enjoyed your concert. Who is your favorite composer?" He would answer, "All of them." He never told them. I would ask him in the car, "Who is really your favorite composer?" He said, "Glenn, when you get to Brahms where else can you go?! From the Brahms *Requiem* to his four symphonies, to the piano concertos."

He used to tell me, "Conductors live a long time, because you exercise every part of your body all the time and that's great. But where you are going to fall apart are your legs." I asked, "Why is that?" He replied, "Because you don't really get the exercise in your legs. Run in place, walk as much as you can, and you may live a long time." When he retired from the university, he was probably seventy-eight, but he went around the world guest-conducting performances. In Athens, Greece, during a break in a rehearsal while conducting the Athens Philharmonic Orchestra, he sat down and died of a heart attack. He was probably eighty-two, or something like that. His wife Mary said, "Glenn, he loved you like a son." I got my church choir, the university choir, and a number of other church choirs together and did the Brahms *Requiem*, in his memory, one afternoon soon after his death. He had a lot of influence on me.

Taken from **The Armchair Conductor:**
How to Lead a Symphony Orchestra in the Privacy
of Your Own Home *by Dan Carlinsky and Ed Goodgold*

> There is a long and impressive list of prominent conductors who beat time to age eighty, eighty-five, or beyond—until time finally beat them. The roster includes Arturo Toscanini, Otto Klemperer, Pierre Monteux, Bruno Walter, Ernest Ansermet, Sir Thomas Beecham, Sir Adrian Boult, Leopold Stokowski, Tullio Serafin, Andre Kostelanetz, Fred Waring, Pablo Casals, Hans Knappertsbusch, and Arthur Fiedler, who in his late seventies began spouting this motto: "He who rests rots."
>
> Why do so many conductors outwit the actuaries? Perhaps it is the occupation itself. "I have an energetic job," said Sir Malcolm Sargent, who could have been speaking for all his fellow conductors. "I spend up to six hours a day waving my arms about. If everyone else did the same, they would stay much healthier. I don't have to play golf to get exercise." His colleague Sir John Barbirolli said the same thing, but in a more earthy fashion. "You know why conductors live so long? Because we perspire so much."

I WILL TELL YOU one of the things I learned from Fabian Sevitsky. During my first week, John Bitter, the dean of music said, "Glenn, I think I just did you a grave injustice. I have scheduled Beethoven's 'Ninth Symphony,' and you don't even have a choir to sing it." I said, "John, you have done the greatest thing for me you could possibly have done. You have given me something to shoot for. If I said, 'Come and join our choir,' people would ask what we are going to do. You don't say, come with me on our trip, people ask where you are going. So when I say we are doing Beethoven's 'Ninth Symphony,' we have a goal." When I recruited people for that choir, I said, "We are going to be privileged to perform Beethoven's 'Ninth Symphony' with the orchestra on December 5th and 6th." I had something to shoot at!

In the rehearsals, when Fabian Sevitsky started working with the orchestra and the choir together, he would never ever reprimand a person in front of everybody, that was a no-no. Then we would go back in his office and he would say, "Glenn, the choir is lagging behind my beat." So I figured out that they were putting the consonants late; they have to be on the beat for the vowel sounds and early for the consonants! We were trying to start the whole word on the beat, but we had to start the consonants ahead of the beat so the vowel sound would be on the beat. I learned that from an instrumentalist, Fabian Sevitsky, my dear friend. If you ever admit that you know it all, get out. Nobody is going to want to be around you! "I am a self-made man," someone said, and another man replied, "Well, that sure relieves God of a lot of responsibility!" The more I learn in life, the more I find out I don't know. In fact, I am embarrassed to think about what I didn't know in my early years. I can't imagine the Keesler Male Chorus winning first place competition in the military, with no more than I knew at that time.

JOHN BITTER retired from the University of Miami in 1963, after I had been there three years. The next year I took the group to Dallas for a concert tour, and the new dean, Bill Lee, was very happy because he wanted us to get out as much as possible. I was directing all-state choruses to encourage high school recruiting, and he was my number one fan! John B. had also been a great supporter, but Bill Lee had a lot of different musical experiences. He had played the piano with Tex Benneke and had played percussion instruments in the Houston Symphony. The Singing Hurricanes were his bag. He thought they were one of the greatest groups that had come down the pike!

Instead of being only a classical music lover of Bach, Beethoven, and Brahms, he was my biggest promoter! He would bring people down to the rehearsal saying, "I want you to see Draper's rehearsal with the Singing Hurricanes. They are experimenting with movement." He initiated a degree program in commercial music, where students spent their senior year in New York City at a music publishing house. Where can you better learn to run a publishing house or be in the music business? Then he had another degree program called Jazz, and he got Jerry Coker from Indiana University to come down to start that program. They had a chance to put it into practice in all the hotels on Miami Beach.

The Singing Hurricanes sang for many conventions, and I mean hundreds. I could have probably organized a group on my own and stayed there and made a living by singing for conventions, because we could make one or two thousand dollars a night, even then. That wasn't what I wanted to do, however. I learned something about payoffs. A certain restaurant chain had just been organized in the mid–1960s, and they were going to have their first convention in Miami. They wanted the Singing Hurricanes to be the entertainment. They bought jackets for every singer and an executive jacket for me to wear. They furnished the bus to take us to and from rehearsals. It was blown up so big that they paid two thousand dollars for the group to sing which, of course, went to the school.

When they paid me the school's two-thousand-dollar check, they handed me another check for two hundred dollars and said, "This is for you." I said, "I can't take it." They said, "What do you mean, you can't take it? It is made out to you." I told them that I couldn't make money on the students. If word got around to the students that I was making money on them, and my incentive for accepting singing opportunities was what I could make out of it, then I was using the students. They said, "Then we will make it out to your wife." I said, "No, you can't do that either. I cannot take your two hundred dollars." I had never been in a situation like that, and the guy said to me, "This is done all the time! You do favors for people, under the table." I said, "There aren't going to be any favors under the table for me." I learned something about the "system" and about myself that I didn't know before. Thank goodness that I was that strong, I always told my kids that you never go wrong going right! I would not want one student to come in and say, "The reason that we gave up our night to study for exams is so that we could help Draper make more money." I could never, ever do that!

The Singing Hurricanes ended up going on four overseas tours for the government in 1961, 1963, 1965, and 1966. When I left in 1968, they were supposed to tour again that summer on another government trip. That was five overseas tours in eight years. That wasn't a bad record was it? Archie Jones was the head of the committee for the overseas tours. He told a story to me at a convention, which I have always loved. He said that in Kansas City there were a lot of church marquees. He saw one church marquee that listed a sermon topic as, "Is There a Hell?" and underneath it said, "Come Out and Hear Our Choir." I have loved that story! I can still hear him laughing about that. He became a really good friend to me, and he said, "Glenn, you really don't have to apply to these tours anymore. We will take you any time you can go."

═══════════════════════════════════

Bill Brett

On an overseas tour, Lounelle once tried to thank a nice German maid at a hotel for lending her a hair dryer, after hers had blown up by plugging it into the socket. You must understand that Lounelle is a true southern belle. Lounelle hails from Dallas, Texas, and she has a bit (Ha! Ha!) of a southern drawl. Lounelle's Dallas, Texas, accent on the German word for "thank you" (*danke schoen*) was not understandable to the maid. A few of us who happened to overhear this international exchange of verbiage explained the word phonetically approaching "daunkeeshayen" to the German maid. As the light bulb of recognition lit in the maid's brain, she started to laugh uncontrollably and commenced telling the rest of the maids how *danke schoen* is pronounced "Texas style."

FIRST UNITED METHODIST CHURCH OF CORAL GABLES

I HAVE ALWAYS LOVED good church choirs, and I have spent my whole life working with choirs. My mother was a pianist and organist in a church in Roanoke, Virginia, where I grew up. In those years, the recordings of the Mormon Tabernacle Choir were the envy of every choir director or every person who wanted to be in that business. I loved the recordings. When I was fourteen years old, I started singing in the Greene Memorial Methodist Church choir in Roanoke, where Mrs. Eula Ligon was the director. Even though I was an instrumentalist in those years, I thought that I would work in churches or with church choirs, at least on a part-time basis. It was my ambition to have a very large, successful church choir, and I used to dream about that. With that in mind, I felt God was leading me into a music ministry.

When I was at Pfeiffer College, I received an invitation to move to Miami. When Lounelle and I first got down there, I was disappointed in the First Methodist Church in Miami that had asked me to come down and visit, but I was very impressed with the university. They offered me the job at the university, and we asked somebody to take us by the First Methodist Church of Coral Gables on that first trip. I was impressed with their beautiful sanctuary, and it had great acoustics. I prayed, *Lord, if you want me to do something, open the doors for me.*

At Pfeiffer College during the spring of 1960, we went on a tour of Florida, and I met a minister by the name of Dr. John H. Hanger while we were in Jacksonville. I told him about the two invitations that I had to go to Florida Southern and also the University of Miami. He said, "Glenn, by all means take the University of Miami. You will have more opportunities there. They have a lot more money and they have a larger student body. The University of Miami has thirty thousand students and Florida Southern has maybe four or five thousand students." That particular spring is when I officially accepted the job to go to the University of Miami.

In the middle of the summer at Lake Junaluska, I received a letter from Dr. Hanger, who was the minister in Jacksonville, Florida. The return address was First Methodist Church, Coral Gables. I opened it and it read, "Now I know why I told you to go to University of Miami! It is because I have just been transferred to Coral Gables at the First United Methodist Church, and I want you to be my choir director." I have never forgotten being so ecstatic in my life! I could not believe that the hand of the Lord had worked like that. Dr. Hanger continued, "It will take me about a year to get this straightened out, but I am going to bring you here. The current director has been here for some time, and I will have to establish myself in the church before I am able to bring in a new director."

In the meantime, the South Miami United Methodist Church heard that I was coming to the University of Miami, and they wrote me a letter to ask if I would be willing to be their choir director. Since the other job was not available yet, I told them that I would love to consider it. They flew me down, I had a rehearsal with their choir, and they offered me the job. I told them about my ambition to be the choral director at the First United Methodist Church in Coral Gables, because I wanted to be very up front with them in that respect.

The University of Miami Choir received the invitation to tour Europe, as I have told you, and I came back from Lake Junaluska just before we left to go on that trip. Dr. Hanger called me and said, "Glenn, I think we have it worked out now. I want you to come over and meet the whole committee Saturday afternoon." On Friday night, I went to the church by myself and knelt at the altar and prayed for the longest time that God would open the door for me to direct the choir at Coral Gables. I just thought it would be one of the greatest things in the world. When I went over there on Saturday we talked about salary and about not being there in the summertime, when I had to be in Junaluska. Some of the members didn't really understand that, but Dr. Hanger said, "If he hadn't been at Lake Junaluska, I would never have known him. It would be a great honor for our church to have him direct the music for the World Methodist Conference at Lake Junaluska, which is the biggest Assembly in the southeast." When I left there, I shook hands with everybody, and left Monday to do our first performances overseas with the military.

As soon as I got to Europe, there was a telegram from Dr. Hanger. It read, "Unable at present to complete deal. Don't give up. We are still going to have you, we just can't do it now. Some complications have come up that we can't explain." I didn't know what to think except, *What can I do? I am overseas and Lounelle is back at home.* As soon as I came back, I called Dr. Hanger and he said, "Some people thought that we needed to give Mrs. W. more advance notice about it because she had been there for twelve or fourteen years as their choir director. She has done a good job and she is loved, and we can't have her feeling that we just kicked her out." I told him that was fine. I went back to the other church and directed the music there. During the wintertime the congregation at Coral Gables called me over and said, "We are now going to officially invite you. Will you accept the position?" I said, "Yes, I absolutely will."

There began an incredible experience for me working with Dr. John H. Hanger. He was the epitome, in my opinion, of a saint. He was one of the most congenial, loving, cooperative, and appreciative ministers that I have ever known. There was not a Sunday that went by that he didn't compliment the choir publicly for the great job they did. He would come on Wednesday nights and tell the choir what a great job they were doing. Unfortunately, Dr. Hanger died in April 1965, three years before I left.

LOUNELLE AND I were meeting a lot of new people in the city, and some of those people went to our church. Like Mr. George Gray, who was on the mayor's committee. Lounelle and I ended up being Martha and George Washington in the Orange Bowl Parade. Someone else invited our choir to sing some things with Lorne Greene on a nationally televised broadcast. The *Ed Sullivan Show* and other things came to being, and the church choir grew from maybe twenty-five people to more than seventy voices. I could hardly wait to get to our choir rehearsals. It was one of the most exhilarating things that I had ever been involved in. I had never had a church choir with seventy-five people in it. That church is still one of the most beautiful churches that I have ever seen. It seats about sixteen hundred people, has a beautiful choir loft and organ, and the curvature of the ceiling lends itself to a beautiful sound. I used to bring the University of Miami Choral Union and blend them with our church choir and as many people in the community that we could come up with and do the *Messiah*, the *Elijah*, the Brahms *Requiem*, and the *Christmas Oratory* by Bach. The acoustics were certainly as good as you could find any place. We made several wonderful friends when we were there.

IN MY SECOND OR THIRD YEAR, the church was going through some financial problems, and I went to a finance committee meeting one night. Mr. Bill F., who I suppose was a lawyer, stood up and said, "Brother Glenn, we love you and the church choir, and we just love the music that you are doing. However, as far as we are concerned, you can sing 'How Great Thou Art' every Sunday and we would absolutely love it. Since we have a budget crunch, we are proposing to drop the $4,000 for music down to maybe $500." I thought, *I can't panic, I can't jump on him in front of everybody. I can't be defensive.* Then I stood up, and I said, "Bill, I really admire that sport coat and that tie you have on. Why did you buy that sport coat and that tie, because they were new? Why aren't you wearing the same tie that you wore before? In my opinion, if I started using 'How Great Thou Art' every Sunday, as beautiful as that is, it would be like eating the same thing for breakfast every morning, over and over and over. How long is it going to be before you would be pleading with me, please don't sing 'How Great Thou Art' one more time? We have to keep abreast of what is going on in the world, otherwise we are behind. If you want me to keep this choir moving forward, you have to keep feeding them new material, new food. You can't rely on the same pancakes, how many times can you eat old pancakes? Never. You would want them hot. If they aren't hot, you won't eat them." Finally, the guy said, "Okay, give him the $4,000 and please sit down, Glenn." I said, "Thank you, gentlemen." Sometimes you have to sell your program, and you have to come up with a better argument than anybody comes up with. You are dealing with the business world, so you have to be able to talk with them intelligently on their level.

That choir was tremendous. Rehearsals were on Thursday nights, and after choir rehearsals we would always go to Chippy's, a coffee shop where you could buy a piece of pie or other desserts, salads, and sandwiches. That was always a great fellowship time for the choir. They would spend anywhere from thirty minutes to an hour after the rehearsal just in fellowship. So we became a really close family.

Lounelle was such an incredible help to me during those years. She was one of the most loved ladies I have ever seen in my life. She has been so supportive and so helpful to me at all times. She types for me, and she helps me write letters. We sit down and discuss things over and over. Sometimes she needs my shoulder and sometimes I need her shoulder. Through those years of raising our children, there were a few times when she didn't get to go on an overseas tour. We did very well then, and knew we could trust each other. Our marriage was incredible, and we felt that God had brought us together and that we were a team. She was just the best, and I can't imagine anybody else being any better than she has been for me and what I need. She has been so loved by choir members that they call her "Lady Lounelle." My school and church choirs, and members everywhere we have been, have absolutely loved her. She has always helped with the robes and she has always helped with calling people and telling them that we missed them.

Bill and Betty Brett
Sang in University of Miami choirs in the early 1960s;
both have been choir directors; Bill is an organist

Lounelle is the rock behind the volcano! She is the steady, soothing choir mom everyone loves. She is the doctor, nurse, stage hand, and seam-stress you could talk to when a compassionate ear was needed. Lounelle is the only woman, other than my wife, who has stayed as beautiful over these last forty years as the day I met her. Lounelle is the perfect compliment to Glenn. She is a wonderful friend who is always there when you need her.

A LOT OF OUR choir people sang at the University of Miami Choral Union, and we would go to football games together on Saturday afternoons when I could get tickets cheaper for the whole group. We would charter a bus and go to the game and then come back to the church and fix steaks for everybody. We also went to retirement homes and sang for the residents. We used to have an Easter Sunrise Service in Coral Gables and, for some odd reason, it fell upon me to direct that big choir made up of people from all the different area churches. After that early sunrise service, we had 8:30, 9:45, and 11:00 services at the church. The male chorus sang at the 8:30 service, and the chancel choir sang at the other two. Christmas Eve services were always very special, as were Thanksgiving, Easter, and Memorial Day services.

I have always been for that family feel and togetherness in choirs. I don't want anybody to be left out. We had many picnics, and it was not uncommon at all for eight to ten couples on any given Sunday in church to say, "Let's go out to so and so." Or you were invited to somebody's place, who were having a big picnic out on the lawn. Miami lent itself so well to outdoor living anyway.

IT WAS HARD for us to leave the University of Miami, very hard. I remember Lounelle crying as we drove out of town that day. Those people in Florida were wonderful and we have been back several times to visit them, and they have invited me to come down and direct music for their revivals and other special times. The Chattanooga Singers have been there five or six times to do concerts.

6

Chattanooga's
Ambassador
to the World

1968–Present

_He doesn't let you get away with being less enthusiastic
in a rehearsal than you would be on stage._

~Kim Cargile

UNIVERSITY OF TENNESSEE, CHATTANOOGA
1968–2002

When we came to Chattanooga, the committee that brought us there were very proud. They had hooked an _Ed Sullivan Show_ guy, they had hooked a guy who had been in the paper as "Hurricane Comes to Chattanooga." Ben Haden had invited Scott Probasco, president of the Sun Trust Bank; Dr. William Masterson, the chancellor of the university; Hugh Huffacker, who owned an insurance company; another bank president; and several educators to a meeting at Christmas at the Mountain City Club, where they presented a unified university and church effort to me. They were all trying to sell me on the pros of coming to Chattanooga. We then scheduled a meeting that afternoon with Dr. Masterson at the university. I went to the school and I said, "You do not know what I can do. Why are you offering me a job?" He replied, "You had a good promoter in Ben Haden. My best person on this campus right now is Barry Jones, the band director, and if you come you will be my other best person. I think what you are going to do with the choirs will exemplify how I want this university to go. Others know us as the people who live in an ivory tower. We do not associate with anybody. We live up on this hill and nobody comes to see us and we do not go to see anybody. I want your choir to go out in this community and all over the world as you have been doing in Miami and get us on the map." Through me, he thought he could accomplish that mission.

Dr. Masterson was a great friend and supporter, and he stayed about four years after I came. When he retired, I had the sweetest letter that you would every read in your life. Yes, the chancellor spoiled me and I didn't have to worry about anybody else, so to speak. I did not take advantage of Dr. Masterson, do not misunderstand me, but other people in my department didn't like me because he hired me. In fact, this past spring, when I was talking about leaving, the provost said to me, "Glenn, you are a rare case, you are the only one that I have ever known who succeeded after being hired by the chancellor. Everybody else looks down on you. The department that you went into hates you, not because of you, but because the chancellor hired you. You must make the decision yourself whether you want to go on a gradual retirement or . . ." I said, "They call me floorboard. I have only one speed, stop or all out. When I leave, I will just leave."

Nevertheless, when I came, I did not have a choir (none at all) at the church or at school, so I had to fend for myself. However, you know what, at the University of Miami I didn't have anything there either. When I went to the Rotary Club in Chattanooga, they recognized me as the guy who came from the *Ed Sullivan Show* and the University of Miami. They had me on a cloud and I wasn't sure I could ever be that big. It could be embarrassing for me. I had to organize a choir. That was what they were paying me to do.

Ben Haden was grateful that I had come, and he was also proud that I was Methodist (instead of Presbyterian). He said, "Now the Methodists will start coming to my church because you are here." Anyone who worked on the staff of the church could not join the church, because he said, "If I ever had to fire them or let them go, then they would stay around and haunt me." I didn't want to join the Presbyterian Church anyway, since I was continuing to work during the summers at the Methodist Assembly at Lake Junaluska. I still belong to the same Methodist Church in Coral Gables, ever since we were in Miami. Coming into school under those conditions was very different from going to Pfeiffer College when you were nobody, or even to Miami.

UTC CHOIRS

NOBODY IN THE MUSIC DEPARTMENT, other than the department head, had a secretary. Soon after I came to the university, Gaye Sellers, who had done my choreography that year, was getting ready to graduate, and she was planning to go to Atlanta to work. When I asked her what she was going to do, she told me and I said, "What do you really want to do?" She said, "What I really want to do is to come back and be your assistant." (Her boyfriend was at the university.) I went to the chancellor's office and I said, "Bill, I need an assistant." He said, "Is that your number one priority?" I said, "Right now, it is my number one priority." He said, "Okay, what shall we pay her?" I told him what I thought we should pay her, and within two weeks he sent me a memorandum, "Hire Gaye Sellers."

The very next year when we were invited to go on our first European tour, the chancellor wanted us to go very much because he said the publicity alone was worth it. He felt that if prospects heard about the university, the students who were trying to decide where they wanted to go to school might say, "Let's go to UTC, their choir is going to Europe." He said, "Glenn, the value of a tour like that is not just the tour itself, it is the fallout!" We were to leave on April 13 and come back on June 14—nine weeks. Dr. Masterson had the students in the choir sign up for a two-hour course, but they went to school four days a week in that class, so they doubled up their time. So by the time we left on April 13, they had already taken their exams and were finished with classes.

WHEN I MOVED to Tennessee I told myself, *One thing for sure, you are not going to ever have five choirs at UTC like you did at Miami. You just kill yourself; you need to enjoy life.* The first choir I organized was the Chamber Singers. They were a little more high brow, and would do Bach or Beethoven. After our first rehearsal, I said, "I'm going to organize a group that we will call a show group, and we will do movement with it. If people in operas can move on stage, why can't a choir? People in musicals can move around, why can't a choir? I am looking for somebody who has had dance experience." The students responded, "Gaye Sellers is your person, right here!"

One young woman asked me how good this choir was going to be. She said, "If it isn't going to be any good, I do not want to be a part of it." I said, "If it is not going to be good, I do not want to be a part of it, either. If I am the director, I want it to be the best." If you want to start something new, start with young people. Their young minds are waiting and, if they like you, they will follow you anywhere.

When we had seventy or eighty singers, I organized another choir. I gave the big choir the name Chattanooga Singers and kept the Chamber Singers, but cut it down to twenty people. Then we had the Singing Mocs, a multi-talented, kick-up-your-heels group. The Chattanooga Singers was the parent organization. They did not do much movement, but they did a lot of variety. Members had to be in the Chattanooga Singers to be in the Singing Mocs. When we went on tours, we used singers taken from all three groups. The Singing Mocs group was the complete opposite of the Chamber Singers. They were a show choir, with organized production, choreography, and costumes, and they sang medleys that fit, key-wise, instead of "and the next number is." Most people had never seen choirs sing medleys like that.

Those singers were very proud. We sang one of our first big concerts at a Rotary Convention in Gatlinburg. Somebody in the Rotary talked them into getting the Singing Mocs from Chattanooga to sing that year. The University of Tennessee, Knoxville Singers had sung for them for years, and they were afraid that we wouldn't be any good; but we were so good that they later asked us to sing for the International Rotary Convention in Atlanta.

Our choirs became very popular. All the service clubs started asking us to sing at their banquets. Then at Christmastime, I said, "Gaye, let's do a Christmas concert on television." Channel 9 invited us to be on a program at Christmastime and we sang for ten minutes. I then got together with the bank, Coca-Cola, and several businesses like that, who sponsored us, and we went on location. However, before we did that, we would record the music in a studio and then go on location and lip-sync it, with costumes. We went to Atlanta and performed "Christmas in the City." We performed another one called "An Old Fashioned Christmas," and we went to the oldest city in Tennessee, Jonesboro, and sang "Silent Night" in a barn. We recorded these television shows at Christmas for ten or twelve years, and it once won the best locally produced television show in the country.

Basically, I had three choral groups and taught choral conducting. For about ten years I taught a music class called Music 111. It was a general course where music majors learned about symphonies, etc. I had 150 to 200 students in that class. I have many people tell me when I meet them that they used to be in my Music 111 class. I met people that way who never sang in my choirs. In the choral conducting class, you had to sign up for a year, first and second semester. I would have anywhere from 10 to 15 students. I think the most I had was around 22, but that was too big because I wanted to see them all conduct, and if I had too many people, I could not get around to them very often. Eight to 10 students was the ideal number in the class and I enjoyed doing that.

Dr. Robert K. Dean
UTC choirs; first president of the choir;
assistant professor of music, Radford University

Glenn had a hard row to hoe when he first came to UTC, at least for a couple of years. He was not welcomed with unanimous open arms. It was not his fault, but they hired him in a round-about fashion, so as not to arouse antagonism among the old guard—which, of course, is exactly what it did. At least, that's the way I perceived it. Before Glenn's arrival, there really wasn't anything such as a choral department per se. You had the option of singing in a small choir, which was geared toward teaching and singing classic literature, but that group performed very irregularly. It was still a European-style conservative curriculum. Glenn always handled this with the utmost discretion. I never heard him say a negative word about any of his colleagues in the department. He just did his own thing, and did it so successfully that any criticism of him just fizzled.

Glenn wanted to take the choir and turn it into a touring and recording, big-time collegiate ensemble. (Which, of course, he did.) Within a year, we were traveling to various regions of the country and were completing a recording. One side of it was the classic repertoire and the other side was the pop stuff for the Singing Mocs. I sang in the Singing Mocs for a couple of years, but my heart really was not in it. Glenn, very typically, accepted that about me and never held it against me that the pop music wasn't "my bag," as we used to say. For one thing, I had two left feet and could never master the dance moves to the point where I felt comfortable. My partner was Alice N., and I think she had sore feet that entire year.

Glenn's acceptance (among some) by the music department was never complete. Many scoffed at the "show biz" aspects of the Singing Mocs. It's like that in any music school. Nevertheless, his power base lay in the upper administration, who were not as affected by jealousies and typical music department sniping. He survived because he attracted good singers to the university and brought great exposure and recognition to the university, and because his choirs sounded good! Even the most jaded faculty members had to admit that his choirs sounded good.

David Fowler
UTC choirs and choir president;
attorney-at-law; a state senator

While I enjoyed the music we sang at UTC (and we sang a variety of music), I think the thing I appreciated most was really the spiritual dimension that Dr. Draper brought in an inoffensive way. He was who Glenn was, so it was not anything that was contrived or forced on anybody. When we would sing some songs, particularly, "When I Survey the Wondrous Cross" which was a favorite, he would stop and talk about the words and say, "When you are trying to sing this, you need to convey the musicality in the context of the spirituality of the song." You could tell it was a very real thing to him. It was not just music. It went beyond having quality music and, as a result when I was there during that period from 1976 to 1980, there was a sense in some ways that the choir was my church, it was my fraternity. Other people found all those things in other places.

Other things that I remember about Glenn are that he was a very demanding person, he expected the best, and I think sometimes he thought we were better than we were. He would want us to put down the music, but we did not know the music. You could not look at your music. It was like walking into your second year Spanish class and being told, "Now say everything in Spanish." However, I forgot my first year Spanish! There were times when, to be honest, it could be frustrating. You did not know the song, yet he wanted you to know it. You were supposed to put your music down, and then you put it down and you couldn't sing it right, so it was a catch-22!

Glenn was also famous for pulling out stuff at the very end and saying, "This is a good piece, we need to have this for the tour." I will never forget one of the things we most enjoyed doing was a spiritual medley and a hymn medley, and I don't think on either of those we ever saw a sheet of music. He would write the words on the board and he would go to each part and sing their part and you would put little pieces of them together. He then would move onto the next part and sing everybody their part. Of course, most of these we knew, we had heard them growing up, but not necessarily all the words, and the rhythms and harmonies might be a little different here and there. He was a very creative guy and would always come up with something!

He was not afraid to do things that I thought were unusual at the time. He came up with the commercial medley. We would be right in the middle of a series of sacred songs or maybe other tunes, and "Now for a commercial from your favorite sponsors." We would sing "Sometimes you feel like a nut and sometimes you don't." So, we would sing all these commercial bits and then we would pick back up where we left off.

He was willing to adapt to the times. We did—it wasn't a rock 'n' roll medley, but it was not just show tunes and old love songs from the '50s. We did "Boogie Fever" and stuff like that, and we wore outrageous pop costumes. We did a little more modern dancing with it, since Glenn was always open to adapting to the style and the trends of music and what was popular, particularly if we would go into high schools. He didn't want to sing "Love Is a Many Splendored Thing" all the time because they had never heard it, and they could care less, and it was boring. Instead, we all put on knickers, suspenders, and wild flowered shirts and sang "Boogie Fever."

Whether you wanted to hear show tunes, classical music, or elevator music like "Love Is a Many Splendored Thing," he would even inject unusual humor. We would sing "Old McDonald's Farm," and Tommy Taylor was the best "dog" I have ever seen in my life. Tommy was my roommate and he could howl. He is a choir director now. I will never forget once when he did that and people would just die laughing, so there was something for everybody. Glenn was able not only to have a good product, but he was able to sell that product to his singers, which made our product even that much better.

There were times that I would come home and be frustrated with Glenn because he had been so demanding or he had been so hard on somebody in practice who was a friend. The next day if he had asked me to walk over nails through fire into a brick wall, as fast as I could I would have said, "Okay." I think he would have been a great general. If we had needed to go to combat, he would have been one of those men that at times you would have loved to hate, but whatever he would have told you to do, you would have been ready to do it. He demanded a lot, but he also knew when to demand, when to stroke, and when to lay off. I will always look back with warm memories on those years.

Dr. Bill W. Stacy
UTC chancellor for the last six years;
a big supporter of Glenn Draper's musical endeavors

He starts with fine, decent Christian values. We used to say, "A good man speaking well," so you have a good man doing what he loves to do. I think you start with some character and decency, and then you look at his musical talents, his repertoire, and the ability to know music and to select it and to put it on. Then third, he is in the showman's business, able to inspire and to cause his kids to perform well, not only musically, but in essence in a kind of show or performance mode. There is just the fact that he loves what he does, and it shows in the sheer exuberance about his directing music and choirs.

Supporting something that is really good is very easy. I was very pleased to relay to him an invitation from the National Prayer Breakfast chairman this past year, and was very proud of their work there. It is a bit strange, honestly, for a choir from a public university being the featured choir at a religious orientation; however, most of the great choral music in the world is religious music. It is not surprising that choral music would have that preponderance or maybe even an overwhelming place in the literature of choral groups; however, out of this university, it still fits. The institution is very comfortable with its former Methodist sponsorship as a small liberal arts school. It changed maybe about the time Glenn got here. They still sanction the chapel so that there could be a Methodist service in there, whether it's a wedding or any other church ordinance. Nevertheless, it is part of our heritage here, so Christian music has more than acceptance. It has a desire and an affirmation, rather than being just tolerated.

Kami Hudson
UTC choirs; assisted with choreography of Singing Mocs;
Glenn Draper Singers

If I had one statement to sum up Dr. Draper, it would be something that he has said quite often that fits him perfectly: "I don't try to take *people* and make *music*. I try to take *music* and make *people*." That is the best statement that I know about him, because that is what he does. I think he is so effective with college students my age because we are trying to find out who we want to be and where we want to be in life. Also, he cares so much, not just for everyone, but for our age group particularly, his caring is genuine.

Robert John Allison Waller
UTC choirs; Lake Junaluska Singers; Glenn Draper Singers

I first met Dr. Draper when I signed up for the Chattanooga Singers in the spring of 1996, and went in for the audition for voice placement. He told me that he really liked my voice, and that was just it. I saw him as a tyrant until our first concert, because he just kept getting onto everyone. There were always one or two in the class singled out because they were troublemakers, and there was usually just cause for that. My case was no exception! However, after the first concert, I really fell in love with the whole situation. On the first day we sang through a piece three times. The first time we just did it without singing notes, just reading the parts. The second time, we sang it "la, la, la," and the third time, we sang it as it was written. The first time we sang it, it was absolutely horrible, but the third time it sounded like we were a recording. It completely fascinated me that he could take five minutes and turn a group of people from all kinds of backgrounds into a tremendous choir.

Anthony J. D'Andrea
UTC director of bands; one of Glenn's closest friends at UTC

Glenn is the busiest person that I have ever met in my life, and he stays young that way. I have never seen anybody handle so many different things as well as he does. He is definitely a people person. He knows what audiences like to hear and he gives it to them. He has been very successful with the kids—works them to death and always has them performing all over the place. Whether you like that style of music is not even a factor. It is just that he is so good at what he does. He is brilliant. He is extremely well-known, and the university is going to miss him when the time comes for him to finally retire. He is quite an unusual and talented man.

Lee Greenwood
Well-known professional performer; admirer of Glenn W. Draper and his music

Upon meeting Glenn Draper, you immediately get the feeling you have known him for a long time. His gentle manner reflects his love for humanity. His excitement for life is infectious and before you know it, you're drawn into his world and become a part of something great. I feel blessed to know Glenn and his music.

Kim Payne Greenwood
UTC choirs; former Miss Tennessee

As I reflect on my time at the University of Tennessee at Chattanooga, those years are packed full of images of Dr. Draper in the rehearsal room, on the concert stage, and on planes to distant lands. Most importantly, those years are full of memories of Dr. Draper's caring, kindness, and his ability to strengthen character in college students at a very vulnerable time in their lives.

Dr. Draper is a truly brilliant, gifted, and giving man. I feel so honored and blessed to have found myself under his tutelage in music as well as in life! He totally lives each day to the fullest and continues to push himself (and those around him) toward personal excellence in every aspect of his life. One day, when our two boys go off to college, I hope they have a wise and caring friend/professor like Dr. Draper, who will take the time to show them the way.

UTC TOURS:
STATESIDE AND OVERSEAS

A CHOIR without concerts or tours is like a boat without a sail, a car without gasoline, or a couple without each other. Music is best created for listening people and not for buildings. One of the main reasons Dr. Masterson wanted me to come to UTC was to organize singing groups who would carry music and goodwill from Chattanooga around the world.

A lumberyard of seats in an empty auditorium does not talk back, and an empty chair never says to another chair, "Check out that sound!" My work was cut out for me at UTC since there was no choir for me to conduct either at school or the First Presbyterian Church.

At school, the only time I could schedule a choir rehearsal was at noon, which was the activities period and the only time that many students had an opportunity to eat lunch. I got hamburgers and drinks and took them to the rehearsal room in Cadek Hall, and it worked!

I promised the choir that I would take them to many places around the world that they had never been. *Who is this man?* they wondered. One of the girls by the name of Susan Martin asked, "How good is this choir going to be? If it's not any good, I don't want to be a part of it." I replied, "If it's not going to be any good, I won't be its director."

On the day before Thanksgiving, we gave our first public performance to a packed hall in the Guerry Student Center. Dr. and Mrs. Masterson, Mr. and Mrs. Polk Smartt, Ben Haden, and a number of people from the First Presbyterian Church were there. I had always said that the best was to come—and it was! I'm grateful to Susan for asking just how good this choir was going to be!

The sensational tours have included: the Rotary Club International Convention; a nine-week all-expense-paid tour to Europe; the Royal Albert Hall in London, England; Carnegie Hall in New York, New York; Olympic Stadium in Moscow, Russia; the White House in Washington, D.C.; the Sydney Opera House in Australia; and the Presidential Prayer Breakfast in Washington, D.C.

THE CHATTANOOGA SINGERS have toured Australia in 1984, 1986, 1988, 1991, 1994, and 1998. Reverend Sir Alan Walker, who was responsible for us going, tried to get as much mileage out of those trips as possible. In 1986 he arranged radio and TV concerts and he had us go to the studios for ABC (the Australian Broadcasting Company in Sydney) and record an hour-long television program before going on to nine other cities, including Canberra and Melbourne. After we had been touring for about a week, we recorded the concert at the Sydney Town Hall, and then a week later we went into a studio and lip-synched that music, which is absolutely easier once you have it recorded. Of course, in a live performance you have to keep in mind that you may have people coughing or sneezing.

On our 1988 tour, we sang in New Zealand first. We then flew from New Zealand to Brisbane, which is quite a bit north of Sydney. Another great thing about that tour was that we stayed the first week in the same homes and they bused us out to different concerts every night. They were holding the World Expo '88 in Brisbane and we sang at that. That was a real experience. On the very first night when we landed in Brisbane, I was staying with some wonderful people and I was so excited about getting there, but sleepy and ready to go to bed so we could get up the next day. We were scheduled to have a concert in Brisbane at a big beautiful church right in the middle of the city. The telephone rang after I had been there about fifteen or twenty minutes, and these two men wanted to come over and talk to me. I said, "Is there any other time that we can do it?" They said, "No. Alan Walker wants to record tomorrow night's concert." I said, "If you mean the first concert, that would be bad! It would be our worst concert." They said, "You try to tell that to Alan Walker down in Sydney." No matter how I protested about that, they recorded the concert. I didn't hear anything more about it, and I didn't even want to ask anything about it. I thought maybe they had forgotten it or it didn't turn out, so they weren't going to do it after all.

The following Sunday afternoon, those two gentlemen said, "Sir Alan is coming up tomorrow and we want to start filming what you recorded the other Saturday night." I said, "I haven't even heard it, so we cannot do that. You have to give me the tape." That night, after the concert, when I got home at ten, they brought me a tape and I sat there and listened to it. I listened to three minutes of it, and I said, "This is not good. This is a poor recording, we didn't do a good job, and I will not film our program to that." They said, "What are you going to do? You have to tell Alan Walker. Do not tell us, as it will not do any good. He is a very strong-willed man who knows many people in Australia." I got him on the phone and I said, "Alan, I just listened to that tape and it's embarrassing. We can do a lot better than that." He said, "Well, we are planning to come up tomorrow and we have the TV people set to film you up in the Blue Mountains of Australia," which is quite a bit west of where we were in Brisbane. I said, "Alan, we cannot do it." He said, "What do you mean, you cannot do it?!" "We are not going to do it," I said, "it will not work." He said, "Pray tell me, what in the world do you have in mind?" I said, "I have in mind doing a live concert in the Sydney Opera House." He said, "Oh my God, that would break us, we could never afford that." I said, "If you got a lot of people you could afford it." He said, "How are you going to get a crowd?" I said, "Every night we will promote the Sydney Opera House concert, but first, you have to call to see what night is available." He said, "What time is good for you?" I said that our last night in Australia would be fantastic. He said, "Okay, let me call you right back." He called back and said, "You are not going to believe this, but that is the only night they have free in the whole month!" I said, "We just need one night. It's like a parking place, you only need one parking place—don't worry about all the parking places you did not get—you don't need them." He said, "Draper, I cannot believe you. You win out again. We are good friends, you understand, and I want to keep that good friendship."

I promoted heavily at all the concerts that we did. I told people that there was one great thing about our tour: "We are going to see you again next week because we are going to be at the Sydney Opera House Sunday night." I asked, "How many people from here would go on a bus—raise your hands," and I got a show of hands every place! That is how we built a crowd to come to that concert. There were about 2,400 people who came to the concert that Sunday. When we got to Sydney, I went over to the opera house just to look it over. I did not know you had to have a guide to take you around, you cannot just ramble around at your own leisure in that place. A man could get lost in there, like getting lost in St. Paul's Cathedral. I met these two people and they escorted me in. We had a bite of lunch there in a little restaurant, and then we went into the hall. It was a beautiful hall, and I thought about all the famous people who had been there, and now the Chattanooga Singers were going to sing there. We came from our rehearsals in our little choir room to singing in this world-famous place.

We went in, and they asked what I needed. I said, "We need some risers," and they asked, "How high?" I said that I didn't know, about nine inches. So he went over to the wall and pushed a button, and risers came up out of the floor. I had never seen anything like that. I asked, "What are the acoustics like?" and he replied, "What do you want them to be like?" I said that I wanted them to be alive. So he pushed some more buttons and these cloudlike fixtures hanging so high up that you don't even notice them, start moving around in different formations so they can focus the sound. He said, "You tell me when you think we have it right." So when I left there, we had the risers coming out of the floor, we had the sound very good, we knew where we would all meet, and we had dressing rooms!

The organ is way up high and you have to climb steps to get up there, but you can watch the director down below on a monitor. Jim Wilson could see me conducting on the monitor. That was a wonderful time—it was one of the best tours I have ever been on in my whole life. After the Sydney Opera House "any old storm shed just won't work anymore." You are willing to pay more rent from now on! You may turn down some places that you don't want to go to, because you say this is not the Sydney Opera House.

On our next trip in 1991, Sir Alan booked us at the Sydney Opera House. However, we didn't have to go out and sell it, and we had a huge crowd of people who paid. One thing I remember about that concert, after it was over several people came running up to me and said, "Oh, we are so glad you sang that song 'Surely the Presence of the Lord Is in This Place,' it is beautiful. When you were here before you sang that in the round with candles and they televised it. We have searched everywhere for that music and have written to your country. We have tried to find recordings of it, but we haven't been able to do it. However, we took your recordings from the television to our church and taught it to our congregation. Every service we have Sunday morning is now closed with the singing of 'Surely the

Presence of the Lord Is in This Place.' We always said if your choir ever comes back to Australia, we would go. That is why we came tonight. We rented four vans to come hear your program." We were very appreciative that they did that.

Lounelle M. Draper
Glenn's wife

On one of our later Australia choir tours we had the privilege of singing in the Sydney Opera House. We were so thrilled because it was a packed house. The people who worked in that particular auditorium were just astounded when they heard this choir from America. When we first came in, they were not cooperative, but once that rehearsal ended and the performance started, they were just in awe. I was sitting beside them, up in the control booth, because I knew the sound and lighting that Glenn would want. They did not allow me to touch the controls, but I could tell them what was coming up.

The Sydney Opera House sits right by the water, and boats come up and dock very close. I had noticed the hammer and sickle emblem on an enormous cruise ship from Russia as I walked in the auditorium that night. It was the first time I had ever seen that up close and personal and not on CNN or in the newspaper. Someone on that particular cruise ship evidently picked up a paper and thought, *I have a free night, I think I will go to this concert because there is an American choir at the Sydney Opera House.* He was a card-carrying Communist. One of Glenn's final numbers was "When I Survey the Wondrous Cross." After the performance was over the man walked up to an usher who, thank the Lord, happened to be a Christian, and said in English, "I want what these singers have. I want what they are singing about, Jesus Christ." This usher led that card-carrying Communist to Christ that night after that concert. The word got back to us through Winifred, the wife of the organizer of the entire tour, Rev. Sir Alan Walker, who had worked so hard on this tour. Sir Walker, knighted by the Queen of England, was the head of evangelism for the Methodist Church around the world.

Dr. Reginald Mallett

My wife and I have been friends of Glenn and Lounelle since the 1960s. I think the major step forward in our friendship was the year 1972. It was in that year that Glenn brought the University of Tennessee Choir, "The Chattanooga Singers," to England. I believe this was Glenn's first English tour. This tour was organized by the Reverend Peter Bolt. Peter is a retired

Methodist minister living in Wales. He, together with another minister, the Reverend Alan Hughes, worked very closely with Glenn in this and subsequent visits to England.

On the occasion of Glenn's first visit, my wife and I were living in Reading where I was in family medical practice. None of our friends there had experienced a visit from an American choir, and the unanimous verdict was that attendance would be small. Knowing what an exciting evening Glenn would present, my wife and I began to get folk interested. We held a series of suppers to which we invited five or six couples, and at which we played some of the records we had collected from Lake Junaluska. Each couple agreed to provide hospitality for one of the singers. Since there were about forty members in the choir, we now had a significant number of people who were involved in the coming concert. Each couple was given ten programmes to pass on to others. The result was that the largest Methodist church in the area was absolutely packed for the night of the concert. Even the balcony, that had not been used in decades, was filled. Everyone was captivated by the singing.

We met Glenn, Lounelle, and the singers at the airport at the beginning of this tour. Reading was to be their first stop. Glenn had brought with him all kinds of equipment such as risers, instruments, etc. It was impossible to find room for all this, together with the choir, in the large bus that would be their base as they travelled across England. Glenn entered a steep learning curve and adapted very quickly. The tour was a triumph, and marked the beginning of a long association with England which experienced other visits both by the University of Chattanooga Choir and the Junaluska Singers.

One such visit stands out very vividly. It was in the early 1970s. On this visit my wife and I took a week's vacation and travelled to each of the venues where Glenn and the Junaluska Singers were appearing. The most memorable event in this tour was in a town that I thought unpromising. The hall where the performance was to take place was rather unattractive, and the concert had not been promoted very well. There were about seventy elderly people present, and they did not appear to show any real enthusiasm. I was, therefore, astonished when Glenn came on with his exuberant bounding energy and his great smile. He and the singers could not have given a more upbeat performance if they were before a crowd of two thousand at Lake Junaluska. Before they were through, that relatively small group of people was absolutely captivated. In this, Glenn showed his sheer genius and commitment. He could so easily have decided to offer a modified low key concert. Instead, he gave the whole works. It was as splendid as anything I have ever heard anywhere! I thought that displayed the character of the man. By his dedication to his music, he created an atmosphere and lifted spirits in what could so easily have been a depressing situation.

Another thing that is worth noting is the way in which Glenn and his singers were greeted with standing ovations. Such are rare in England outside political rallies. Even for great musicals in London's West End, standing ovations are rare. Glenn, however, regularly brought his audiences to their feet in delight and even rapture.

James H. Cooley Jr.
UTC choirs and past president; Glenn Draper Singers;
church choir director

Concert experiences are fantastic, no matter where you are in the States or overseas. An experience of being with Glenn that stands out in my mind was the first tour to Australia that he did in May 1984. As Glenn loves to say, "Music is a universal language," and true enough it is very universal, and I will never forget flying into the country of Australia that morning. We had flown out of Honolulu on a Boeing 747 at midnight the night before and, of course, it was a long flight with time changes. As we were on approach into Sydney, Australia, seeing Sydney harbor and other sights, our group of about forty gathered and sang "The Majesty and Glory of Your Name." It was a thrilling experience, and I will never, ever forget that. That was a ministry opportunity. I guess that is the amazing thing about Glenn, I see how the Lord planted him in a secular university, at UTC, but he never compromised his witness for Christ. I look back on that five-year span of being a Chattanooga Singer, and I look at all that I learned in terms of leadership and music. However, I really look back then and think, *God, you gave me an opportunity to be a missionary for a while*—He really did—*and to help touch people's lives and bring joy to them*. That was a great time coming into Sydney with the people who got to share in that experience.

Another time that I will never forget, and I think this speaks to the love that Glenn has for people and his singers, when we were in England and had pulled into a small town, we had the afternoon to mill around. At the midpoint of the hour we were supposed to be back on the bus to leave. Well, there we were having a great time, and we met at our appointed time, everybody piled on the bus, and we pulled out. We had a counting-off system, where we accounted for everybody. We got about twenty to thirty minutes down the road, and somebody from the back of the bus said, "Where is Randy?" It turned out that one of our basses was not on the bus. It was as if one of our sheep was missing. We turned around and went back. By the time we got back to this tiny English hamlet, it was absolutely pouring down rain, and we were all dry on the bus. I remember as we drove up, we could see Randy in the distance; he was crouched over, holding something over his head trying to keep dry.

We pulled up and he was thrilled to see us, but I will never forget Glenn's response. Glenn always sat in the front of the bus. Randy got on the bus and he was soaking wet. Nevertheless, Glenn put his arm around him and hugged him. I thought to myself, *Good night, he is remarkable, that is totally remarkable!* He would have done that for the best singer or the worst singer. It would not have mattered—that is his love for people and his commitment to the people he works with. I have never forgotten that.

I guess another story that I have to tell is very unusual. In March of 1992, I returned to sing for a tour as one of the "senior citizens." My time at UTC was really from 1980 to 1985, but Glenn had another tour in March 1992, and I was thirty-two years old then. He called me and said, "I could really use you." My dad was still living, but had been diagnosed with cancer in October of 1991. I knew that this might be my last opportunity to do a tour with Glenn Draper, so I said, "I need to do this!"

We were in a concert one night in a Methodist church somewhere in England, and the choir was split. That was nothing new. You will see the most creative formations with Glenn Draper. Anyway, half the group was on the bottom floor and half of us were upstairs in the balcony. We were all singing together in a circle around the organ, and the back of my knees were against the organ bench. I thought that the organ bench was firmly placed and that it was not going anywhere. During one of the breaks in one of the songs, when the whole choir was not singing—remember I am getting to be an old man, I'm not eighteen to twenty-two anymore—I leaned back against that bench. As I leaned back, hoping to be propped up, the bench went backwards, and I went with it. Lori Beth P. was singing a solo, "I Am a Poor, Wayfaring Stranger, Traveling Through This World of Woe." I fell into the organ and it played baaaaaaaaaa! I fell right into the organ, how do you get out of that? I was helpless. The beauty of the story is this: Glenn was on the lower floor, so he couldn't see me, and then he hears this organ and this banging around. The organ was on and it was making these tones, but he knows there is no organist up there! Who is playing the organ? All Glenn knew was that the organ was playing! However, when I fell into the organ, the note that I hit was right on the pitch that she was singing! So it was not a totally dissident sound because it was on the right pitch. I was pulled out of the organ by a couple of girls. I have tried to forget that story, but it is hilarious! I just wish it had happened to somebody else besides me. That was a comical thing that happened that night, and Glenn says to this day that I am the only guy who could fall into an organ and come out on the right pitch! Nothing ever stopped, we just continued like nothing ever happened!

Kim Cargile

One of my favorite experiences with Glenn was in Rio de Janeiro. They have the big Christo statue up on Christ Mountain that you can see from all over the city. We were determined that we were going to get up there. No one knew you had to have reservations on the shuttle bus that takes you up there. They did not have seats for most of us. Glenn looked at me and said, "Kim, we are going up that mountain!" He got us a taxi and a bunch of us piled in it like sardines, and we got up there before the other people who rode the bus and paid more money than we did. The cab driver waited for us, so we stayed up there as long as we wanted for less money than those who were scrambling around to get on that bus. We always joke about that when we meet an obstacle. He will say, "We are going up that mountain!" It reminds us of a fun day.

The first Indonesian trip, of all the trips that I have been on, was the most life-changing because of the people. I have never met people like that in my entire life. We went there thinking we were going to minister to them, but they ministered to us more than we ever did to them. Christianity is all about showing love, and I have never met people in my entire life who just love you unconditionally even though they had never met you before. We were from across an ocean, but they treated us like royalty. However, the weird thing is that tends to be the case (but not to that extent) anywhere we go overseas.

Everyone thinks his choruses are the grandest thing ever. A scripture talks about a prophet without honor in his own hometown, referring to Jesus. However, it is really true, because Chattanooga has no idea really of the extent of what Glenn Draper does, especially overseas. If they could ever go to England and see those packed halls, or Australia where we sang at the Sydney Opera House, they would see how popular he is. There is a really neat family from Sheffield, England, who follows us. They are our own little groupies. The first concert we do during our England tours they are there, they take their vacations while we are there, and they follow wherever we go in the country. They started coming in 1994, and every time we have been since, which I guess is maybe four times. They come here to see us too. It is just amazing how Glenn has made those contacts through Lake Junaluska that gets him many overseas trips.

Jim Wilson
Pianist and accompanist, First Presbyterian Church
and overseas tours; Glenn Draper Singers; Glenn's close friend

We were in England somewhere, in the middle of a concert doing a long piece of music. The last part of it really picked up in volume and intensity, and it occurred to Glenn suddenly in the middle of the piece that it would be great to have the organ playing the last part of it. It just happened that the organ was upstairs, and there was an accapella section in the middle of this piece of music. Glenn points to me and says, "Go up and play the organ," and I went racing upstairs carrying my music, sat at the organ, got the stops pulled, and by the time we were at that place in the music, I was ready to go with the organ.

I will never forget the trip to Australia, at the Sydney Opera House, where we sang a couple of different times. The first time I had the opportunity to practice some on the organ when there was no one there, and that was a unique situation because that almost never happens. When we did the concert, I had played the organ on some pieces, but the organ is very high up and the stage area is below. You can see the organ console well up on the wall, and to get there you have to go up a staircase and walk a catwalk. It takes forever to get up there to it. Timing was not a problem, it was just so far away and I was very concerned about staying with him. When I got up there, I found that there was a television monitor focused on him and another on the choir and then there was an audio monitor, so I could hear the sound simultaneously. It worked out well. That was a breathtaking experience.

Stacie Caraway Coder
UTC choirs; Lake Junaluska Singers; First Presbyterian Church choir;
Glenn Draper Singers; attorney-at-law

When we are going on tours and must change planes and reservations and not pay any fees, Glenn will stand in the back and watch the ticket agents at the counter and predict which one will be the most cooperative. He will wait and let people go in front of him until he gets that one agent he has chosen, then he will go forward. It is amazing, it never fails. The rest of us will be in the other line. He watches their countenance, he watches how they deal with people, and then, like I said, the rest of us will be asking for the exact same thing in other lines. However, he will get it and the rest of us are trapped in the airport for the next two days. He doesn't flounder, and I think that is another sign that the Lord is with him.

Bob and Dorothy McDowell
First Presbyterian Church choir; Glenn Draper Singers tours

Now that we are retired, we said yes to a trip overseas. It was one of the most enjoyable trips that I have been on (and I have been overseas several times), just to see how the Lord works through Glenn. No one can say no to Glenn. As he says, you never know whether you can have something unless you ask. We got to the hotel in England where we were to spend the night, and there were no rooms for us. He had made the reservations through his secretary, Rosie, but evidently they were made through the headquarters and not through this particular hotel in England. They had booked all the rooms. Glenn said, "I have a group here, they are tired, they are sleepy. We need rooms." They said, "But we are all booked up!" Glenn said, "You must un-book." They said, "You can go about four blocks to another hotel and we can put you up there." He said, "No, this is the hotel where we booked, this is where we stay." The hotel phoned ahead to whatever group was coming in and told them that they would have to go to the other hotel, and they found every one of us a room. We said, "Praise the Lord," because we were tired.

Glenn does these kinds of things. He doesn't get angry about it, he is just so firm in what he says. They listen to him, and I think the Lord just steps in and says, *you have to say yes to this man.* Glenn does not back down, no matter what they tell him. He is a wonderful person to travel with because he cares about the group. He wants to make sure that everyone is comfortable and he will call to ask if everything is all right. When he has twenty-five to thirty people, which is a lot to care for, he cares about them all.

Eliot McDowell
Member of UTC choirs; Glenn Draper Singers tours

We were on one international trip and something happened to one of Dr. Draper's teeth, he had chipped it or lost a crown. We thought, *Okay, we are going to be without Dr. Draper for at least the rest of the day.* Two hours later we were back rehearsing. Somebody had found a dentist for him and got him in right away. Nothing stops the man—feast, famine, or whatever. We were in Indonesia and, because of the small planes that they had, we sent half the choir on one flight and half came later. The first shift was Dr. Draper, Kim [Cargile], and all the men except two who had remained behind to be the protectors of the women. We got up bright and early in the morning and were on the plane by 6:30. We jetted over to a new church that they had just built in Indonesia. While we were there, Glenn said, "Okay, we are going to do some male chorus stuff." He didn't have a stitch of music on him, and he said, "La, la, la, la . . . I want you guys to sing that." After about an hour, we had it down, and I had never seen him that happy. Just having that male chorus sound is where I think his roots are.

Dot Carter

We did a two-hour concert every night on tours, and it was never the same concert twice—never. Most people would be just absolutely frightened to have to go through that much music. I will never forget the first time he asked me to go to Florida with them. He said to come by the university and pick up a pack of music, and it was 180 songs that I had to memorize in two weeks because he would not allow us to use music. I nearly passed out because I had been a choral director and I had just never been with a director like this.

Robert J. A. Waller

On a tour, Glenn is absolutely notorious about having a list of songs before the concert starts, and then when you are on stage he will say something to Kim (Cargile) that no one in the choir can hear, and suddenly everything is changed completely. It has made us wonderful, because we can hear a measure of piano accompaniment at the beginning and we can sing it. He knows the keys of everything. The way it works is, if you sing this song, it can go into one of these other two songs, and you know that because he will tell you it could go into this or this. You have to pay attention constantly. For any concert, I (and other singers who are a bit more seasoned) pay attention to what he says the first song is. After that we listen to what we are going to end with especially, but all the stuff in the middle is up in the air—you just hold on and pray. We always pull it off wonderfully, because he never makes us do something that we do not know, that we can't pull off. He has a tremendous amount of faith in us, and I think because of that we live up to it.

Martin W. Hamby Jr.
UTC choirs and Lake Junaluska accompanist for seven years;
a Christian music arranger; Glenn's close friend

Glenn does not use his camera on tours very much, and I always wondered why. As I get a little older, I think I probably know; he was too busy enjoying the trips and the students, without trying to capture them on film. I think that would have detracted from the pleasure that he was having then. I just have so much admiration for him and for what he does and how he lives his life. I asked him once why he takes the trips, and especially why he likes to return to the same places. He gave me an answer that I really was not expecting, and that I have never forgotten. He said, "To see the looks on the faces of the kids that see this for the first time." That really motivates him to be a facilitator and to open up worlds for young minds. That is a very admirable trait.

Jay Lifford
UTC choirs; Lake Junaluska Singers; Glenn Draper Singers

I remember one experience on my first trip to England in 1997, when we went to this huge Gloucester cathedral. We were inside looking around, and there was a beautiful altar in the middle of the rotunda, and Glenn said, "Wouldn't it be great to sing right there?" We thought they would not let us do that! Well, that was the last time I ever underestimated Glenn Draper. He talked to the priest or whoever was over it, and convinced him to let us sing a few numbers in the round in the middle of the altar. We gathered around and sang the Rachmaninoff "Ave Maria," and the Biebl "Ave Maria." I remember singing that song, there is a big chord at the end of it, and when we finished the chord you could hear it right above us, and it touched all of us. It got so quiet in the whole cathedral, nobody clapped, nobody did anything, and Glenn just looked around and he said, "Just kneel and pray if you'd like, and then go back to the bus. However, I want you to take your time. I want all of you to sit here and when you think you are ready to go back to the bus, we will be waiting for you. Just take a moment, and if you are a praying person, pray, because I can feel God's presence." We all just sat there quietly.

I didn't really know God at all then, but I remember tears streaming down my face because it was just an awesome experience. We all went back to the bus. It was amazing because our morale was not very good on that day up to that point. We were just not getting along. We didn't like each other, but that experience solved that problem. It was exactly what we needed at just the right time. I have always felt that God's hand is on Glenn. I have read that if you want to take on a God-sized task, you have to ask God's help. Glenn's whole life has been a God-sized task, he always wants to do something that somebody told him he could not do. I just feel like God has really anointed him and has been with him. After six years of being with Glenn, I'm convinced of it now!

FIRST PRESBYTERIAN CHURCH
1968–2001

Choir

Robert H. Shipp

David Cooper, in his well-written *Catalyst for Christ, 150 Years. First Presbyterian Church Chattanooga, Tennessee*, wrote, "Mr. (Ben) Haden's preaching brought dynamic change to the ministry at the corner of

McCallie and Douglas in 1967 but Dr. Draper and his music, beginning in 1968, dramatically underpinned that preaching with spirit and warmth. Instead of good music just being presented, the congregation became involved in it, altering the whole tenor of worship."

Ben Haden
Minister of First Presbyterian Church thirty-one years;
radio and TV evangelist, with "Changed Lives" radio program;
Glenn's close friend

One day I was at the Kiwanis Club in Miami as a guest speaker, and Glenn and I happened to be in the men's room at the same time. I recognized him and remembered that I had met him back in my first week in Miami. I said, "Glenn, I have lost my choir director, who was both organist and choir director, and I would like for you to be my choir director. The pay is $300 per month." Glenn looked at me and said, "I would like to come, but in all frankness, my brother and I have the very rare privilege of supporting both our parents in retirement." I thought I was back in God's country. I had not heard that since I was a child. In any event, that was the first time I tried to hire him. I didn't argue with him because there was no argument with that.

When I came to Chattanooga in 1967, I did know who I wanted as my choir director. They had an opera coach as their choir director for forty-six years, and between the time I accepted the call and reported to duty he had died of emphysema, so the vacancy was there. I called Glenn and he asked, "What kind of choir do you have?" I said, "Well, we have a quartet, and they have sung here for twenty-five years. They sing at the Synagogue on Friday nights and they sing here Sunday mornings. There are a couple of people who sit in with them, so I guess you could say that we have a choir of four." He said, "That is not a whole lot!" I knew I had my man when he said that. I told him, "I want the quality of the Mormon Tabernacle Choir, and I want music that people like and can sing. I know you are the man."

I kept calling him on the telephone. I knew Glenn was the right man, and I knew you did not build a church on preaching. I can show you one church after another where no matter how good the preaching is, the music program nearly offsets it. I got Glenn and his younger son, Dean (who was then five) to come up and look at the situation and meet with the committee. He went back and talked with his wife, and they prayed a lot about the possible move. She told some people there was a crazy man in Chattanooga trying to get them to move from Miami. Lounelle said, "I can't stand it any longer, I am going up and look at this situation." She is not an aggressive woman, but she came alone to look this thing over so she could discount it. She met with the committee and asked all the questions. She walked off the plane and told Glenn, "I have never been so royally treated in my whole life." Then when they put their house on the market, they thought that would be the last test. In a poor real estate market, the house sold the same day and they got their price, no argument—so they came.

We had a separator wall in the church, four or five feet high. The choir sat behind it in loose chairs and did their nails, combed their hair, or took notes because they couldn't be seen from out front and they could not see the service, except when they rose. They were in the pit. Of course, the students in the balcony were seeing them the whole time. There was one woman in that quartet who had a voice that was so high that when she sang with the quartet and with the congregation singing, she was louder than the entire congregation. We did not get rid of the quartet and it took me eighteen months to get the separator lowered to where they became part of the worship service.

======

AFTER I FIRST CAME, we had eleven people in the choir the first Sunday and nineteen the second, and people thought, *Golly, a miracle has taken place!* The choir loft used to have steps that went down to the organ. I had to put one foot on one side and one foot on another place to direct the choir. The next Sunday I went down in the kitchen and got a stool, put it down in that hole, and stood on it when I directed the church choir. However, from the congregation, it looked like I was standing on the pulpit, almost on the Bible. In this conservative Presbyterian church, it caused quite a stir to see this young whippersnapper standing on the pulpit. I said, "When we 'stand on the promises,' it doesn't mean literally," so I had a few times that were like that.

======

Dolores Cooley
A member of the quartet at First Presbyterian Church;
later a choir member for several years

Ben Haden had just come [to First Presbyterian Church], and the soprano soloist did not care for his preaching, so she left with no warning. I knew the tenor soloist in the church quartet. I had sung in the opera with him, and he called me and asked if I could come help them out as they needed a soprano soloist in the quartet. Glenn came shortly after that in 1968. Glenn, Lounelle, and I immediately hit it off from the very beginning. The Drapers said to me, "Dolores, where do we start?" I told Ben Haden we would build a choir! I said, "You will really have to promote it, Glenn, because this church has never had a choir and they are so traditional." I knew he had many barriers to overcome because I had been in this city all my life. Glenn had an advantage since he was also connected with the university. He could get some college kids to come over and start singing who weren't connected with the church. He did not try to take anybody away from their own church, and steadily we started having different ones come. He put out the word in the church congregation that we needed people to come join the choir. Before you knew it, the choir began to build slowly. The quartet stayed intact, however, the four of us had to take turns going to both services and singing at 8:30 and 11:00 and being there for all the services. Glenn's personality and his witness were just so dynamic and sincere that it did not take long to build up the choir.

I STARTED REHEARSALS Sunday morning at 10:00, before the 11:00 service, and had a Sunday school class. Ben said, "Glenn, you cannot do that. This is a really big Sunday school church, and they have to go to Sunday school." I said, "We will let our choir have its own Sunday school class followed by a rehearsal." We also had a rehearsal Wednesday nights. If the rehearsal started at 7:30, I would say the rehearsal will start at 7:29 and will be over at 9:16, and the choir members knew exactly when they were going to rehearse. Ben started and ended his midweek services with an alarm clock, and if he was in the middle of a sentence, he would stop and have a benediction and we were out of there. He used to say, "How dare preachers take advantage of people in the name of Christianity? We don't have that right because they are busy too, and I know because I was a businessman." We saw eye to eye on many things.

Ben never got into my business. We never had a meeting on what I was going to sing Sunday morning, nor did I ever ask him what he was going to preach Sunday, because if he had told me, I guarantee you he would not have preached it. Sometimes he changed his mind coming down the steps from his office going to the church. It was that fast. Ben said that he was in California at a meeting of ministers, and they were discussing church organization and all the things that go into making up a church, and they got around to the relationship of the choir director. One minister said, "I spend an hour a week with my choir director; another minister said, I spend a half-hour every morning." They spend all this time just preparing all these worship services so that everything fits. They came to Ben and asked him, "How much time do you and Glenn spend together?" He said, "Frankly, we don't spend any time. I have never asked him and he has never asked me." They said, "How do you explain that?" He answered, "Well, we are a couple of crap-shooters." That is how it works, and it just blew their mind. They couldn't believe it—they spent hours and money and time, and here he didn't know what we sang until it was over. I didn't know what he was preaching on until it was over. My relationship with him was very good.

Robert H. Shipp

Glenn had some questions about his decision to come to Tennessee. David Cooper tells about some of those problems in his book *Catalyst for Christ*:

> In the first few weeks after arriving in Chattanooga, Dr. Draper tried to interest anyone who would listen in joining a choir being built from the nucleus of the quartet. It was a struggle. He tried to put a spark in weak congregational singing by having warmups before the service, but a number of people frowned on that. He worried that the members of the quartet saw their nice arrangement being tampered with by a "slave driver." The organ was malfunctioning on a regular basis. By the time the October mission's conference had arrived, Dr. Draper was discouraged. He wrote a note that he never shared with anybody, stating his fears that he had misread the Lord's leading, that he had made a big mistake by coming to Chattanooga.
>
> But gradually the numbers in the choir increased. Dolores Cooley's husband, Jim, joined her; Jim Sasse's wife, Carolyn, joined him; Bill and Janice Leetch came; Dan Patrick came; Cecil Clark signed up; the Kessel family joined in; and others did too. Some of his UC choral students sang with their professor on Sunday, as well. A new organ was planned.
>
> As the choir began to grow, as the program at the university began to take shape, as his family began to settle in, a peace came over Glenn and he tore up his note. His ministries on both sides of McCallie Avenue began to meet with success. The success he had experienced so many times before. The success he knew came from a faithful God.

Dolores Cooley

Those were glory days for the First Presbyterian Church. Ben had just come and was making a tremendous impact on the city and people were coming to that church in droves. Glenn was building up the choir, and he had his university group, the Chattanooga Singers, and the Singing Mocs began to be known, and they were singing for everything in the city! It really became the focal point—it was a real ministry for me and it was the highlight of my life. Opportunities opened from being at First Presbyterian that I probably would have never had the opportunity to do—to go all over the country, sing at big conventions, and conferences. It was just a very special time.

Glenn has helped so many people at First Presbyterian that I am sure many people do not even realize. I was kind of on the inside and did know about some situations. We did have many of the wealthier people in Chattanooga, but being a downtown church, we had some very poor people who came in off the street. A few found their way to the front, and if they wanted to sing, Glenn would always make sure that they had the chance to sing and that they would fit in okay, and he would take them in.

Dr. John "Jack" T. Evans
Long time member and former president of
First Presbyterian Church choir; a retired physician

Glenn in music is every bit in his field as good as Ben Haden was in his, a good combination, but tough. People sometimes ask Glenn, "Do you get together with Ben on Friday or Saturday night, or Wednesday night before rehearsal and decide what he is going to preach on, and then try to correlate your music with what he is going to preach?" Well, neither one of them knew what they were going to do Sunday. Ben certainly did not know what he was going to preach Sunday. He often changed at the last minute, and it just worked out that, so often what Glenn chose for the music, just went so well with what Ben chose for his message. It always worked out. We had more people congratulate us when it had nothing to with humans. It just worked.

Ben Haden

Glenn is the only man whom I have ever met who likes everything from boogie to Bach, and I believe equally. I think Glenn is a genius. He took a group of people, which was no choir, and made it into a choir. In subsequent years at Christmas, I have heard, back to back, the Christmas concerts of the Mormon Tabernacle Choir and of the First Presbyterian, and I think he beat them. I think Glenn has opened more hearts to the Lord through music than I have done through preaching.

Sarah Lovell
First Presbyterian Church choir member;
UTC choir; Glenn Draper Singers tours

I grew up (and at age nineteen, am still growing up) at the First Presbyterian Church. Dr. Draper had been the director there since I could remember, so I have always looked up to the choir and wanted to be a part of it. I sang in Kings Kids, the children's group, for ten years. I kept singing, and when I was too old to be in it and I had adult parts, I would just help out. I then took a year off from singing since we do not have a youth choir at First Presbyterian, and tried to join the adult choir when I was thirteen and in the eighth grade. I had to audition with Dr. Draper in the beginning of the summer and he said, "Well, I do not think your voice is strong enough yet. We are going to take the summer off and then you can join in the fall." When I started singing in the choir, he would always tell me the story about how when he was fourteen years old he walked for three miles and got on the bus and then had to walk to the church to get to choir rehearsals. He just really encouraged me, and I wanted to keep coming. I decided later that I wanted to be a teacher, and through his influence I decided to be a music education teacher, teaching choruses at either a middle school or a high school.

Christmas Concerts

IN 1968, when I first went to the First Presbyterian Church, I told Ben I wanted to do a Christmas concert and he said, "Glenn, I do not want you to be embarrassed, but nobody comes to concerts here." I replied, "Ben, I have to try and I am going to do the *Messiah.*" Ben said, "Just take my warning, there is not going to be anybody here." The night of the concert the church was filled with people. Choirs from the university and the First Presbyterian Church joined, forty-five to fifty people must have probably been singing that first time. I had an organist from the Methodist college in Athens, Tennessee Wesleyan. The next year they let me hire an orchestra which added a new dimension.

After about three years of doing the *Messiah*, I decided to do a potpourri Christmas concert that was a little more difficult because I had to fit different kinds of Christmas music together. Ben started televising the Christmas concerts. Miss Tennessee, Kim Payne, who sang in my UTC choir, met Lee Greenwood on a tour while watching our Christmas concert on television in Thule, Greenland. They later married. My point is, Ben always thought big. He wanted to be the first one to do anything. Our broadcasts had to be timed down to the second, and we had to be dressed in exactly the right outfits. Then I started doing medleys for television. The choir would sing one number and the orchestra would play a number, then they would combine to do a number. We did that for about thirty years, I guess.

Jean Hanlin audited one of my classes and listened to some rehearsals for the Christmas concert, and she talked her husband, Carey, president of Provident Life into coming to the Christmas concert. The next day Carey came up after church and said, "Glenn, that Christmas concert was fabulous." I said, "You're with Provident Life Insurance Company, aren't you? What would you think about your company sponsoring the broadcast?" He said, "Well, I don't know, but I think it is a great idea." He called me the next day and said, "By the way, we want to sponsor next year's Christmas concert," and they continued that for thirteen to fifteen years.

At our last Christmas concert in 2002, we had 88 people in the orchestra and 155 people in the choir. It was a joint effort of the church, the Adventist university orchestra, and UTC, and resulted in a huge production. The Christmas concerts provided a great incentive to people who didn't even sing in our choir. They would practice and sing for our Christmas service and remain as choir members. After Christmas and in the spring of the year, we would join together and do works, either on the campus or at the church, and that relationship stayed forever.

Robert H. Shipp

"An outstanding musical Christmas program has been a tradition at First Presbyterian Church . . . with Dr. Draper combining his church and school singers and conducting an orchestra," writes David Cooper in his book, *Catalyst for Christ*. "The programs have usually been at 8:00 P.M. and have been standing-room-only performances, most with overflow audiences watching on closed circuit television in the fellowship hall. To obtain seats, many have found arrival at six P.M. necessary. Those have enjoyed watching the last minute rehearsals. They have shown the edited tapes on Chattanooga television on Christmas Eve and Christmas day. The broadcasts have also been carried on the Armed Forces Television Network around the globe."

WHEN YOU ARE in the performance area or you prepare sermons, you cannot preach last week's sermon. You have to come up with something new. This is what causes burnout in some people. Sundays start coming every five days, and the same is true when you do Christmas concerts. How many times can you sing "Silent Night" without starting with the fifth verse first, or singing one verse in minor to make it different, so people will say, "Well, I never heard that before." We have been doing a Christmas concert at the First Presbyterian Church, and every year they televise it.

After I had done several yearly performances, I could not just use a particular number for a close or a beginning, I had to have some variety. I was looking for an ending, and I heard Norman Luboff's recording of an arrangement of the Doxology, which says "Praise God From Whom All Blessings Flow." I went to school and asked Gaye Sellers to try to find Norman Luboff. She found him at home in Los Angeles, and I asked him if he ever published his arrangement of the Doxology. He started laughing and replied, "No, I didn't publish it. I never thought it would sell." I asked him if he had a copy since I wanted to use it in a Christmas concert. He said, "Glenn, I just moved into a new house and all my music is stacked in the garage or up in the attic, and I have no idea where anything is." I told him I would really like to have that arrangement, but since he didn't publish it, I was unable to buy it from a music distributor. He said he would try to find it.

One week went by, two weeks went by, and the third week we got this big package in the mail from Norman Luboff. It contained a hundred copies of his arrangement for the choir with full orchestration. I couldn't believe it! We sang that as the closing, and it was a sensation. People had never heard that arrangement of it. It was something that we had never done before.

You have to keep coming up with new things. I made a friend out of Norman Luboff. I said, "Norm, what do I owe you?" He replied, "Not a thing, just send me a tape of your recording." I sent him a copy and he sent me back a letter that said it sounded really good, I appreciate your hard work, let's keep in touch, etc. I told him I would love to record that some-time, and he said, "Do it. I don't have any intention of ever publishing it since I do not think it would really sell anyway." Norman Luboff has since passed away, and if I can just outlive my audiences, I can repeat the same music and performances, but I can't count on that.

GLENN DRAPER SINGERS
1985–Present

DOWN DEEP INSIDE, when I was a kid years ago or when I was in college, hearing the Robert Shaw Chorale or Fred Waring's Pennsylvanians, I thought, *Someday I am going to have a group like that.* On November 30, 1985, we did the first performance of the Glenn Draper Singers at the Tivoli Theater in Chattanooga, and we had a huge crowd. The Glenn Draper Singers hadn't done a recording then, and didn't do any recordings until 1989. We sang for the National Religious Broadcasters Convention in Washington, D.C., in 1988, and I was flooded with requests for recordings from radio stations all over America, but I did not have any recordings at that time.

When we were in a recording session at Lake Junaluska in the late 1980s, the recording engineer, Jim Deal, and Al Miller, one of the singers, said, "Glenn, we want to talk to you after we finish recording." Al had been in the Junaluska Singers for ten years. When we finished recording about 10:30 P.M., I said, "Guys, I'm tired. How about tomorrow?" They said, "No, it won't take long, come into my [Jim Deal's] office," which was in his van. Jim said, "We think you ought to organize your own group. You owe it to yourself because of all the work that you have put into it. Nobody else has many of these arrangements that you do, they are yours, and you owe it to us. We have followed you around all this time." I said, "Well guys, would you join me?" They said, "Yeah, this group would go with you anywhere."

That year after we went to the White House for a Christmas concert, our family was on the airplane going to Dallas from Chattanooga on Christmas Day, and Glenn Wright said to me, "Dad, you must do these recordings. When you do concerts, within three seconds you cannot even bring it back. That sound is gone, and is all in people's minds and soon forgotten. You must do recordings because five, ten, or fifteen years from now when you are gone, I want to be able to play these recordings for my friends and say, 'This is what my daddy's choir sounded like.'"

Lounelle had just read the riot act to me about slowing down and doing too many things and killing myself. She said, "I know you love us, but you have to show it. You are in too many things . . ." I said "Okay, Honey, I understand." After she fell asleep, Glenn said to me, "Daddy, who are some men you think would be great for the recordings?" I made up a list and when we got to Dallas, he called Jim Deal, the recording engineer, and all the guys and told them to come to First Presbyterian Church on the second of January, and then Thursday, Friday, and Saturday we would do recordings. Not one guy said, "I cannot come." Not one guy said, "How much are you going to pay me?" They all said, "I will be there." Glenn and Dean put up some tithe money and we recorded "Glenn and the Men" and "Heavenly Light." "Heavenly Light" was mixed because I had some women come in after a day and a half and we recorded a lot of music with them. That is how the Glenn Draper Singers began recording. [At the time of this publication, twenty CDs by the Glenn Draper Singers have been recorded.]

In March 1994, I took thirty-two Glenn Draper Singers to England, and it was probably one of the best singing groups that I have ever had. They were all top-notch singers who had sung with me in the past. We did not have a concert in London on the last night, so Jim and Noveita Wilson, Lounelle, and I had planned to go out on the town, have dinner, or go to a concert. Our wives said that they were too tired to go, so Jim and I decided to go to St. Paul's Cathedral instead. I said, "Evensong usually starts at 5:00, so why don't we get there about 4:30?"

We took the railway and got there around half past four. They were taking the seats and TV cameras down so I asked someone what was happening. They said they moved the service to four instead of five because the BBC wanted to televise it. The organist was playing so I said, "Jim, why don't we just sit here and relax awhile?" I saw them bring out a conductor's stand and, in a matter of minutes, they rolled a piano in and put it beside the music stand.

Soon we were informed that London's two-hundred voice Bach Festival Choir was going to rehearse the *St. Matthew Passion* at six o'clock. Within fifteen minutes a lot of people started coming in. They made one more announcement, "You have five minutes to leave through the front door." So we got up and pretended to go toward the door, except we walked way around the choir and came up where the men were, and both

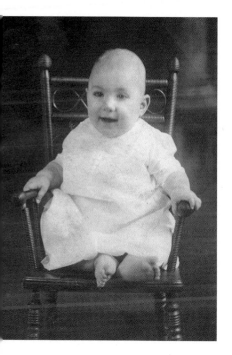

Top left: Glenn at nine months old. **Top right:** *The Draper brothers in 1936. Clockwise from top left: Glenn, Gene, Douglas, and William.* **Bottom:** *The Draper family, 1945. Back row: William, Glenn. Front row: Douglas, Jack, Carter Lois, and Gene.*

Top: *Glenn and Julius Walthall in their band uniforms at Andrew Lewis High School in Salem, Virginia.* **Bottom:** *Glenn with his high school quartet. Left to right: Lowell Eller, Thomas Tobey, Julius Walthall, and Glenn Draper.*

Top: *Glenn's high school dance band. Glenn is playing the trombone in the front row. To his left, Julius Walthall is playing clarinet, and brother Gene can be seen in the back row on the trumpet.*
Bottom left: *Glenn in 1946, walking the six-mile route to attend choir and band rehearsal.*
Bottom right: *Glenn's twenty-first-year portrait. The aspiring conductor wanted to direct his own choral groups.*

Top: In 1949, the Golden Tone Quartet was the first integrated quartet at Indiana University. Left to right: Gary Pittenger, Hardy Leiburg, Glenn Draper, and Bill Smith. **Bottom:** "The Aristocrats" missed by two percentage points being named the best barbershop quartet in the Air Force worldwide. Left to right: Charles Poole, Gerald Strickland, Glenn Draper, and Roger Hinkley.

Top: *The Keesler Mixed Chorus and Orchestra performed Handel's* Messiah *on NBC's national radio broadcast as Glenn conducted, 1953.* **Bottom:** *Left to right: General Parks, Glenn Draper, General Carpenter, and Chaplain Hanna gathered after the 1953 performance of the* Messiah *at Keesler Air Force Base.*

Top: The world-famous Keesler Male Chorus. **Bottom:** *Airman First Class Glenn W. Draper at his desk as music director at Keesler Air Force Base, early 1950s.*

*Top: The Pfeiffer College Male Chorus. Jerry Thomas, pictured third from right on the front row, went on to found the Singing Men of America, which now boasts chapters of male choruses throughout the country. **Bottom:** The Draper brothers, October 1956. Left to right: Douglas, William, Gene, and Glenn.*

Top left: *Glenn and Lounelle on one of their first dates at the SMU Tri-Delta Christmas party, December 1955.* **Top right:** *Lounelle Mayes's engagement photo, 1956.* **Bottom:** *Count and Pauline Mayes, Lounelle, Glenn, and Carter Lois and Jack Draper at Glenn and Lounelle's wedding, November 24, 1956.*

Top: *Just married! Glenn and Lounelle, November 24, 1956.* **Bottom left:** *Evangelist Billy Graham came over from Montreat, North Carolina, to speak at Lake Junaluska during Glenn's first year there in 1956.* **Bottom right:** *Glenn and Lounelle with young Glenn II in Miami, 1960.*

Top: *The Singing Hurricanes of the University of Miami visited Thule, Greenland, in 1963.*
Bottom: *The University of Miami Choral Union and Orchestra performed Handel's* Messiah *at the Dade County Auditorium in 1965.*

Top: Glenn Draper greeted Ed Sullivan before the Singing Hurricanes appeared on the Ed Sullivan Show *in 1965.* **Bottom:** *The Singing Hurricanes chatted with Pat Boone after their performance at the Miss Universe Pageant in 1966.*

Top: *The Junaluska Singers' first year with twelve members was 1968.* **Bottom:** *The choir of First Presbyterian Church, Chattanooga, 1972.*

It was a glad reunion on June 13, 1971, when Lounelle and the boys welcomed Glenn home from a nine-week European Tour with the Singing Mocs.

Top: *The Singing Mocs performed for President Gerald Ford during his visit to Chattanooga in 1974.* **Bottom:** *The Singing Mocs performed an open-air concert in Hamm, Germany, Chattanooga's sister city, in 1976.*

Top: *The Junaluska Singers posed before the famous cross on the lake in 1977.* **Bottom:** *The Singing Mocs stopped at Trafalgar Square during their tour of London in 1978.*

Top: *The Singing Mocs' Christmas special was named "Best Locally Produced Television Show" by* Reader's Digest *and* Guideposts *in 1977.* **Bottom left:** *Glenn with Mitch Miller in 1985.* **Bottom right:** *Dean Draper II pretended to be a conductor like his grandfather Glenn as he watched his Christmas special on television in 1993.*

The Draper family at home in 1984. Left to right: Dean, Glenn, dog Hershey, Lounelle, and Glenn Wright II.

Top: *The Junaluska Singers filmed a television show called "Goin' Country" with Sheriff Glenn in 1982.* **Bottom:** *The Junaluska Singers. This group was also known as the "Miracle Singers of 1984."*

Top: The Chattanooga Singers posed for this publicity photo in 1984. Glenn's son Dean is pictured sixth from left in the second row. **Bottom:** The combined choirs of the University of Tennessee, Chattanooga, and First Presbyterian Church, Chattanooga, performed Handel's Messiah at the Tivoli Theater in 1985.

Top: *The Chattanooga Singers performed at the famous Town Hall in Melbourne, Australia, in May 1986.* **Bottom:** *The Chattanooga Singers performed at the Crystal Cathedral in Garden Grove California, in 1988.*

The Junaluska Singers at Lake Junaluska in 1987 with the Memorial Chapel in the background.

The Glenn Draper Singers performed a Christmas concert for Ronald and Nancy Reagan at the White House in December 1988.

Top left: Glenn and Lounelle visited England in 1989. **Top right:** Glenn Wright II, Glenn, and Dean hit the slopes in Snowmass, Colorado, in 1988. **Bottom:** Glenn and Lounelle with Count Mayes and their grandchildren at their home in 1989. Their grandchildren are, left to right: Dean, Avery, Cal and Wright (sitting on Count Mayes's lap), Sandi, and Riley.

The Glenn Draper Singers performed a second Christmas concert at the White House, this time for George and Barbara Bush, in December 1989.

Top: The Junaluska Singers gave a "down home" concert in 1991. **Bottom:** The Chattanooga Singers performed at the Sydney Opera House as part of their 1986 and 1991 Australia tours.

Top: The Glenn Draper Singers gathered in front of St. Basil's Cathedral in Moscow, where they sang for a Billy Graham Crusade. *Bottom:* Lounelle, Glenn Wright II, and Glenn with Billy Graham at Olympic Stadium in 1992.

Top: *The Junaluska Singers performed at the World Methodist Conference in Rio de Janeiro, Brazil, in August 1996.* **Bottom:** *The Junaluska Singers performed on an Alaskan cruise in 1996.*

Top: *Nineteen ninety-seven marked the fiftieth reunion of Young Roanoke Sings. Left to right: Glenn Draper, Buddy Philips, Redge Hutchison, and Julius Walthall.* **Bottom left:** *Glenn met again with Robert Shaw at his choral workshop in New York City in 1998.* **Bottom right:** *Glenn and Lounelle with their dog, Sport, in front of their Signal Mountain home.*

Top: The Glenn Draper Singers performed at the Chataqua Music Center in New York state on August 23, 2000. Accompanist Kim Cargile is standing to Glenn's right. **Bottom:** *The Chattanooga Singers appeared at the Presidential Prayer Breakfast in January 2001.*

Lounelle and Glenn went on a horseback ride in Banff, Canada, in 2001.

Top: Glenn conducted the choir and orchestra at First Presbyterian Church, Chattanooga, on his *first Sunday before he resigned, December 2, 2001.* **Bottom:** *The Glenn Draper Singers at their White House performance, December 20, 2002.*

Top: *Glenn conducting the choir and orchestra at First Presbyterian Church in Chattanooga.*
Bottom: *The Draper family posed for this portrait during their visit to the White House on December 20, 2002.*

of us ducked into the bass section and sat down quickly and hoped that nobody would notice what had happened. Sure enough, the conductor came in, greeted everyone, and started on page one. Everybody started singing while seated, and after about fifteen minutes he had us stand.

I said, "Jim, this is a good time for us to leave since everybody is standing and we will not be that noticeable." He said, "How are we going to get out of here?" I answered, "Well, let's go out the way they came in, through those corridors." We saw a door, but it was locked. We turned left, and the only place to go, except to go back into the hall itself, was down into the crypt area. It was dimly lit and tombstones were all over the place. We wondered how we were going to get out of there. No exit was visible, but I did see some steps on the side of the wall. We climbed them until we found a huge open window and we jumped into the courtyard. We thought, *Now we are free.* The only problem was, the gate out of that place was locked, so I said, "Jim, we are this far, we are going to get out of here." I hoisted him up on my hands to the top of a ledge, and he jumped and landed down on the street. I climbed up the sides and pulled myself up. That is how we got out of that place!

I was determined that the night was not yet over. We went into a Japanese bookstore right across the street and asked them if they knew anything about a concert series on the Thames River at the Royal Festival Hall. They told us what subway to catch, and after we arrived there Jim said, "You know, we will never get in. We don't have any tickets." I said, "Jim, you know better than that." We saw three long lines of people waiting to try to get tickets, and from the looks of things they weren't having any success. However, there was a very short line on the end that could have been a reserved ticket pickup window. I got in that line and said, "I would like two tickets." The attendant asked, "For tonight's concert?" I said, "Oh yes, I know it will be wonderful, I can hardly wait to hear it." She looked around for a minute and found two tickets that I am assuming someone had just turned in, and she sold them to me. We walked in and left the rest of those people standing out there who never got in. I didn't know how that worked, but you never know until you try.

Afterwards we told that story to Lounelle and Noveita and they laughed about our escapades, but we did not tell them about everything all at once. Gradually, we told them how we ended up in the crypt and how we got out of there. Of course, if you told that to an Englishman he would just die, because we defied their authority. [I told part of this story to Dr. Reginald Mallett, from England, when I interviewed him, and he refused to believe that this had occurred because of the security around the national treasures in St. Paul's Cathedral. I verified the experience with Jim Wilson.—Editor]

The Glenn Draper Singers have sung at the Billy Graham crusades, Moscow, and other places. We have had maybe twelve overseas trips, to England, Australia, Russia, Estonia, Finland, and Indonesia. From now on, all of my overseas trips will be the Glenn Draper Singers. However, in a sense that is what I have been preparing for. I have been training myself all this time to get my own singing group. We did a concert in Cullman, Alabama, on February 7, 2003. The lady who invited us is a sister of Zach Wamp, a member of the U.S. House of Representatives, who invited us to sing for the Presidential Prayer Breakfast. She heard our recordings and wanted our group to be there. I have trips to Florida, North Carolina, Texas, Georgia, the White House, and a recording session with Lee Greenwood scheduled. I will be busy, but I do not want to be on the road all the time.

LAKE JUNALUSKA
1956–Present

WHEN I FIRST STARTED at Lake Junaluska, we had a big volunteer choir that flourished for a while. We had to sing for the coronation of the Queen and things like that, and sometimes I would add a few extra voices. However, I had a quartet only for about ten years until 1967. In 1967, one guy from the University of Miami and his girlfriend, who was a soprano, wanted to come up just to sing with us in the quartet. Three girls, Lynn Duke, Jean Peacock, and Ann Peacock were the others.

Early in the summer of 1967 Dr. Potts, the new executive director who loved music, wanted to start an artist series on a weekend night with a vocal soloist or a piano solo, but the people did not support it at all. The last concert was scheduled to take place, and he and I were standing in front of the auditorium and I said, "Dr. Potts, we lost a lot of money this summer, didn't we?" He said, "Yeah, about $10,000." I said, "If you will give me that $10,000 and let me hire twelve really good singers, I think you can recoup that by us doing the kind of music that I think people like to hear." He thought about it and said, "Glenn, you go do it, but don't you tell a soul."

The next spring I was in Miami, so I went to Lake Junaluska in February and auditioned. Nancye "Scooter" Formo, who was one of the first to audition. That summer we showed up with twelve people. You will not believe the hassle that I got from people criticizing me for spending money that the lake "did not have." Dr. Potts said, "Glenn, we will weather this storm, they are on my case too." In fact, a former judge talked to me recently. He said, "Glenn, I do not know how you have done it all these years, but I have been your admirer. I remember the days when the committee meetings used to try to figure out how they could get rid of you because they thought you were going to break the lake. The only thing that shut them up was that the auditorium started filling with people. Then they had to back off." They were eating their words, because what we had set out to accomplish was taking place.

We took the first tour with a group in January 1971, to Florida. Bishop Henley was the bishop of the Methodist church in Florida, and he called me and asked if it would it be possible to bring the twelve singers to Florida. He had three congregations in Tampa, Orlando, and Tallahassee. We set up a weekend, I got the singers, and we all flew down there and sang. It was quite successful. That was the first tour of the Junaluska Singers. One thing just led to a half dozen others. We did many recordings in those years, and they were the glory years of getting started. That is when people stayed for a long time. "Scooter" Formo, Frank Calhoun, Charles Middleton, Ron Whittemore, Al Miller, and Sara Smith Youngblood all were with me for nine to ten years. It is not that way now because it is a different ball game.

I wanted to get more singers, because we could sing some things a lot better with sixteen than we would ever sing with twelve. We were over in Rockhill, South Carolina, and I told Dr. Mel Harbin, the assembly director at the time, that we needed to get a bass player and a drummer to play for the concert that we were doing. I said, "Look how much better we sound with a bass player and a drummer. How did we do without them?" So I got him to hire a couple of kids to come to Lake Junaluska for the summer that first time. The next summer, about 1983 or 1984, I took the money that he was giving me for that and hired additional singers instead of the drummer and bass player. When we went to sixteen singers, the difference was incredible, but we still received criticism.

One guy who almost wrecked our ship was someone that got on the executive committee from Kentucky. I never met him, but I talked to him on the telephone. He was trying to force me to use 75 percent Methodists in the Junaluska Singers and several other people climbed on his band-wagon. I said, "I can't believe you are asking me to do that. I will never go down on my standards for singers, and it does not matter whether they are Methodist or what." I do ask them if they are Christian. When they sing "This Is My Story," I want to make sure they have one. I said, "If you stand a Methodist, an Episcopalian, and a Lutheran up, and the Lutheran has the best voice, which one would you hire? I am hiring the Lutheran, I do not care whether he is a Methodist or not." One thing for sure, you cannot have a committee put a chorus together, it has to be the idea of one person. I believe that more now than I have ever believed it, whether I am right or wrong is beside the point. A committee cannot direct a choir.

Junaluska has offered me a wider scope of meeting people than any other organization you can imagine. I have met people from India, Africa, Asia, Japan—from almost everywhere. I sat on the stage with Jimmy Carter, and I recall Richard Nixon saying that we were one of the finest groups he had heard from that stage. I heard Billy Graham say, "If Cliff Barrows ever leaves me, Glenn Draper is the man to direct my music."

Eddie Fox called me last week and said, "Glenn, in Estonia they want to know if you will come to sing for the dedication of a big Methodist building right on the ocean." I said we were supposed to go to Australia. He called Australia and talked to Ken Anderson, who is sponsoring our trip next spring to Australia, to see if he would postpone it to next fall. My point is, there is this network of people all over, calling from everywhere. A man just called and wanted to know if we would come to South Africa and sing in 2006. Where else could you have those contacts? Being at First Presbyterian Church, never; being at any other church, never; being at any school, never. It is a crazy quirk. I have been at a Methodist church in the summer and a Presbyterian church in the winter. Tell me, how do you explain that? I then worked at a secular, state-supported university.

I feel that this is my calling. I know that to some people that would sound trite, but my calling at Junaluska is not just to do better music, or to educate people about music, that has never been in my plan. It is to sing music that people consider to be worshipful, and that they are going to like. Knowing that there are different kinds of people out there, I have to do different types of music. The elite musicians dislike me for that because they say I am letting down musical standards; but I say, "Whose standards? My standards or yours?"

Dr. James B. Buskirk
Retired minister; lecturer/evangelist;
visiting minister at Lake Junaluska for many years

Glenn is fantastic in his teaching, he knows what he is doing musically and he can do the cognitive part of it. He can put it together with such expertise when he brings people here to Junaluska, and we just wonder where he gets them since they are so excellent. He is absolutely a magnet who attracts all these young adult people who come here to sing, and he makes them work hard. Many young adults do not want to work that hard. Let me tell you, they get impacted with the Lord Jesus Christ and they leave here different people. They come to sing because they live to spend their lives serving God and they want to do it with their voices, etc. He is just invaluable to the kingdom of God because he can do that.

Sara Smith Youngblood

One of the things that I did every year was plant a pitiful little garden outside the singers' lodge at Lake Junaluska in the shape of a heart, but people drove over it and terrible things happened to it. The garden never did much because it was in a spot that was damp and had too little sun. After I had been singing in college at Miami for two years, I was having vocal trouble and decided that I should retire from the singers and find another job. We were on a tour (one of those weekend things that we did during the year), and I told Glenn that I thought I probably would not come back. It was turning out to be a sad weekend.

Then Glenn got everybody together when we were about ready to depart to another place where we were going to sing that night. He had something behind his back and said, "Sara, you must come back." I said, "I am not feeling good and I am not singing well," and he replied, "You must come back." He brought some pots and seeds from behind his back, and he said, "Who else is going to plant the memorial garden?" Well, I came back.

Dr. Melton E. "Mel" Harbin
Retired from ministry; executive director,
Lake Junaluska Methodist Assembly

I first met Glenn back in the late 1950s when I was the pastor at Memorial Church in Thomasville, North Carolina, and he was at Pfeiffer College. When I came to Junaluska as director of the Assembly in 1977, he was director of music for Junaluska and had twelve singers. We became very close friends right away and traveled with them a lot, taking the Junaluska Singers over the jurisdiction and several mission trips to Panama and other areas. Later, on a mission trip to Jamaica, St. Thomas, and St. Johns, we were very fortunate to be able to contact a pilot in Miami who took all twenty-six of us on a small plane, and we hopped all over those islands.

I will tell you one incident that happened on that trip, as testimony to Glenn's influence with the Junaluska Singers. We were traveling with them for nearly two weeks, and we came back to a church in Florida for one last concert. We had in that entourage a young lady twenty-seven years of age, who had never made any commitment to Christ. The last concert that evening, she came to where my wife and I were sitting and said, "Mel, you are a minister aren't you?" I said, "Yes, I am." She said, "I need to talk to you," so we went into another room and she said, "I have never made a profession of faith in Christ. I have learned on this trip that you can be a Christian and be a happy, wholesome person and have a good time. I want to know Christ, will you help me?" I asked her to make a commitment. We had prayer, and then she shared that experience with the singers.

This is a testimony to Glenn Draper's influence and what he did. None of us can ever measure the total influence that Glenn Draper has had over hundreds and perhaps thousands of people who have come to Junaluska through his wonderful witness and testimony. This influence is not only in directing the singers, but through the life he lives and the personality that he exhibits. He is a true, godly person, who loves the Lord and loves people and is just a great friend.

Charles Middleton
First African-American singer at Junaluska;
assistant church choir director; Glenn Draper Singers

I did not read music quite to the point that Glenn wanted, and he tested me out in Stuart Auditorium. I was standing on the stage and he had me sing a piece, and I thought he was trying to get a feel on how I could sing, but now I realize that is not what he was looking at. He was looking at what *feel* I had for the music. He has a sixth sense about the way things should be and how to present it. Glenn had me sing, and I kept singing, then he would tell me to sing again in a different way. I tried to jazz it up and present it to him differently. He went all the way to the back of Stuart Auditorium and listened. He put his hand to his ear and said, "Do it again!" So I did it again, I guess I did it about four or five times. He came up to me and said, "You know, Charles, people come to Lake Junaluska for all kinds of reasons, the least of which are the conferences. They are looking for inspiration."

I came from a Baptist background with shouting and all that involved. Glenn gave me a different point of view of people and their emotions and what they feel. He said, "What you are going to be doing is singing for people who have never been in this auditorium with a black person singing as a staff person, so it is going to be a selling job." I was older and I had been in the military and had been exposed to racism. This was during the '60s when civil rights were just coming out. Glenn said, "Your musical skills are not as good as I would like for them to be." He never said I did not have good musical skills. The way he presented it to me was that he was going to put me in the water and either I sink or swim! That was a challenge to me. I did not know what Lake Junaluska was, it didn't mean anything to me, I just thought it was a job. I said, "Okay fine," and he said, "I will be in touch with Frank [Calhoun] and let you know what my decision is."

I went the entire spring wondering, *Am I going to get this job?* Frank Calhoun, being the person he is said, "Charles, I would not sweat it. I would concentrate more on your academics." He brought me back into focus. Then I heard from Glenn through Frank, and I also got a letter saying to come to Lake Junaluska. Glenn reminded me when I got there that this was my test. You see, he was aware enough to allow me to know that, rather than to put me up against an obstacle and let me try to surmount it without any tools. I knew I was in a setting that was predominately white except clergy and the staff at the lake, and I was on display more than just as a singer, since I was a black person. I can admit that sometimes it became agonizing for me because I could look in people's eyes and imagine what they were thinking. I could see the disdain.

Yet as time went on, those glares and that feeling of intimidation changed, and I thought, *Yes, I could handle it.* During that time, with the racial climate in the country and me being the only black person and about five years older than most of the singers [it was unusual that] a young singer, Carol D., and I befriended each other. We spent late hours talking and walking around the lake, nothing romantic at all. Still, some residents apparently went back to the Assembly and said something about our being out at that time of night. That heightened my awareness that I was still black and I was still at Lake Junaluska; however, Glenn never said anything about it. Although I knew he was aware of it, he made me feel like I was an adult and it was my choice to make. I felt comfortable, even then! As for his wife, Lounelle, she just embraced everybody. Friends of mine who came from Paine College would say that Glenn and Lounelle were different. I would ask, "What do you mean by different?" They said, "They accept everybody!"

Glenn accepts you on your own merits and maybe molds what he would like to have out of that. He allows you to be and takes you to a different place. I was allowed while I was at Lake Junaluska to grow tremendously, and I became very fond of Lake Junaluska and the people who were there.

I went on to stay with Glenn for ten years and we went on many trips and tours where we had lots of fun and lots of events that we remember. I owe so much to John Murphy, Scooter [Nancye Formo], and Frank Calhoun, because they shared my life while I was growing and assimilating into a culture that was not my own. I began to learn that I do not have to go all the way [in a culture that is not mine]. I can make a choice that something in one culture is good and something in my own culture is good, and then bring all these things together. My life has been more richly shared.

The kinds of things we did at the lake would vary. We learned a phenomenal amount of music. Glenn's famous saying was, "Take the edge off when you are singing." In a vocal production you want to give as pleasant a tone as possible, and when you sing a twangy note, he wants you to take that edge off. Blend in yourself, and you get a smooth sound rather than a twang. He puts cutesy kinds of things into your head and then you begin to adjust and think, *Okay fine—he doesn't want the edge and he wants a smoother sound and he does not want the warble,* and then you become a different singer. You begin to learn more, experience more, learn to read music, and how to blend the sounds.

We started with six to eight singers when I was there in 1967, then the following year he added four more. The next nine years I was there we had twelve singers, then he added four more. I thought that our sound was great with twelve people, but the sound is magnificent with sixteen, it is like a full one hundred person chorus. In his theory, you take one hundred people and make them sound like one person, not one person and try to make them sound like a hundred—but *one*. I have based my singing [and directing] on that, you blend into the group. It is like a hand, you never look at your hand and say, "Well, I have a little finger," or "I have an index finger," you say, "I have a hand."

Linda Powers Bilanchone

When my husband, Vic, received his master's degree in music from the University of Miami, we found ourselves lunching at a restaurant on South Dixie Highway across from the university campus. Vic was discussing job possibilities for the fall when Glenn interrupted with his usual intense, "Hey, man," and asked Vic if he could play the bass. He said if Vic could play the bass, there might be a job for him with the Junaluska Singers for the summer. He added that enough people from the southeast pass through there in a summer that Vic would surely meet someone who might hire him permanently in the fall. As much as I had done earlier in response to an invitation to imitate Marilyn Monroe, Vic said, "Yes, I could probably plunk out a few notes." In fact, he did become a Junaluska Singer (who played the bass occasionally), and he did find a permanent job (at Paine College), and that was the first of several beautiful summers that we and our children spent at Lake Junaluska.

Jay Lifford

We [the Junaluska Singers] are not here for the money. The camaraderie of the group is what keeps the singers coming back. It is not to take anything away from Glenn or who he is, we all love him very much, but it's the family that you develop.

Sara Smith Youngblood

One of my biggest regrets is that Glenn specializes in the male chorus sound, and I cannot hear a male chorus to this day without wanting to lie down and cry. He never let the women sing anything like that. We would do this cutesy stuff, but there were things that he would have the men sing that were just so wonderful. I just always wondered, *Why can't we [women] do that?* Well, it is because it was his repertoire, and it was what he did with the Keesler Male Chorus. He had all this great music [for the men] and he just adores the men's sound. Maybe there wasn't anything out there that was that beautiful [for the women]. Still, to this day when I hear the men sing, I think, *Why couldn't we [the women] have done something with all that deep harmony and all that beauty?* The men are always better than the women. He complains about them more than he would the women. Nevertheless, his [main] interest is in the men.

═══════════════════════════════════

Jay Craig
UTC choirs; Lake Junaluska Singers; Glenn Draper Singers

Glenn asked me to come up to Junaluska and fill in, and I absolutely loved it! I fell in love with the place and the people, and it gave me a chance to see Glenn with a different hat on. I think that what I respect most about Glenn Draper is that he is a man who can wear versatile hats. He is with his singers at the university and he is on their level, a very excellent level. But then he goes to Junaluska and it is just a whole different caliber of singers. He also has his church choir that is a different group, and then he has his select group of singers.

Since I have been away, I have sung in other choirs, and my church choir is fabulous, but I think leaving him makes you appreciate Glenn Draper that much more. I do not know how to put it into words, but the sound is just one of those things that you must experience! The sound that he can create is like none other. I know that part of it is the caliber of singers that he chooses and attracts. I love to sing with the smaller groups, I like working with sixteen, that is my favorite. He can get that group of folks to become united and to focus on one thing which is God, and to blend Glenn's talents and abilities with ours. It just meshes, and I just cannot put it into words. It is an experience that you must have yourself.

═══════════════════════════════════

Jennifer Odom
Lake Junaluska Singers; Glenn Draper Singers;
music major University of North Carolina, Greeneville

It is a lot about the music, but it is a lot about the love and spirit within the group that makes it successful. It is definitely a sound—a Junaluska sound. Although the groups change and the people change, it is a sound that people identify with through the years because it stays close enough to that same core sound that he wants. The energy that Glenn has to keep everyone going and working is another reason that he is so successful. He never stops, he is always finding more to do and give and perform and sing. It is definitely a divine gift, an anointment. I often say that nowhere else would you find what we do here at Junaluska or what he does with his concerts. There is a combination of all these different styles and all this variety in one concert. If we are doing a concert in a church, we will do largely Christian, sacred music, but he will throw in other things that will be of interest to that audience.

Kelly T. Wilson
Lake Junaluska Singers; Glenn Draper Singers;
music major at Converse College

Number one, I think that he is determined. You know that the second that you have told Glenn Draper "no," you have just sealed your own death sentence. That is a big part of it, but I also think that he is anointed by the Holy Spirit. Sure, there are lots of people who know how to cross their *t*'s and dot their *i*'s better than he does, and he will say that, but, I believe that he is anointed. I know him purely from the Lake Junaluska standpoint, but I know this is true across the board, at school and church. I doubt that anyone else could have made out of this place [what he has]. All you have to do is look around and see the impact, not only of Glenn, but of what the Junaluska Singers have made on the world. I think that is not earthly power, that is divine work.

It is a cliché to say, but I think that he loves what he does. He could not do this all the time and not love it. The singers certainly are not in it for the money or the success. He took me out for ice-cream last night, and I said this to him, "There are few people who you can be so angry with that you want to positively shake, and then you can walk out of the rehearsal room and still love."

Laurie Harper Evans
Lake Junaluska Singer for seven years; church choir director

As I think of my years with the Junaluska Singers under the direction of Glenn Draper, a huge smile spreads across my face. Glenn's love of music and for God was exemplified through his leadership. I grew to love Glenn and his family very much, and will always cherish my years at the lake. My twin sister, Lisa, and I auditioned for Glenn in his home when we were nineteen years old. We sang for Glenn and performed our comedy routine (the Chipmunks seemed to be his favorite) and that day started seven wonderful years as members of the Junaluska Singers.

Singing with Glenn and the Junaluska Singers was life changing. The dearest friends I have are friends that I made there. It gave me a strong foundation in my music that I draw on in so many facets of my career. The spiritual growth I experienced was incredible. The beauty of the lake is still comforting and peaceful. And, most of all, Glenn Draper has a place in my heart that is full of joy, admiration, gratitude, and love. Glenn has blessed my life so much and I thank God for Glenn's friendship and inspiration.

7

The Different FACES *of*
GLENN DRAPER

Every person has a special place in his life.

~JENNIFER ODOM

AS A HUSBAND

Lounelle M. Draper

G lenn and I met in the fall of 1955 at Southern Methodist University. I went there to audition for the concert choir at SMU, and when I walked in for my audition (which was held by the choral director, Dean Orville B., who was also the dean of music), Glenn was sitting there and I was introduced to him. On that weekend, a girlfriend of Glenn's (whom he had dated off and on for seven years and who had come to Dallas when she found out that Glenn was going to be attending the university there) was given two tickets to a fashion show. She took Glenn to the fashion show and I was modeling. The first time I came out, Glenn said, "I've seen that girl before." The second time I came out, Glenn said, "I know where I have seen her. She auditioned for the concert choir Monday." The third time I came out, he made some kind of a remark, and the girl said, "Why don't you date her?" On Monday of the next week, I ran into him on the front steps of the auditorium on the SMU campus and he asked me for a date. I told him that I had already accepted a date for that particular night and he said, "Well, I hope you have a miserable time." I was kind of taken

121

back. The next time I saw him, he said, "I am so sorry I said that to you, but I still hope you had a miserable time." I knew then that I had met a very competitive man.

He asked me to sing a solo in his church, which I accepted, and we began dating a little bit. A Sunday night came up and he asked me to sing in a large, city-wide choral festival at his church, and I told him I would be glad to sing in the choir. He did not ask me for a date that night, he just asked me to sing, so I accepted a date with someone else for nine o'clock on that evening. When he turned around after the offertory, I was gone because the service was very long and it was close to nine. On Monday morning when I had some communication with him, he was furious. I said, "I am so sorry, but you had never asked me for a date." He said, "Well, I just assumed we had a date." I said, "I must apologize, I just didn't know that at all."

We did begin dating more, and I fell head over heels in love, and the months went on until spring and very close to school letting out, and I knew he had accepted a position as director of music at Lake Junaluska, North Carolina. I thought perhaps I would never see him again. He had made no commitment whatsoever toward me, other than the fact that one night he was following me home from SMU and he kept blinking his head-lights, three times, three times. I thought something was wrong with my taillights. I stopped and I went around to his car and said, "What's wrong, why are you doing that?" He said, "It means I love you, I love you, I love you." I did have that kind of commitment, but that was about it.

I accepted a job as a camp counselor in Hunt, Texas, where I had been a camper for a number of summers and was now old enough to be a coun-selor. I dated that summer and I think Glenn might have dated a couple of girls at Lake Junaluska that summer, but we did write, and at the end of the summer he wanted me to join him in North Carolina. My parents thought it would be great, so I flew up and saw Junaluska for the first time in my life in the summer of 1956. We drove from Junaluska to Roanoke, Virginia, where I met his mother and father, and it was there, where his mother was proposed to by his father in the parlor of the old home that she used to live in, that Glenn proposed to me. We married November 24, 1956.

Married life began on the Pfeiffer College campus in Misenheimer, North Carolina. It wasn't long before I realized the honeymoon was over. However, like Glenn says, "We are always going to be on our honeymoon." I knew I was sharing him for the rest of my life with countless young men and women who would be singing in his choirs. They became a big part of my life and I adored them.

What I saw in Glenn from the get-go was his enthusiasm. You know that word is derived from the Greek enthousia, or "possessed by God." Glenn was ordained by God to be a choral director and to be in the Lord's work. God has always had his hand on Glenn's life, and I think he has had a special anointing of the Holy Spirit. At Pfeiffer I began to see Glenn's dreams come true. People in his Air Force days had already recognized it and had already seen this. People in his college days at Marion, Indiana University, and SMU had also already recognized this, but I then began to recognize it in full. I saw him take a group of young men at Pfeiffer College where about four out of the forty had musical training, and within a couple of months he made them into one of the finest male choruses you would ever hope to hear. It was like he waved a magic wand and this miracle happened. Spiritually speaking, we knew that it was God's gift to him that enabled it to happen. The choir received an invitation to sing for *Voice of America* in New York after he had been there only a few months. My eyes were wide open, but I couldn't believe what this man could achieve so rapidly with his concert choir as well as the male chorus at Pfeiffer College.

We were employed by Pfeiffer College for four years, and I say "we" because I served as the assistant to the president's secretary and as a speech and drama teacher, my major at SMU. Glenn always kidded me about that because I never did get rid of my Texas accent, combine that with four years in North Carolina, and now thirty-three years in Tennessee, and it just gets worse. Anyway, it was a great four years.

After his third year at Pfeiffer College, Glenn was offered a position at the University of Miami, but he turned the position down and we had one more year with our wonderful students at Pfeiffer College. They were seniors that year. The Lord then moved us to the University of Miami, where life took on entirely new dimensions because we had gone from Misenheimer to a huge city, Miami. The added dimensions were a lot of glamour and glitter, and his groups, the Singing Hurricanes, the Male Chorus, and his concert choirs who were asked to share billings with established stars for benefits that would come to Miami Beach and Miami. He shared billings with Liberace, Mike Douglas, Frank Sutton, and Lorne Greene of the old *Bonanza* show. He did a benefit at the Fontainebleau Hotel with Prince Philip, who was the honored guest. Our souvenir for the evening was a navy blue leather menu with gold cord going down the back and side and Prince Philip's picture framed into the front cover. It was quite a night, and it was quite a life.

I had the opportunity to sing for a portion of three filming seasons on the old *Jackie Gleason Show*. I was one of the voices for the June Taylor dancers. The women in this small ensemble were never seen on camera, because we were in a soundproof cubicle at the side of the orchestra which was conducted by Sammy Spear. Mr. Gleason was wonderful to every lady who had anything to do with the taping or filming of the show. He would give flowers or a potted plant each Saturday night, no matter what role you had. If you were a seamstress, a makeup artist, or a singer, you received a gift from Mr. Gleason.

It was easy to be up there in the clouds with all the glitter and glamour, however I would have to come back down to earth and be the mother I was supposed to be, and loved being, to two little boys. I had to change those diapers, fix those meals, and play with those children. It was a great life in Miami and I watched my husband have a tremendous witness for Jesus Christ in a very cosmopolitan university. I would say about a third of the students were unbelievers, a third were Catholic, and a third were Protestant, and he always had a witness for Christ. He could go in a USO bar with his singers and sing the "Lord's Prayer," with everybody just sitting there, some half-boozed and others getting ready to be boozed up.

I remember one time overseas, I think it was in Taiwan, two missionaries came up to him and said, "We cannot thank you enough for your witness to Christ with the servicemen who are stationed here in the Far East. They said that you have made our work easier with your witness for Christ." I think, too, that the key to Glenn's success is that he has always put the Lord first and God has protected him. God has protected him in a secular university; God has protected him here in a state-supported university for thirty-three years, where he has never failed to have devotions with his students prior to concerts, sing sacred music, and to tell them what the words in the sacred music really mean.

To point out what a strong light he has been, I want to share one thing that touched my heart that I will never forget. After we had been away from the University of Miami for maybe five or six years, we went back for a visit. On a Saturday morning Glenn said, "I have to go back to my old rehearsal hall." I said, "Okay, let's go reminisce." In that rehearsal hall that particular Saturday morning, they were having a guitar clinic, and there must have been twenty-five guitarists there with a leading player directing the clinic in all the innovative, wonderful ways guitars could be played with some new music. We listened for a few minutes and kind of peeked into his old office and then turned our backs and began to walk out. We were just about a quarter of the way across a beautifully landscaped area between the choral and band room and orchestra rooms, when a young man came running up behind us and said, "Are you Glenn Draper?" Glenn, said, "Yes, I am." He said, "You don't know me, I was in the guitar clinic a few minutes ago, and I ran out when I recognized you. I want to thank you for something. Although this is six or seven years later from the time you were at the University of Miami, I want you to know that the light you had for Jesus Christ on this campus has continued. We have a tremendously strong contingency of very wonderful Christian faculty members and students on this campus which resulted from your zealousness for Christ when you were a professor here." I mean, tears just came to my eyes—this is six or seven years later and it has caught on, it has not been extinguished. God has his light everywhere, but I know this is why Glenn's life has been successful, because he has honored the Lord. I feel, musically speaking, that

God has orchestrated every heartbeat of his life as well as mine. I feel that he put us together.

My choir director in Dallas was Glen Johnson. He was the director I grew up under in my graded choir system at First United Methodist Church there. God prepared me to be a choir director's wife and I don't think that any other lady could have understood Glenn like I do, had music not been my background. I feel that the Lord is first in his life. I almost feel sometimes like music and all his choirs are second, and I am third along with our wonderful sons. Glenn says I am wrong in that, but sometimes I feel it. I kid him about it. He loves his choirs.

I got to know, under difficult circumstances, the old girlfriend whom Glenn had dated off and on for seven years. Her husband and my father were in a nursing home at the same time in Dallas. Her husband had a number of strokes, and my dad was not well either, so we really got acquainted. She said something to me that I will never forget. She said, "I honestly believe that when Glenn stops conducting, he will die shortly afterwards." This could be very true. It is so much his life. Also, conductors who continue to be quite active in their senior years get a wonderful workout in the upper body. Blood is pumping really well, and they often perspire quite a lot, so they are getting a good aerobic workout.

Conductors have been interviewed around the world, and they attribute their longevity to these very facts. I think it was Arthur Fiedler who handed his baton over to a champion wrestler, turned on some music, and said, "See how long you can keep just a normal beat pattern to a normal piece of music." After about nine minutes, the champion wrestler was laid out on the sofa totally exhausted. I think it was Leonard Bernstein who said a very active conductor will burn as much energy during a concert as a pro baseball pitcher would if he pitched three games a week, which he would never dream of doing. That speaks loud and clear on the workout that your active conductors get. Marilyn, his old girlfriend, may be correct about that, but I hope not. I frankly think he will "go up" conducting!

Now I'll say some things that I know about Glenn personally and that as a wife aggravate me, although they are not big things. Glenn's mind is continually turning and turning. Sometimes we can be talking about one subject, for example, "What would you like to do in May?" He will throw out two or three options, like another choir tour, and after the choir tour maybe a trip to Myrtle Beach. Then suddenly he will jump to September without my knowing it, and he is talking about a possible trip to Germany. I'm thinking that the trip to Germany is in May, which we had just been talking about, but he has jumped the track to September. That is hard for me because I am very organized and it is frustrating for me sometimes to stay on the same wavelength with him. That is just one example of the many, many times that this has happened.

I have never seen so much energy in one person. Sometimes I will say, "I'm really tired, I think I will lie down." He can lie down for twenty minutes and then go for another twelve hours. He can just go nonstop; we have all seen this, and singers have seen this in recording sessions and rehearsals. He may be a seventy-four-year-old man, but he has the same energy level, and sometimes a higher energy level, than his freshmen do. That is outstanding, and his new singers at Junaluska, the rookies, or his new freshmen at UTC, their mouths sometimes just fall open. They cannot believe the energy in this man, or what he can accomplish in a short period of time.

As to his character, I could trust my husband to the end of the world. When my children were younger and I did not travel as much with him, I knew he could be trusted. I want to tell you, talk about beautiful girls, he has had beautiful girls under his direction: first runner-up Miss America; Miss Miami; Miss Florida; Miss Virginia; Miss South Carolina; Miss Chattanooga; second runner-up Miss Tennessee; fourth runner-up Miss Tennessee; such beautiful girls! It is just wonderful to know that I have a husband of such high character and our sons have a father of high character.

He is one of the most loving people I have ever met in my life, and he does stay in touch with friends from as far back as grade school, junior high, and high school. There will just be a sporadic telephone call out of the blue from him, it's like the Lord will have laid that person on his heart. I remember one lady who was a former classmate whom he called out of the blue because she was just on his heart, and Glenn had come to find out by that call that she had terminal cancer. It lifted her spirits to hear from him, but that is the kind of man Glenn is. No matter how busy he is, he makes time for everyone.

He is sensitive, he is tender, and at the same time he can be a tyrant in a rehearsal. I mean, if somebody is not doing something right and he has already corrected it three times, watch out! He never would do that with me because he knows I could walk out, and he has to live with me. He can be ferocious in a rehearsal, but I don't mean cussing mad. Glenn does not curse. I think one time he came back from Junaluska, after working with a Christian professional singing group all summer, to our church choir here in Chattanooga, and the sopranos weren't getting a part and he was upset with them. He meant to say, "Sopranos, you're not worth a *dang*," and he accidentally said, "Sopranos, you're not worth a *damn*." He didn't even realize he said it until my mouth flew open and the eyes of one of the elders sitting in the choir were enormous. When he realized what he said, he was so embarrassed, he just about died. He said, "I meant to say *dang*, I meant to say *dang*." We all doubled over laughing because we knew it was totally out of character for Glenn Draper.

He is a merciful person. I remember when a girl named Amy B. received a traffic ticket, she was very upset because she didn't have the money to pay for it. Glenn pulled the money out of his pocket and gave it to her, and she started crying. She was so grateful. I remember on a trip to New Orleans with the Singing Hurricanes, that the place where we were supposed to have performed told us that our black students could not have a room and we would have to find housing for them somewhere else. Glenn said, "Then we are not singing here." We all met together as a choir and decided that we would just go into New Orleans and stay in a hotel at our own expense and have a free night. One of the singers, a girl named Lydia M., told Glenn she didn't have the money to pay a hotel bill and Glenn told her, "Don't worry, I will pay your hotel bill for you." He has been very generous in many ways with his students.

Our minister told us one time something that I thought was so great. He said, "If you are going to witness to a waitress about Jesus Christ and His love for that waitress, leave her a big tip after you have witnessed to her. You should not leave a little tip, leave her a big tip. That speaks loud and clear, and has many dimensions to it. If you are going to witness for Christ, you help those students out, you don't just teach them to sing, and you don't just witness to them, but you help them when they need help."

Many of our students, when the great overseas tour opportunities came up, wouldn't have the money to go if Glenn did not raise the funds on their behalf. We think it is a worthy cause, because they get to see the world, and they get to see our Christianity in full force and our witness throughout the world. They become a part of that sometimes when they are not even Christians themselves, when standing there singing about Christ. We have had a number of students through the years whose lives have been changed. Some we have not found out about until years later when they will appear at one of our performances and say, "You don't realize it, but after I left the university and got out in the real world, I gave my life to Christ."

Character-wise, I hold my husband in the highest esteem. As busy a man as he has been, he has been a wonderful husband. We are close, and he is very tuned into my moods and to when I am low. We recently had a rough year. My sister-in-law, Sarah (who was like a sister), died of lung cancer. Then my dad had numerous hospital visits with pneumonia, and more and more medical problems began happening, and a few months later he went to be with the Lord. It was quite a time, but God has seen us through it. I thank God for a strong body and a high energy level, not just for myself and what we as a family have been through in the past year, but to keep up a little bit with Glenn Draper.

As for our life here in Chattanooga, Glenn and I both love changing seasons. People think we are crazy, but we love snow, the crystals of ice, and the sledding. When the weather forecasters say we have inclement weather coming and we may get four inches of snow, we jump up and down cheering. I start making homemade vegetable soup and we gather wood for the fireplace and get hot dogs to roast in the fireplace. Other people say we are crazy. I can remember one time, when the whole city of Chattanooga was iced over and they called off everything, Glenn said, "We are never free on a Wednesday night, we are always at a church choir rehearsal. Let's go to a movie." We were on Signal Mountain and "we slid down that road" and drove to the only theater open way across the city. We were the only two moviegoers in there, and then the power went out. We left the movie to try to get back up the icy, mountain road, but Glenn made it seem easy.

QUEEN LOUNELLE is loved and respected by her husband, sons, grand-children, singers, and friends more than anyone I have ever known. As her husband, it's been forty-seven years of "paradise."

AS A FATHER

Dean E. Draper
UTC choirs; the younger son;
owner of insurance company, the Dean Draper Company

When I tell people that my name is Dean Draper, everybody always says, "Oh, I love your dad, my daughters think your dad . . ., my son thinks your dad . . ., we heard your dad's group in who knows where, and we listen to Ben Haden and to your dad . . ., we've been to Lake Junaluska, etc." It is very rare that I call on anyone, especially in the business profession, who does not know or know of Dad. Where it benefits me is that they all like him. It is not like when you mention someone like Bill Clinton, where you would have different connotations, they either hate him or love him; but when you think of Glenn Draper, he is loved univer-sally by people. The only people who don't love him are people who are jealous because they have never made it. Let's face it, in the music profes-sion, it is very difficult to make a healthy living. It is not a profession you choose because you want to make a lot of money. Dad is one of the few people who went into a profession that is not money oriented and has been successful, not only financially, but also succeeded in regards to making a name for himself, impacting a lot of people's lives, and going to places where other people can never get in because he is the ultimate networker. He knows how to meet people in the right places. People who are in that profession are frequently jealous and if you are good, some-body is always going to try and shoot you down.

Dad's brother Gene, to whom he was very close, had a major influence on my brother and me because he chose the profession of sales for a Fortune 500 company, the largest legal publishing company in the world, Commerce Clearing House (CCH), and brought my brother and me into that business when we got out of college. He and my dad were very much alike in regard to the fact that they are very positive, very focused, very congenial, and very talented. The highest award the company gives is the Gene Draper Award, named after my uncle. He was their number one salesman, the best in the nation for that company, for close to thirty years. Glenn and I were able to follow into that company, but that shows you that if Dad had chosen that profession how successful he would have been because he and his brother, Gene, were two peas in a pod. They had that ambition, that excitement about life, that talent.

Dad's gift was not only in people, but also in music. Dad has a tremendous amount of God-given talent. I do not know of anyone personally who has the kind of ear that he has. I don't understand it. No one can explain his energy. His ear for music, and being able to create a sound from ordinary people to make them be one in sound is something I have never heard from any other choir director. I have never seen people gather around one person and want to do their best, not only to please God but to please that director. I am sure that Robert Shaw would be an example of another person. I think Dad and Robert Shaw were different in the fact that, in my opinion, Dad is more of a person who really cares about the individual. He knows everyone's birthday, and he makes a point to connect with everyone with whom he is involved. I think people love him more for that than they do for his talent, because he is such a people person. He really cares about individuals.

We believe in the power of prayer in our family, and in a personal relationship with Jesus Christ. I have been studying some different theology with regards to Protestantism and Catholic faith. We look at the difference in the Protestant church, and sure we have our differences, but the theology of salvation by grace is the same. There is a process of growing for a new believer, it will take time, but they will become more and more like their Savior because he is in us and changing us. It takes longer for some and it doesn't take as long for others.

Where the public sees the outside, the success and the impact that he has had through his talent, my brother Glenn and I benefitted from the hands-on experience of a real father. About four years ago I gave a speech for a group of our insurance people. One of the biggest parts of that speech was the impact that Dad has had on my life and all the stories and his sayings, like, "Make friends before you need them" and "Swing hard, you might hit something." When we were kids growing up, Dad was very actively involved [in our lives], even though he was just as busy then as he is now. In the 1960s in Miami he always found time to be with his children. I mean not just watching TV but out doing things with us like playing with us or taking us to Miami Hurricane football games, and thus he was very much involved in our lives. We used to play football constantly in the backyard, and in Miami in the 1960s, as it probably is today, lawns were manicured and people just pruned and cared so much about their yards. However, ours looked like a goat ranch in the backyard because we played football all the time. Dad was always quarterback for both teams. One of the neighbors said, "Dr. Draper, your yard is looking really rough out there." I am sure the neighbor was a little unkind about it because he felt it brought down neighborhood value since the backyard was pretty torn up. My dad replied, "I'm not raising grass, I'm raising men." That was Dad's desire for Glenn and me, he wanted to raise men.

Around 1971, during a weekend trip to a church camp, our family went out to the lake to swim. My brother and I took turns swinging and jumping into the water from a rope that hung from a large tree limb. I somehow managed to get my leg tangled in the rope and found myself dangling upside down about twenty feet over the rocks below. Within minutes my father had climbed the tree, wedged his way in between two limbs, and untangled me. When he brought me down from the tree, he said, "Dean, you have two choices, you can either go back to the cabin, or you can climb back on that rope and try it again." My father had the wisdom to know what a critical decision this was during my passage into manhood. Would I stare fear down, or would I succumb to it? I must have swung from that rope ten more times that day, and I will never forget the lesson he taught me.

I have pictures in one of my annuals, I think from the ninth grade, where I had just scored a basket. You can see me with the ball, just as it left my hand and scored, and in the background you can see my dad in the bleachers with his hand raised up. I remember that because this was at 3:30 in the afternoon. How many men are there to watch their kids play basketball in the middle of a workday? There was my dad in those bleachers watching that game, and I think about that and what that's done to me. As a father, I want to be the same way, so I never miss my children's games. I want to be there for them because my dad was there for me, and I know what it meant to me that he cared enough to take time out of his schedule, which was so busy and has always been busy, to be involved in our lives. I don't fully understand how he did it, especially now that I am almost forty, but he did it. He was very busy with work and had so many different things going all the time, yet he always found time to be at home with us, and really be actively involved in our lives.

We benefitted from my parents having a marriage that is literally made in heaven. They fit just like a hand in a glove. You don't see many couples who are married forty-something years still holding hands and still actively building that relationship and taking trips together. I hardly ever heard a cross word between my parents. It just didn't happen, and nothing went on behind closed doors that we didn't know. They have a wonderful, happy relationship. They found each other, and each found the right person. My dad needed somebody who had the energy that my mother has and he found it. My mother needed somebody she could support and encourage and be a helpmate to and be the housewife, the home executive, and he found that in her. She found a man who could lead her and always provide for her and take care of her and make her feel special. It's unimaginable that they could have ended up with anybody else. They are that perfect and people see it. The students see it, the choir sees it, and it encourages others to look at themselves and say, "What are we looking for in a mate?" Everyone would say, "Boy, I would love to have that kind of relationship." They have it, and Glenn and I have benefitted from their happy marriage and from their home. The gospel was never jammed down our throats. We were led to Christ at a young age in a loving manner, and we saw our parents going to church and we were at church because they were there. We never felt dragged to church, it was just something you did.

I benefitted from singing in Dad's groups. I'm not a good singer (Dad would tell you that if he was being honest with you), I have a choir voice. I look back at those days from 1979 to 1984 as the happiest days of my life. I was singing in the Chattanooga Singers and the Singing Mocs, because it was our own fraternity. It is a secular university, but Christians were drawn and are still drawn to that choir because of my dad and the spiritual impact that he has in the community. So many parents want to send their kids to sing with Glenn Draper because they know they will be involved in an organization where they are going to get Christian leadership and feel loved, and be a part of something where they are not going to be off partying or causing trouble. There will be no hazing or partying, it's going to be wonderful Christian love, with travel experiences. I had that, and I look back on those five years as just incredible years of Christian growth and Christian fellowship experience in regard to travel, building relationships, and learning all about life.

I will be honest with you, being under Dad in regards to singing is not easy; he is not a typical let's-just-get-out-there-and-sing kind of guy. He is a perfectionist in regards to himself and in regards to others. He will pull you, very often beyond where you want to go. You really have to be sold on what he is trying to accomplish in order to really be a part of it. Many people, I'm sure, have dropped out because it is just too hard. If you want to really sing and make it sound good and be the best you can be, and be willing to be pulled, then you are singing for Glenn Draper. That is where you want to be. You left choir rehearsals tired.

There were some really funny instances and there were instances where you saw his genius. He could pick out someone who sounded good or bad out of fifty people. He could spot it. I mean, he knew if he heard something wrong. He didn't have to say, "Where is that coming from?" because he knew the person who was doing it. If something sounded good, he knew. He has an ear like I have never understood from any other musician. He can hear very clearly if there is something that is not in sync or is not tweaked right. He is looking for perfection, he is looking for this unity of sound where you are literally taking fifty to one hundred voices and making them one voice, and if something is not right, I can assure you that he knows it. You might be embarrassed. There have been people who have been embarrassed, but he doesn't intend to embarrass anybody. He just wants to root out the wrong sound, not root out that person. People have gotten their feelings hurt, and I'm sure I also did in the past.

You have to look at the big picture, what we were all trying to accomplish. We were trying to become one voice, and when we would sing, you would have people standing on their feet and giving you a standing ovation. You would have people with tears in their eyes, so you knew it was all worth it. You just knew because in the Chattanooga Singers and in the Singing Mocs, which I was a part of, when you were done, people had heard something they had never heard the likes of before. Usually, they are coming to some convention or they are coming to some church thing or to something going on in their community, and the choir is very often going to be a just side show. The choir is going to sing, and everyone is thinking, *Okay, now it's time to get out of here.* However, once we started singing, you cannot imagine the immediate silence and attention we received at the high schools, colleges, and everywhere we performed. It was just remarkable. I remember one instance when we were on the bus and ready to leave after singing at a high school in Asheville, North Carolina, in the early 1980s. The principal ran on the bus and said, "I have to tell you, we have never had an assembly like that where people have been completely silent and then rose in a standing ovation. Our high school kids are usually chattering, goofing off, and wanting to get out of there." That was very typical when we sang.

My favorite story of being in the Chattanooga Singers under Dad was in 1984, when we went to Hawaii and then on to Australia. While we were in Hawaii, we wanted to do a luau when we had some free time. We got on the tour bus to go out to the part of the island where they were doing the luau, and the Hawaiian girl who was the tour guide was telling funny jokes, but some of them were a little off-color. Who would know about the Chattanooga Singers, from a secular school? As we were returning, she said, "Tell me what you all do." We told her that we were part of the university, etc. She said, "Why don't you sing a song? I would love to hear something." Of course, she was expecting to hear maybe a patriotic number, maybe something from the stage, or a show tune, but we sang the most beautiful song, "The Majesty and Glory of Your Name." We sang it in harmony without any accompaniment, and it was beautiful. She broke down and cried. She was someone who was just there to make a living and have fun and tell a couple of off-color jokes, but she cried. When we got off that bus, she was hugging and kissing people, and tears were flowing. You just saw the impact. You see, it all starts with Christ. My dad is definitely an excellent conduit, and the love of Christ flows through my dad to singers to impact even one single life. I will never forget that because I thought, *This is what it is all about.* Of course, on that tour we had the opportunity to sing to tremendous numbers of people, but what touched me was that one life that was touched. That is Dad's life. He has touched so many people wherever he has gone.

The other thing that I often thought about was Dad outside of the entertainment spectrum. One was that he was such an opportunist, very much being in the right place at the right time, and that is not always accidental. Glenn and I have often told a story (and I even wrote an article for an insurance trade journal that was published across the country and mentioned this story and how it relates to my profession) in regards to being in the right place at the right time. Dad, Glenn, and I and another friend of ours in Miami in 1967 or 1968, were out in the driveway in Dad's convertible listening to the pre-game show for the second Super Bowl, Green Bay against Oakland Raiders, at the Orange Bowl. The Orange Bowl was only a couple of miles from our house, and we were saying, "Gosh, I would do anything to be at that game with the mighty Green Bay Packers—Vince Lombardi, Paul Hornung—all of these incredible people." Dad said, "Well, why don't we just drive over to the stadium and get a closer look?" We got in the car, not expecting anything, thinking we will just listen to it on the radio while we are sitting at the stadium and it will almost be like we are there. We drove over there and, sure enough, because everyone was already parked we found a parking place literally within seventy-five feet of the actual stadium. We got out and said, "Let's walk up and see what we can see." We could see the corner of the end zone, and actually see some of the play going on. It was the first quarter, and with about seventy-four thousand fans cheering, we couldn't believe it. Out of the blue a man comes rushing out of the stadium with his wife and his kids in tow. This is the first quarter, and I mean this guy is headed out somewhere, something is going on, an emergency or something. Dad runs up to him, and says, "What's wrong?" The man says, "I have been called out on an emergency, I'm a doctor," and Dad said, "Do you mind if we have your tickets?" How many dads would have said, "Let's just go there?" When you are right there, things happen. He was just always that way.

Dad is so personable, he never met anyone he didn't like. He is not afraid of anybody, and he never met a stranger. Tom Landry, the Dallas Cowboys coach, was sitting maybe thirteen rows behind us, and my brother Glenn says, "Tom Landry is back there." You know, this was the heyday of the Cowboys Super Bowls, and Dad says, "I'll take you back there to meet him." (As if he knows him.) In the middle of the game, Tom Landry was trying to watch the Cotton Bowl and Dad says, "Tom, Glenn Draper, I want you to meet my boys, Dean and Glenn," and of course, Tom Landry says, "Glad to meet you." Dad knew that we would never forget that.

Not long ago I was watching the Chattanooga AA baseball game with my sons, and Tommy LaSorda, the famous Dodgers manager, was at the game because we were playing one of the Dodgers farm teams. I told my kids, "That's Tommy LaSorda," but they already knew who he was. Anyone who follows baseball knows that this guy is famous, probably one of the most famous managers of all time. You know what I did? I ran back to my car and got my camera, but I couldn't find anyone who had film. I finally found some, came back sweating with my camera, got my boys (they had caught two foul baseballs), and I said, "We are going to meet Tommy LaSorda." We ran down there, and I said, "Tommy, these are my sons, Dean and Riley, and I want you to meet them and they want to meet you. Can I get your picture with them?" He was very gracious and let us do it. The reason I did that was because my dad had done that for Glenn and me. I said to my boys, "You don't understand this now, but someday you will remember this. You are going to have the picture, you are going to have the autographed baseball, and you will know that your dad went out of his way because he wanted you to meet somebody you wouldn't forget." It is amazing how that filters down. You see that in your dad and you want to be like that also.

When it comes to music, I think back to the stories of when Dad came to UTC, but I have only heard this through him and through others like Gaye Sellers Slaten. He came onto a campus that had no choir, and he started going to the student center and shaking hands with students who didn't know him at all and telling them, "I want you to come sing with me! We are going to go to Europe. I'm going to take you all over the world." Within one year, in 1971, they took a nine-week tour to Europe. It was written up in the paper, and was the biggest news in Chattanooga, because back in the late 1960s those things didn't happen. You didn't take choral groups all over the United States or out of the country. Within one year, we were making albums. It is hard to understand, but it all starts with his incredible amount of enthusiasm and focus, and what I would call ambition. He has such vision about what and where he wants to go. There is an old saying, "The world makes way for a person who knows where he is going." Well, Dad knows where he is going and it seems like everything parts out of his way and lets him move forward. I have never seen anything like it.

The thing that amazes me now is the fact that he is seventy-four years old, but you would think he is forty-four. He has the same energy and enthusiasm and ambition he did thirty years ago, and he still has to have something going all the time. I know that probably drives my mom crazy. He can go from the Glenn Draper Singers, to the Junaluska Singers, to the Chattanooga Singers, to the Singing Mocs, to First Presbyterian, and then to conferences and things that don't even involve those activities. He can turn on a dime, and can concentrate on one particular thing. He can shift continually into different areas and focus totally on that area, not just once a week, but several times during a day. I don't know how he does it. That is exhausting even thinking about it. But he can, he is very driven. He had four offices—at home, the university, the church, and Lake Junaluska. It's just difficult to put your finger on how this man does it at seventy-four, I don't know—he is an enigma. He acts like he is just starting out in his career with so much energy and enthusiasm.

I believe the people, aside from the immediate family, who are impacted most by my father are those who have been under his directorship. I think from the church choir to the Junaluska Singers to students at UTC, there are thousands upon thousands of lives that have been influenced not only toward music, but toward Christ, toward positive thinking, everything you can think of as positive, because of the direct correlation of being under him. I think the greatest outpouring I saw of the evidence of that was one of the reunions we had for the Chattanooga Singers, probably in 1998. There is a giant scrapbook filled with pictures and letters from former students over a thirty-year period, beginning in 1968. One scrapbook was from singers of the past who could not come to the reunion, so they mailed letters. I cried when I read about all the students who are living all over the country, some are still in music, some have gone into professional music, some have made popular recording tapes, some are in different ministries, dentistry, you name it. The people who wrote those letters in that scrapbook said, "Glenn, the love was incredible and the impact that you had on my life made those the happiest years of my life." All the letters seemed to have a common theme, he just has affected so many lives.

There is an old saying, "We can all count the number of seeds in a single apple, but only God can count the number of apples that comes from a single seed." Well, I look at Dad's ministry and Dad is that seed, and wonder how many of the apples throughout this country have grown because of that one seed, because of the way Dad has impacted them. Because of his impact, how have those people impacted others? He is definitely unique. When you meet Glenn Draper you will meet somebody unlike anyone you have ever met before. Unbelievable, and believe me I have benefitted from that as a person, as a Christian, as a businessman, as a father, as a husband, it has all been a positive impact on my life. My brother would say the same thing. I think anyone you talk to would say the same thing. Where could he have gone, if he had chosen the secular route? He really chose the church route but he had opportunities to join the music scene in New York. When I think of that, one of the positives would be that Dad would be famous, Dad would be one of those guys who made it to the Radio City Music Hall, something just gigantic. I also think of the negative impact of all that might have been possible. Even without the negative, what would that have done for our family? What kind of lifestyle would we have had growing up?

I have a tape of him on the *Ed Sullivan Show*. When I play that tape of Dad's group singing on the *Ed Sullivan Show* to some of my buddies and coworkers, they say, "Your dad was on the *Ed Sullivan Show*?! The Beatles were on the *Ed Sullivan Show*! Your dad sang for the Miss Universe Pageant, your dad did this, and that." It must have been an incredibly exciting time for my father when he was in Miami. They were doing USO tours, and he was meeting famous people because Miami was such an entertainment mecca. He really walked away from that. Of course, he would say it was the smartest thing he ever did, and it was the safest thing he ever did in regards to getting out of Miami.

Dad has always had his act together. He does not believe in owing for anything. He could be one of the chapters in "The Millionaire Next Door"—lived the frugal life, didn't earn a fortune, was wise with his money, invested regularly, bought a house, and stayed there. He has had the same house since 1968, pays cash for things, and is always so wise with his money. He is not a big spender because that is not where his happiness lies.

We always had everything we needed, but what we had was more valuable than money, we had the time and hands-on attention from our father. I wouldn't trade that for anything in the world. He was an incredible provider and we never had to worry about anything. I am thankful that we never had to worry about whether Dad was going to be out of work or whether he was going to lose money. He just took care of things. He handled that part of his life equally as well as his business life, which is not very common. He had the spiritual, the business, the family, and the financial parts of his life always in tune. I can't even say that I have done that. Not many people can say that they have kept all those things in line with each other and done well with all of them. It is very difficult, and I think part of it is a God-given gift and wisdom. He has a tremendous amount of wisdom, but I also think it has to do with the incredible amount of energy that he has. I used to say he could just do it all! So much is written about Glenn Draper, the director, but it is Glenn Draper, the father, who influenced me the most.

AS A MUSICAL GENIUS

Dr. Robert D. Andrews
First Presbyterian Church choir member for many years;
provost, Oxford Graduate School

When I came home after the first couple of Sundays with Glenn, I said, "This guy knows how to pull music out of people." That is the key to the whole thing. People ask me about the choir and I say, "If you played college football you can play for a routine coach or you can play for Bear Bryant, and you know the difference." It is the quality of a leader that has that genius to pull people beyond their own capabilities and stretch them beyond what they are able to do. I recognize that in him. I had recognized it before in two or three other people. Usually if you meet one like him in a lifetime, your life is rich.

You recognize that quality, and it is like other qualities that you read about that everybody can recognize, but nobody can quantify. I don't think I can quantify it, but I just recognize that in a person and I want to be a part of that person's organization because it rubs off. As a youth pastor in Chicago, I had a pastor who was a "pastor's pastor." I went in and talked with him and said, "I want to be on your staff, I will be the janitor, I don't care, I just want to be on your staff. You are a pastor's pastor." Through the years, I have watched young people come and Glenn makes them stars. He is not interested in making himself a star. He makes them stars, one after another after another. He brings them into UTC and four years later we are all sorry to see them graduate, but a lot of them stay right here and they sing at Junaluska and then they become recording stars or they go on to opera, or do whatever they do. I have seen it over and over again. He is the same kind of person who recognizes talent in a person, pulls it out of them, then turns them loose and lets them go do their own thing.

I know one of the characteristics of the kind of genius personality that we are talking about with Glenn, Bear Bryant, Lou Holtz, etc., is somebody who is at the top of their game, and is teaching other people and is being copied. One of those characteristics is that they are youth oriented. They have a young mind, and they don't talk down to people. They pull people up, and when you are around a person like that, you go away feeling better. I made up my mind a long time ago that I didn't want to just envy those people for being that way, I wanted to emulate their style, figure out what it is, and I wanted to leave people feeling good for having met me, too. Glenn has taught me how to leave people feeling good.

You hear in sales, every person has a sign on their forehead, "Make me feel important." With Glenn it is not a practiced thing, it is not a gimmick. If you tell Glenn your birthday, he will tell it back to you five years from now. He has a gift with numbers. It is ironic that he will remember your birth date, but he might miss your name. If you go to a concert, or sing in a concert with him, he knows who is there. A week later he will thank you for being there.

That reminds me of another quality that I have observed in the personality type that we are talking about, the genius personality. They are sometimes lonely. I don't think Glenn would ever admit he is lonely, but I see an amazing response from him to praise. If you just say something nice to him, there is just an amazing response, he lights up. I think it is because he takes a lot of heat as a music director. They never can sing the right mix of music for some people. I have noticed that about him and I have known several people like him whom I have managed to get close to and one of the things you can do is just say, "That was wonderful, that was really good."

AS AN INSPIRATION

David Fowler

At UTC after we had sung in a school, I was one of the people cleaning up and getting things organized, and a man came up to me and said he was the janitor and had stuck around to listen to us. He was apologetic for listening, and said how much it had meant to him since his wife was very sick. He sure wished that she could have heard that music because it would have encouraged her and lifted her spirits. I said, "You just take an album," but he said he didn't have the money to pay for it. I said, "Take the album, and if you can ever pay for it, just send us the money, but don't worry about it, you take this home to your wife." Sure enough, about two weeks later we had arrived at home from the tour and this note came with five dollars and he said what it had meant to his wife to hear that music and thanks for just letting him have it. What a ministry—I remember sharing that with the whole choir. So there was a sense that what we did was not just entertainment either.

We had another lady, in a church in Dallas, who had wandered in off the streets. She heard us singing and had come in and listened to our rehearsal. We saw her in the back, and she said she was going through a divorce, her husband had left her, and things were a mess, so I invited her to come back that night. The bottom line was that it was another one of those things that had moved her and gave her a sense of encouragement and comfort. So there were a lot of little things that we did that went beyond representing the university and just singing good music. I felt like we ministered and encouraged people. When we were in Jackson, Tennessee, another choir member and I stayed the night in a home with two small children. Our hostess said that her husband was out of town, and she was sorry he couldn't make it, etc. The next morning we came down for breakfast and she started crying and said, "I just sensed that your choir has a very strong spiritual dimension to it, and actually my husband has been seeing another woman and we are in the process of a divorce, and I don't know what to do. Would you ask your choir to pray for my family?" I shared her story and request with the choir that morning on the bus, and we all prayed for her.

I had Glenn and his choir come to the state legislature twice to sing. I think when he celebrated his thirtieth anniversary at UTC, we passed a resolution honoring him, and then again about two years ago. I wanted the legislature to appreciate that we really had a commodity in the person of Glenn Draper. Many times a prophet is not honored in his own country, but we have something here that a lot of people wish they could say they have. They sang a short concert before the session started. The clerk for the state senate, generally a nice, but crusty guy, had been around there for thirty years or so and had seen a little bit of everything, heard the music. He actually had tears in his eyes after they sang "Amazing Grace." He came up to me and said, "I have never heard that song sung in such a meaningful and powerful way as I just heard it." To see this guy crying was kind of like seeing Vince Lombardi with a tear in his eye.

We also had another individual in the senate who is probably one of the most liberal of the senators. I would say he would probably concede that, just as I would concede that I am the most conservative of the senators. Glenn and the choir sang an accappella arrangement of "The Lord's Prayer" for our invocation. We always start each session with a prayer and have various ministers come pray, but it was the first time anybody had ever sung our invocation. The senator came up to me afterwards and said, "That was really special, it was the most meaningful invocation that I think we have had." He had been there a long time, and was not much for hearing the preachers. Many times he didn't even come in while we said the prayers, but that had touched him in a way that no minister had touched him. The way in which that familiar prayer was sung was really a holy moment, and even those who didn't share the Christian faith also found it to be a meaningful, holy moment.

Merlin E. Johnson
Retired Methodist church minister of music;
Glenn's friend for many years

I hear the criticisms here every year, "Oh, we have heard it before, it's the same as last year. Just like it was ten years ago." I don't know how many we have heard, probably forty years' worth almost, and I don't know if it is just me, but I don't even remember what it was last year. I feel the electricity of that night. I know for a fact that when we stood up to participate, I was involved totally and was probably singing too loudly because I was so inspired when we sang "God Bless America" or the national anthem, or whatever we sang as a congregation. Not too many people around me really were singing. What that means is that a lot of people don't know how to sing anymore, because they have only watched TV. What Glenn offers to people, and of course they are already talented musicians or developing talent, is the opportunity to be a performer like you see on TV, instead of sitting there watching TV. We're supposed to be the worshipers, not the observers, not the TV couch potatoes who are sitting there being entertained. We are to be the entertainers. If we state it properly, we are God's entertainers. We are doing what He expects us to do. That is what I think the singers are able to communicate to people and I know it is what Glenn is trying to do. He turns around and directs the congregation with as much fervor as he does the singers, if not more.

Glenn Wright Draper II
Glenn's older son; church elder;
financial planner with Merrill Lynch

Wherever they would show up to sing, the people would be just mesmerized, just amazed at the beautiful sound, the energy, and the heart of the singers. That was always a joy, no matter where we went on a tour, to watch the countenance of the people as they were lifted up to new heights of praise and adoration of God. You just can't describe it. All my life I saw that, and it made us so proud that he was our dad and how God had gifted him. That was always so exciting to see. I knew before they started to sing that this was going to be the response that you were going to see because it was always that way. Ever since childhood, I could see music melt the hearts of people. You would all of a sudden see their countenances just brighten up, and it was like they were so refreshed. Dad has a unique ability to keep things moving; he is an impatient person, but at the same time he is thinking about how people are thinking to keep them from being bored.

STORIES

Julius Walthall

I think Glenn and his mother were very close. She was very involved in church events. My family was Methodist, but Glenn was a Wesleyan Methodist and more of a fundamentalist. When I first met Glenn, he had never been to a movie, he didn't drink Cokes, wouldn't go anywhere near playing cards, or anything like that. I contaminated him and took him to his first movie, *Moon Over Burma* with Clark Gable.

About 1945, my summer job was digging out a basement in an older house. I was working like crazy when his mother drove him by. Glenn got out of the car and said, "Come on with us and spend a week at High Point at a camp meeting." We used to have tent meetings but I had never been to a camp meeting. I had been working pretty hard, and anything to get a break from that sounded really good. I asked my employer if I could take a week off, and we went the next day to the meeting somewhere near High Point, North Carolina. It was a rather pleasant experience. There were cabins for the men and women, and all the normal things you might think of at a religious camp meeting.

At one point, Glenn and I sneaked away to the Greensboro–High Point Airport and had our first airplane ride. This is another thing, Glenn would always have just a little bit of money. We paid a guy five dollars to take us both up in a yellow Piper Cub, I can still remember it. The pilot took us up and he would say, "Ya'll all right back there?" "Yeah, we are all right." We kept egging him on to do something, a rollover, a dive, and he did all the tricks that he had nerve enough to do and we just had a great time. That was our first airplane ride. We had a lot of firsts together.

Dot Carter

In 1996, Glenn's choir had been invited to sing at the Olympics in Atlanta, and he was at Lake Junaluska. The rest of us who were going to be a part of that choir drove down and parked at the last MARTA Station, where we were told we could park. When he and other singers from Junaluska arrived in Atlanta, there were no parking places at MARTA, and he began to run around to see if he could find a place. He looked over on the other side of the tracks where there was a hardware store, and he went over and started talking to the manager. The man told him, "Don't even come asking for a parking place, because I'm not letting anybody park here." Glenn said, "But you just don't really understand, sir. I have a choir and we are supposed to be singing at the First Methodist Church downtown and I have got to park." The man insisted that he could not park there. About that time, Glenn began to show him posters and CDs. Glenn had shown him one that had been recorded a few years before, and on the back cover was a picture of Glenn and the singers with President and Mrs. Reagan when they had sung at the White House. The fellow said, "You know President Reagan?" Glenn said, "We have sung at the White House for him before." With that, the man said, "Any friend of Ronald Reagan is a friend of mine and you can park anywhere on my lot." Everybody says that Glenn has angels on each shoulder.

Jennifer Odom

What I personally love about Glenn is that he remembers the little moments that you share with him. For example, we were in Rio in Brazil, and were singing "Shine on Us." The guys were singing it and the girls were sitting down. At some point, he and I made eye contact during that song while they were singing. It was just a really special service, with the whole power of singing in this place, with all these people making it a really blessed sort of moment, and we had eye contact. It was just as if we knew what the other was thinking. Every time that song is sung, and this was forever ago, no telling how many times he has done that song, if I am there, he looks at me. He finds me and we make eye contact, and he will say "Brazil" or "Rio." That is just precious, like he remembers those moments. Of course, he is going to call you on your birthday. He never fails to remember everyone's birthday. Another example is that he may be walking right there in front of the auditorium, and he will see somebody he hasn't seen in forty years. He will say, "How are you doing, John? I haven't seen you in forty years, on December 20, wasn't it?" Every person has a special place in his life.

Lounelle M. Draper

Glenn's Air Force male chorus had sung on the *Ed Sullivan Show* twice. When he and I went to New York City, just to have some fun, Glenn said, "I have got to see Ed Sullivan again." We went to the Ed Sullivan Theater without tickets and we couldn't get in, so he went up to the page at the front door and said, "Please let us in, I want to see him again. My Air Force choir performed on his show twice." The page said, "Absolutely not, you are not allowed in without tickets." Glenn took me to an alley that runs behind the Ed Sullivan Theater and he knew that there was a men's rest room with one door that opens to the back alley. He walked in that door, cleared out the rest room, and brought me through the men's rest room, and we came in on stage. It was before the *Ed Sullivan Show* started, and there was Ed Sullivan just sitting on stage looking through his notes. Glenn walked right up to him and said, "Do you remember me? I'm Glenn Draper," and, of course, he remembered Glenn and they stood and talked. We saw the rest of the show, and it was wonderful. Of course, Glenn had to walk out the front door right past that page who said, "How did you get in here?" Glenn said, "I will never tell!"

Charles V. Perry
First Presbyterian Church choir member for many years

The four of us used to go to Birmingham to hear a concert at Thanksgiving. One time when we were coming back from Birmingham maybe fifteen years ago, the Drapers wanted to stop at a chair factory and pick out a recliner. We stopped and Glenn bought a recliner, and he took it out to put it in the back of the station wagon. It was raining a little bit, just enough to bother us. I went back in the store and told Lounelle that there was no way Glenn was going to get that recliner in the station wagon, not without breaking it down or tearing it up, or something. When I came back out, he already had the door shut and the recliner was inside. I turned to Lounelle and said, "Well, Glenn has the recliner in the station wagon, it's time to go." That was one of the funniest experiences that we had with them. The reason I am telling this is because of his persistence and his determination. He is one of a kind, and with his determination and persistence he will not stop when he thinks he is right and when he knows he can do something. If there are no tickets to a ball game, he will find a way to get in.

Bob B. Davis

Glenn would come to my house in Gastonia, North Carolina, and when my dad heard that Glenn was coming, he would say, "Mabel, you better cook a couple more chickens, Draper is coming!" If there was food anywhere, Glenn Draper thought the food was for him. It didn't make any difference where it was or what, he went after food and ate like it was going out of style.

I remember the time that Glenn came to my wedding in Washington, D.C., and I was late getting packed. The wedding was to start in about an hour and we were leaving right from there, so Glenn said, "I'll help you." We went over to the laundromat in the apartment complex and Glenn started dumping soap into the dryer and threw the clothes into the dryer and turned it on with all that soap in there. When we finally opened up the dryer, there was mucky soap on my dirty clothes. That is how fast paced Glenn was, and I wasn't paying any attention because I was so excited!

Glenn Wright Draper II

We were talking about Dad being a perfectionist and making sure you do things right. I was probably four or five years old and we were in North Carolina, at Lake Junaluska, and we went somewhere maybe ten miles away. I stole a little bag of peanuts, but didn't even realize what I was doing. We got back to the house and I was opening the little bag of peanuts, and my dad came over to me and picked me up and said, "Where did you get these?" and it scared me to death. I said, "Dad, I got them at the filling station in the Lance jar." He said, "We are going back there right now." We got in that car and drove ten miles to take a five-cent package of peanuts back. The man said I could have them, but Dad said, "No, I am going to teach my son right from wrong." Another time I remember when I was a little older, I got a dime out of a phone booth. As a kid, we would stick our finger in the coin return hoping to find some money. I told my dad, and he made me return it. I asked him why, since the person had left it there. He said, "Son, if it is not yours, don't take it."

AS A COMPETITOR

THERE IS A LOT of competition in all of us. In fact, it is said that competition is what makes the world go around, and maybe that is true. People see someone else with a bigger ship than they have and they want to have one bigger than that. "The tallest building in the world," why do they say that? Well, somebody took pains to try and build the tallest building to make it a little taller than somebody else has built. An old saying is, "Keeping up with the Joneses." I found that the Joneses have trouble just keeping up with themselves. I have always been interested in and loved music. I organized a quartet when I was in the sixth grade, when my voice changed, and we sang for a lot of different things. When I started high school, I found three other guys and we started singing together and sang together for all four years. In fact, we even sang at our graduation. That quartet was called The Andrew Lewis High School Quartet. There was a group in town called the Young Roanoke Sings, and I also organized a quartet in that group.

When I transferred to Indiana University after singing with the college quartet and traveling one summer throughout the midwest, my brother and I and a couple of other guys formed another quartet. But I heard a local group on campus called the Jordanaires, and they were very good. I had a problem because I knew that the other guys and my brother would never win any championships. I had to dismiss that quartet and organize another one in order to be competitive with the Jordanaires. I found Hardy Leiberg in the choir who was a tremendous second tenor, and a guy from upstate Indiana, Gary Pittenger, who sang first tenor, and Bill Smith, an African-American, who sang bass. That was in 1950, so you can imagine the feeling around some places, but they were the best voices to put in that quartet. There was a number called "Halls of Ivy" that was extremely popular. I wrote an arrangement of that for the quartet in 1950 for us to sing and compete with the Jordanaires. That arrangement attracted immediate attention for our quartet.

We also caught the eye of a businessman from Bedford, Indiana, Bill LuAllen, who was in the rock quarrying business. He owned a Lincoln Continental, and he loaned us his car on weekends to go to Michigan, Chicago, Detroit, and Toledo, Ohio, to sing. That quartet traveled all over creation, singing programs. It was through the necessity of being competitive that I had to ditch my own brother and two other guys, who were both buddies, in order to compete with the best on the campus. I never forgot what I was after. I have often told people that I couldn't even pass my own audition for the Junaluska Singers. They think I am kidding, but I am really serious about that. I probably don't have the kind of voice now that I would choose for a group like that. I have a good ear, can sing their parts, and let them know how I want it to sound, but as for me sounding good, that is another story. That is what competition does to you.

THE HUMOROUS SIDE

Lounelle M. Draper

Glenn bought a brand-new Buick for our first date, and he was so proud of that car. Once we were driving down a central expressway after our classes in Dallas, and a very inebriated older man sideswiped us. The impact was just a sudden shock to us. Thank the Lord, I had on a mouton fur coat because a piece of the chrome from the steering wheel broke off and went through the fur coat and into the chest area. Had it not been for the coat and the sweater and blouse I had on, it would have pierced my flesh but I was protected by that coat. Glenn's reaction to the impact was so sudden, I had already found out what a fast-moving man this young man was. He jumped out of the car and immediately went around to the driver of the other car and to gaze at what had been done to his new car. In the meantime, I looked to my left and Glenn's pants were in the seat that he had just vacated. Even the pants legs had gone over the seat and were down on the floor by the accelerator and the brake. I thought he had jumped out of his pants! He moved so quickly anyway, that I thought he had jumped right out of his pants. Unbeknownst to me, before Glenn had ever picked me up after classes that afternoon, he had put his dry cleaning in the back seat of the car. I didn't realize that it was his dry cleaning from the back seat that had flipped over the front seat. It was then that I first realized that I was with a man with boundless energy, who was a very fast mover.

Frank Calhoun
Lake Junaluska Singers for ten years

The first summer I was in the quartet at Lake Junaluska, Glenn had an old Cadillac. They called it rattle saddle, and it really rattled. Glenn and Lounelle, my wife and I, and my parents went up on Mt. Mitchell for a picnic. We got up there and Glenn ran out of gas on top of Mt. Mitchell. We started back and he didn't have any gas in that car. That was the scariest ride I ever had, he just drove that thing all the way back down the mountain without a drop of gas in it and, of course, he didn't have any power steering and I'm not sure about the brakes. I don't know how he did it, but it was a very wild ride and I sure was praying all the way. We were really glad to get to the bottom. I think he drives because he has to get there and he points that car and away he goes.

Kathy Tugman
UTC choirs; First Presbyterian Church choir;
Glenn Draper Singers; writes, arranges, and records music

Mel Madaris and I went over to Lake Junaluska because Glenn had invited us to sing. It was our first time there, and Glenn wanted to show us the Blue Ridge Parkway at night. We got in the car, except we knew how Glenn drives, so I made Mel get in the front. While Glenn was driving that car we were both praying, *Dear Lord, if you ever get us out of this car we will never get in the car with Glenn Draper again.* He was just flying around those curves in the dark and I was holding on in the back seat and said, "I really do need to get home to my children." That same trip, he would back up the driveway at Junaluska and it felt like we were going forty-five or fifty miles an hour. Glenn and driving are something I try to stay away from. Everything else about him I love.

Ben Haden

It's rare is to find a perfectionist who is a people person and Glenn is a perfectionist who can get more good sounds out of bad singers, than anyone I know. I made an announcement during church and I didn't notice until the end of the announcement how the choir was chuckling. By request, I had said, "We need choir members, it doesn't make any difference whether you can sing or not." The choir was giggling and almost hysterical by the end of it. I didn't even know what the joke was, however they knew what a perfectionist he was. Anyway, my wife volunteered. During practice one night, Glenn, who has a wonderful ear, said, "There is a perfectly horrible sound that I am hearing over in this area, but I can't quite spot the person." My wife said, "I am the person. I have been asked out of other choirs before," and she walked out. I am sure Glenn said he was sorry, but he never changed what he said. She had only responded to her husband's announcement, "You don't have to be able to sing."

Jay Craig

There was one summer rehearsal at Lake Junaluska where Glenn was really working us like horses and dogs. Back then, in the early 1990s, he would do morning, noon, and night rehearsals—I mean, you had only a couple of hours rest time. During that rehearsal, he had just had it with the altos. He kicked the altos out. We were working on "And the Glory of the Lord," from the *Messiah*, and he kicked the altos out and carried on with the rehearsal. He is great about cuing in different sections when their time comes, so as he was directing he cued the altos, but there were no altos! That really frustrated him, because he said, "Oh Lord," and he was making all kinds of moaning noises. We all wanted to cut up and laugh, but we were afraid, we didn't want to get kicked out. Come to find out, all the altos ran up to the log house where the Drapers lived to see Lounelle. They wanted to prepare Lounelle so that when Glenn came in the door, she could calm him down, and it worked! They were kicked out just for that rehearsal! It all became something to laugh about. It all blew over, and one thing you have to learn to do with Glenn Draper is to let it come in one ear, but some things have to go out the other ear. You cannot take Glenn personally. He doesn't mean harm when he says some of the things he says.

Kim Cargile

Sometimes Glenn puts his toes on the very edge of the stage and the rest of his feet are hanging off. We were somewhere in North Carolina in 1999 with the Junaluska Singers, singing at a university when we did two back-to-back concerts. When I went out for the second one, I thought they had moved the piano closer to the edge of the stage. I felt like I didn't have as much room. Glenn a lot of times will come over behind me to tell me something, or to get me to stand up and take a bow. Well, the second concert he stood up and moved out of the way for me to stand up and take a bow, and he fell probably five or six feet at least, and landed right on his shoulder and just bounced. It scared me to death. He got up and shook and made sure everything was okay, and said, "Keep going—don't stop!" We were all just freaking out because we thought, *This is the end of Glenn.* I started the next song, he got back up on the stage, and the whole audience went nuts. He was sore for a few days, but that would have killed most anybody else. They would have broken something.

Dr. Thomas Hammett
First Presbyterian Church choir member, seven years;
Rivermont Presbyterian Church choir director, six years

I remember the night we were doing Beethoven's "Ninth," and Glenn came out to take the choral bow and acknowledge everybody and, being the absent-minded professor, turned and stepped right through the foot lights and landed spread-eagle there on the stage floor. He apparently fell on a couple of the light bulbs, and they crashed and sparks went everywhere and smoke started rising. I thought that was it, I thought we had lost the night. He got up and dusted himself off and waved to the crowd again, then smiled and went on.

Todd Gaither
UTC choirs; Junaluska Singers; Glenn Draper Singers;
choir director, Covenant Presbyterian Church

If there is a place to trip or fall, Glenn will do it. We were at the World Expo '88 in Australia, and we were singing "The Majesty and Glory of Your Name." As he is directing, he will always try to get us to empathize with the lyrics to interpret the best we can. There is a phrase in that song that says "Little children praise him perfectly." We were on an outside stage, and Glenn was off to the side at ground level. There were people all around the stage. Glenn said something like "little children" while we were singing that part because he wanted us to look at the little children and, as he did, he stepped back on one of the "little children." We couldn't keep from laughing.

Sara Smith Youngblood

Glenn was very protective of his female singers. We were at a very old school auditorium in Marion, North Carolina, but I don't remember whether something had fallen through or if the best the church could do was to put us in a high school that was very old and in seriously bad shape. There were very high ceilings in the rooms that we were changing in, and a bat appeared and flew through somebody's hair, and some screaming ensued. I didn't scream, because I am not a screamer, but Glenn came rushing in, covering his eyes, hitting at that bat with his folder. He wasn't going to look, but he was trying to knock the bat down, while being very gentlemanly. He wasn't going to see us in our slips.

Charles Middleton

When we were first at Lake Junaluska we would dress up and Glenn would say, "Do you have a blue blazer?" I had one but it had lines in it, so it was a hodgepodge of a uniform. We all had gray pants, my gray was kind of dark, but we put it together, trying to look somewhat uniform. Sitting around we would get ideas, *Maybe we could get the conference to give us some money to buy blazers and buy dresses for the ladies, just a simple A-line.* Then we got the idea, *Why don't we buy our own? We could have a bake sale.* So I guess for three or four weeks we had bake sales. I baked twenty-three lemon meringue pies and also some cakes in one night. We also had watermelon sales and a western North Carolina couple gave us a cash donation.

In Asheville, we went to a store called Ivy's and looked at some powder blue blazers. This was the late 1960s. I was much heavier then, but they had my size, and we told the salesperson that we needed six blazers and ties. The guy said, "Okay," and Glenn asked, "How much is this blazer?" The blazer was $55, and Glenn said, "Well, can you give us a discount on it?" The salesman said, "I can give you $5 off," so they added up the amount of money it was going to cost, and Glenn said, "Man, can you give us a little more off that?" He told him all about Lake Junaluska, and what we were doing there. He said, "If you would come up to Lake Junaluska you can see that striking view of the mountains looking across the lake . . ." and he created all this image. The salesperson said, "Sir, I have been to Lake Junaluska and I have seen it, but I can't give you anymore. You will have to talk to my manager." He couldn't find the store manager, so here we sat, Glenn, myself, and two of the other male singers, sitting in this guy's office on a Saturday, and the salesman said, "You know the reason Ivy's exists is to make a profit." Glenn said, "Oh yes, I know that. My father-in-law has a store in Dallas," and he told him all about it. "You just don't realize what Lake Junaluska does for people," and he went through the whole story again. The salesman said, "I will let you have them for $35 each." Glenn moved up in his chair and said, "You know the Lake Junaluska Singers . . ." and on and on. Glenn kept saying, "I just know they will look great in them, and it will be great advertising for Ivy's." The guy said, "You have the knife in my back and you are still sticking me!" Glenn said, "No, I don't want to do that, I want to invite you out to the lake and to the Fourth of July concert." The guy said, "Okay, I will give them to you for $25." We said, "Let's go, Glenn, that's great." Glenn, said "Okay, fine, thank you. Please come to the lake," and he invited him to the concert.

After we got that great deal, we had a lot of traffic returning to Junaluska because of road construction. Traffic was very bad and really backed up. At that time, we had a lot of grass in the median, and all these people were in line, waiting their turn to move up. Glenn said, "Well, nobody is using this," referring to the median. We were sitting in the backseat like kids, and Lounelle was sitting on the right side, waving at the people as we went by. We would get to a point where water was too high, so Glenn would have Lounelle ask the people to let us in. There was no road rage at that time! One time, she said, "I'm sorry, we have a concert at Lake Junaluska," and they said, "Lake Junaluska, I know that. You can cut in." Then we would get past that point and we would get in the median again. There were no bounds for Glenn. We were embarrassed, but it wasn't embarrassing to Glenn; however, I learned from that. *These people don't know you. You will see them this time and then you may never see them again, so why be embarrassed?*

Sara Smith Youngblood

We were in the chapel [at Junaluska] recording, and we have electronic chimes that ring around the lake. We were deep into the recording and the chimes came on and he was hysterical! He said, "Got to do something, got to do something!" I said, "Okay." He wasn't saying it to me specifically, but everybody was running around like a chicken and he was getting hot under the collar! I was vaguely aware that they came from Stewart Auditorium somewhere, and I knew they were plugged in somewhere backstage, so I just looked around and unplugged them. He just couldn't believe that I figured it out. I said, "Well Glenn, it's just a dumb 'ole machine, you know."

8

PERFECT MESSAGE *or* PERFECT MUSIC?

Glenn Draper is constantly thrilled, and I think that part of his success is because he never ceases being thrilled by the sound of music and the words and what they say.

~SARA SMITH YOUNGBLOOD

Robert H. Shipp

Three people whom I interviewed sang for both Glenn W. Draper and Robert Shaw for a number of years, so they would appear to be quite qualified to make comparisons between the two choral directors. Both directors have had very distinguished careers, but had quite diverse approaches to their interpretation of the words and music. Robert Shaw used words almost incidentally to the music, whereas Glenn Draper puts great emphasis on the power and meaning of words set to music. The audience is all important to Glenn Draper, but Shaw viewed the audience as almost unnecessary. It follows that communication of emotions through the text and visual overtones is Glenn's forte; however, Robert Shaw valued the importance of exactness of the beat and the accuracy of complying with the composer's intent. The passages that I have selected from Mussulman's book and the words of Charles Middleton and Dr. Thomas Hammett elaborate on the significant differences between the two directors. Other, even more pronounced, differences in their lifestyle and ideology can be deduced from reading the passages quoted from Mussulman, Middleton, and Hammett.

151

In *Dear People . . . Robert Shaw a Biography* by Joseph A. Mussulman, the author writes:

> Gordon Berger, formerly director of choral organizations at the University of Oklahoma, had moved to New York early in 1941 to join Waring's Pennsylvanians. Purely for the fun of it, he had started a community chorus of about sixty young singers at Norman Vincent Peale's Marble Collegiate Church. In September Berger invited Shaw to guest conduct one number in a concert, and Shaw instantly became so enthusiastic about the group that Berger offered to share with him the job of developing it. Together they decided on a new name for the group—The Collegiate Chorale. Properly speaking, the word collegiate in the church's name referred to a collegium of ministers, not an educational institution, and the noun chorale denoted the tune of a German Lutheran hymn, but the phrase sounded youthful and euphonious, and it was different enough to attract attention.
>
> Berger and Shaw set out to recruit more members. On October 7 they placed a two-line ad in the newspapers announcing auditions at the Waring studios. At the same time Shaw sent a letter, on Waring's stationery, to local alumni of the "all-city" choruses conducted annually by Peter Wilhousky, supervisor of vocal music in the public schools:
>
>> Under the sponsorship of the Marble Collegiate Church of Manhattan, I have undertaken the responsibility of forming and directing the Collegiate Chorale, a mixed choir of one hundred fifty young singers, amateur and professional, to be selected by competitive auditions.
>>
>> The purpose of the Collegiate Chorale is the development of artistry and musicianship among its members, as well as the pleasure it may afford them and their audiences. Its attention will be very largely directed to the acappella literature of the Christian tradition. But, in addition, there will be an emphasis upon contemporary American music, with reference to radio techniques, modern interpretations, and the general artistic demands of the field of professional entertainment.
>
> Lured by what appeared to be an invitation from Fred Waring, nearly 500 people showed up for the auditions . . . Shaw finally chose 185 of them.
>
> One of the most conspicuous features of the Chorale was the proportion among the sections: three basses for every two tenors, three altos for every two sopranos, and twenty more men than women. Another was its youth: ages ranged from seventeen to seventy, but the average was twenty-six.
>
> Rehearsals got under way on a Monday evening early in November. Shaw waded into the music with the same intensity that had inspired his fledgling

Glee Club only three years before. After the second rehearsal Dr. (Norman Vincent) Peale summoned Shaw and presented a few requests in behalf of the Consistory: "Trim the group to 100 members; be sure that fifty percent are members of the Marble Collegiate Church; drop the Catholics, the Jews, and the Negroes; and oh, yes, kindly refrain from profanity during rehearsals."

Shaw hadn't given a thought to the racial and religious diversity of the group until Dr. Peale mentioned it, whereupon it struck him as a rather admirable thing. He and his flock abruptly moved, name and all, to more hospitable quarters. "This shall be for music" was their motto. "These songs for love of singing!"

After rehearsals Shaw and a few of the gang would bound off down the street to the nearest late-night beanery for a lively postmortem over sandwiches and beer. The talk was always about the music, the music, the music.

Robert Shaw frequently used letters to communicate with his chorale members. He always talked about harmony, melody, rhythms, tone, dynamics, intervals, etc. For example, the last paragraph of a letter written November, 19, 1946, and quoted in Mussulman's book, reads as follows:

> I believe then, that spirit in music is not the wholesale emotional orgasm that weeps appropriately in public, but rather the marshaling of one's keenest, most critical consciousness, till one hears in terms of values and the movements of values, until the most pedestrian minutiae of pitch and rhythm are heard inwardly in relation to adjacent minutiae; and finally in relation to wholes of form, tonality and intent.

Middleton and Hammett, elaborate below about some of the distinctions between these two fine directors. However, even though they sang for Shaw for three years and seventeen years respectively, I wonder if they could possibly interpret the above paragraph quoted from Robert Shaw?

Charles Middleton

I sang with Robert Shaw for three years. Glenn is text, the meaning of the text, and how you express it with the notes to the audience. He looks at the aesthetics of the music. Robert Shaw is very technical. When you get into that mold with him, it is almost like you are learning to walk and you walk in a certain direction and your steps are measured, when you put your foot down it is measured. The end of phrases automatically comes. With Glenn there is more of a creative [mood]—bringing all the soul out of you. Glenn communicates to that one person who is sitting there, and if nobody else gets it then that is the purpose for that one person. Robert Shaw measured everything, but with Glenn, although it is measured, since even God likes right notes, it is what you communicate—your facial expressions, etc. When you see the smiles on peoples faces when you say a certain phrase, you know you have communicated that idea to them. It amazes me how Glenn can do that.

He can put together a group of songs, simple hymns, and arrange them in a way that tells a story from the beginning to the end and he creates an imagery, a mosaic that you see. He will start with "Crown Him with Many Crowns" and will go all the way to the cross and "He Lives," and that to me begins to show a story—none of the hymns or the music are there just because of the tunes, they are there because of what they say. He starts with one and it goes to another, logical progression in text and the music has to also embellish the text, but the music is not as significant as the text.

Dr. Thomas Hammett

I was at Florida State University (FSU) from 1976 to 1979 under the guidance of my major professor Clayton Krehbiel. Clayton had served as associate conductor and tenor soloist for the Robert Shaw Chorale. He was also Robert's dearest personal friend. Clayton opened the door for me to meet Mr. Shaw, which subsequently led to my audition for the Atlanta Symphony Orchestra Chorus and Chamber Choir. I moved from Tallahassee to Dalton, Georgia, where I taught school and commuted the one hundred miles to Atlanta for rehearsals, concerts, and recordings. I spent the next seventeen seasons, on and off, under the baton of the maestro. In addition to the many concerts and Telarc recordings (which earned at least a half-dozen Grammy Awards) there were the tours to New York. In 1980, we performed the Brahms, Berlioz, and Verdi *Requiems* in three sequential evenings at Carnegie Hall, which truly astonished the critics. Later there was the trip to Lincoln Center. It was with this background, combined with my educational doctorate from FSU, that allowed me to become somewhat of an elitist, chorally speaking, and I felt that the major classical works were the only literature worthy to perform.

Due to many pressing demands of family and job responsibilities in Chattanooga, my years in Atlanta came to a close. It was about that same time that my family also made the decision to change church affiliation. Glenn had been after me for perhaps ten to fifteen years to join him at First Presbyterian Church, which we finally did. I sang under Glenn's direction for about six years before assuming the music director position at Rivermont Presbyterian Church where I currently lead music.

What I experienced under Glenn at First Presbyterian was extraordinary, and I think the main thing I realized was what a tremendously dedicated Christian man Glenn Draper is. Glenn and I share a similar philosophy concerning church music: music is primarily a tool to serve our ministry of the gospel, both in our local congregations and through whatever doors God opens for us to the world. Too often, I have witnessed the opposite approach to music, both in the concert hall as well as in the church. From the opposite view, the church, the chorus, and individual musicians become the tool which serves the music and the composer. I have heard many conductors say that the important thing we must do is to make sure we do exactly what Mozart or Bach intended. It is as if the humble musicians must sacrifice and dedicate all to create perfect rhythm, beautiful tone, clean diction, and stirring dynamics and thus "perfect music" . . . for art's sake.

I think music becomes almost secondary with Glenn. Music is his tool and his medium—his paint and canvas—because what he is doing is getting the message out. It is the Christian message; it is the gospel, and it is the way of life that he lives.

I loved Robert Shaw, in fact, I wrote a poem entitled "Like a Father," after his passing. His death was very personal to me, and a great loss. Tears still come to my eyes when I hear our recordings on the radio or remember special times with the Atlanta Symphony Orchestra Chorus (ASOC). Perhaps no one had a more profound effect on my life than the maestro, but as in any relationship, all was not perfect. I recall one night in Atlanta with the Symphony Chorus, when we had finished warming up and the ushers were about to open the doors for the audience to come in. Mr. Shaw came forward for one of his last-minute intimate talks with the 250-voice chorus and said, "I don't really mind those people being out there, but the music happens here, between us, and they are just sort of out there listening in. They don't really belong." I thought, *Wow, what an opposite approach.* For Glenn and all of us who subscribe to the Draper philosophy, the audience is why we are there! It is the feeding, the inspiring, and all the things we do for them that validates our work.

It has been my good fortune, privilege, and pleasure to grow into a special friendship with Glenn Draper. It is with regret that I reflect on my days of choral snobbery and would negatively judge the minor imperfections of Glenn's local volunteer and student choral groups. I thought the choreographed "Hi Neighbor" approach to choral music was a bit "cheesy" and unworthy of serious consideration. I have run with the greatest choral musicians on earth, and I have looked back over my shoulder with some who saw Glenn as "running behind the pack." What we didn't realize was that Glenn had already lapped the pack and was coming around the track to pass us again! Glenn and his singers have spent fifty years doing what 95 percent of choral musicians and conductors only dream about doing. He has toured the world numerous times, made a stack of CD recordings, and sung before kings and presidents; but most importantly, he has served the people of God with choral music in a respectable, professional manner. I count my blessings to have been a small part in his ministry and now to perpetuate a similar style and musical approach.

9

And the BEAT GOES ON

*Glenn has an uncanny way of surrounding himself
with positive people—good people.*

~CHARLES MIDDLETON

THE SUCCESS OF DR. GLENN W. DRAPER

Robert H. Shipp

This section is excerpted from *Success is a Journey: 7 steps to Achieving Success in the Business of Life* by Jeffery J. Mayer. After many years of observing successful people, the author shares a "list of the skills, talents, and characteristics you'll find in successful people."

1. "Successful People Have a Dream."
2. ". . . Have Ambition."
3. ". . . Are Strongly Motivated Toward Achievement."
4. ". . . Are Focused."
5. ". . . Learn How to Get Things Done."
6. ". . . Take Responsibility for Their Actions."
7. ". . . Look for Solutions to Problems."
8. ". . . Make Decisions."
9. ". . . Have the Courage to Admit They've Made a Mistake."
10. ". . . Are Self-Reliant."
11. ". . . Have Specific Knowledge, Training, and/or Skills and Talents."

12. ". . . Work with and Cooperate with Other People."
13. ". . . Are Enthusiastic."

While reading through the following responses to my interview question, "Why is Glenn Draper so successful?" determine how many of the above attributes Glenn W. Draper epitomizes.

Bill and Betty Brett

Glenn lives what he "preaches." He is a Christian man who leads by example. Youth can relate to that. He effervesces positive vibes. There isn't a negative bone in his body! Anyone who has any life in him is positively energized by just being around Glenn. Can you imagine what happens when a group of willing, enthusiastic, college-age, young men and women are infused with this kind of a role model? Yes . . . you witness an explosion of latent talent that comes out of an individual multiplied by the number of people within the choir. Glenn picks the best of the best, not only for talent, but for character and congeniality. This not only gives the special groups their ability for top performances, but also inspires those not yet chosen to dig down deeper to become part of the top groups.

Linda Powers Bilanchone

Glenn Draper is the embodiment of singleness of purpose and bound-less energy—a powerful combination. If that isn't enough, he has a memory that makes the rest of us look like we're going through life in a fog.

Rev. Daniel H. Taylor Jr.
UTC choirs; Glenn Draper Singers; minister in Knoxville, Tennessee

I think Glenn is passionate about music, "obsessed" might be a better word. It is interesting to watch him, it is almost like music is always on Glenn's mind. I have been on buses with him where he was just sitting there and looking out the window, but then I noticed by watching his hand that he was directing. There is something running through his mind. Sometimes he is practicing something that he is going to do, or he is working through a program.

Glenn also cares about putting out a very good product. He cares about the craft he has—he cares about music. He wants the audience to come out of there enjoying what they heard. He used to talk about using a scatter gun approach, with all kind of music in a program, so that if a person stayed around long enough, there would be something in the concert that he or she would like. I think he has a drive to take music everywhere. He wants people to experience music and to enjoy it.

Frank Calhoun

I think Glenn has a sound in his head, a sound that he wants. He can hear the voices and select those voices that will create the choral sound that he is looking for. It has changed through the years, of course, as the group has grown. Glenn has a very quick mind and he is able to put things like all the popular medleys together. He and Lounelle both have a gift for creating a camaraderie in the group. Glenn believes in what he is doing, and I believe he doesn't expect anything of anybody else that he doesn't expect of himself. He doesn't like the word "no." If you tell Glenn it can't be done, he will prove you wrong.

Dr. John "Jack" T. Evans

His love of the Lord. He doesn't do it for himself or for glory for himself, he does everything for the glory of the Lord. He is well trained, he is an extrovert, and he demands the most of himself and every choir member whether they are getting paid or not. There is something about the dynamics of Glenn that is absolutely different from any music director that I have ever seen. (I was a music major for a while.) His enthusiasm carries over to the choir, but unless you have some musical background, there is no way to keep up with Glenn.

He may have as many as ten people in his choir at one time who are capable of directing the choir because they are choral music directors in high schools or other places, so he is surrounded by good musicians. Glenn attracts top class singers and musicians, such as Kim Cargile, Judy Glass, and Jim Wilson. We have had several from our choir go to be choir directors in other churches because the training under him is just so valuable.

He has enthusiasm for all kinds of music. When one of our congregation will stop him and say they particularly enjoyed a number that they did that day, he will tell them not to get used to it because next Sunday the music may be something totally different. He is very eclectic in what he is going to choose to sing. I think most of the choir has been trained in classics, but he does all kinds of music.

Kathy Tugman

Glenn just doesn't make you sing to be good. He brings the spirit into the music. He makes it worshipful. That has been the greater part of my worship because he says, "Sing what the song means. It is not just for making pretty noises, but to listen to the words. Sing those words with emotion." Another reason that Glenn is so effective is that his music touches people. He is incredibly energetic and focused on what he wants to do. He has so many things that he wants to do that there is just not enough time to do it all; however, he manages to get it done if he gets something in his head. He is a planner, and he can come up with a show or a program in a very short time.

His memory is incredible. Glenn remembers my birthday and everybody else's birthdays. He remembers all the music that he has done, and that serves him and his music ministry very well. His music is successful because of his sincerity and his belief that God is universal. He is not swayed in any particular direction or by people's bigotry, and he believes that everybody is loved by God. He is such a loving, loving person and he promotes that love within the groups he is in, the groups he puts together, the choirs, and the singers. Love has a lot to do with his success.

Dr. James B. Buskirk

The essence of what I can tell you about Glenn is that he does something probably better than anybody I know in our church, unless it is a minister at First United Methodist where I just retired, but this may be technical. There is a reason why we praise and worship before we preach. The right side of the brain is called the "effective brain," and the left side is called the "carpenter brain." In theological and ministerial language, the right side of the brain is the spirit side and the left side is the reasoning side. When we praise, we sing using the right sides of our brains. We sing before we preach, so that opens up the spirit side of the brain and then the sermon opens up the reasoning side, so we deal with "whole wits rather than half-wits."

Glenn is particularly capable of opening up a congregation to God and to the Holy Spirit like few people I know. He does it with old hymns, they have excellent content and theology, and he does it with a rhythm and a skip and delight, and you could dance to a lot of the songs that they do. It absolutely intrigues young adults and young people. He is a man for all ages and a man for all seasons. He is a professor in college, a director of music in a church (First Presbyterian), but his ministry has been primarily in the United Methodist Church. He spans two denominations and not many people do that. Not many ministers or ministers of worship are professors, and he does that as well as anybody. He is also able to span two age groups—there is a different thought process and a different emotional engagement for youth and young adults compared to older adults—Glenn can bridge that gap.

Kim Cargile

I think it is an anointing from God. You have a lot of talented directors out there who can get an incredible choral sound, but they don't have the communication skills. I have never in my life seen anyone who loves people the way he does. He will go out and talk to a rock. He is so friendly, he never meets a stranger. Glenn just loves people and he communicates that in his music. He is not just there to get the perfect choral sound, all he is worried about is communicating to the audience. Glenn has more energy than anybody I've ever seen in my entire life. You couple that with the musical ability that he obviously has, and he is a musical genius. I have learned everything I know from him.

You put all of that together, the energy level, the musical ability, the love of people and it is just an anointing of the Lord, because his main focus is communicating Jesus Christ to that audience. He knows that if you have a boring product, no matter how good the message is, they are going to sit there and be half asleep. Glenn does anything he has to do to keep people awake. That is what is lacking in most choirs. You can get a beautiful sound or have beautiful music, but there is often a lack of energy and a lack of communicating with the audience. A choir is the mirror of its director. Most universities are concerned about music theory and what a certain chord is, but they never really teach their students how to get up there and sell it. You don't normally learn that in a university setting.

Todd Gaither

Glenn is successful in different ways, not just musically. He has a family who loves him dearly and grandchildren who think he is the greatest, so he has been successful with his family. Lounelle and Glenn have a wonderful relationship and he also has great relationships with his extended family, students, and people who have sung with him. I believe he loves a lot. He loves greatly and he nurtures those around him and builds them up. He is incredibly talented musically and he has shared his love and passion for music with everybody who sings with him. Glenn demands a certain level of expertise and performance from those who sing with him, which drives and propels them to want to do that for him, and then they become a part of something that is great! That is a good feeling, a sense of accomplishment, and a sense that you are a part of a meaningful thing.

We talk a lot about our singing not necessarily being a performance, but a form of a ministry. There are a lot of people in the audience who will be touched by a particular song that is just right for them at that time. It is powerful to be a part of that. He brings a lot of enthusiasm, a lot of passion, a lot of drive, and an endless amount of energy, to his music. I am thirty years younger than Glenn and he still can outwork me.

Glenn is educated, he has learned a lot and studied extensively about music, and I think he is able to interpret music in a way and communicate how he wants that music interpreted so that it has a vast impact on the people who hear it. When you hear choral music in that way, it is moving!

Glenn might be one of the better salesmen I know! There are two sides to that, he has to sell himself and the groups, and then he sells the singers to join him to do these things. There are a lot of telephone calls, a lot of talking, a lot of relying on old relationships, and building new relationships.

Charlie Flatt
First Presbyterian Church member;
the Ed Fest has been held on his farm for seventeen years

I think Glenn is successful because he puts the Lord first. He wants to glorify the Lord Jesus and he can do it in music. I would give anything in the world if I could sing. If I thought I could mouth it, I would be in his choir just because I like the enthusiasm. I have been in sales all my life, and in order to be a successful salesman you have to love people. Glenn would be a fabulous salesman. If he would give up some of what he has and concentrate on one facet, there is no telling where he could go. He is in demand everywhere he goes. He has been to the White House numerous times and been overseas many, many times. I have met some of the people he visits when he goes to England, I have heard how they talk about him and how much they love him and can't wait until the next time he comes.

Lounelle is so devoted to Glenn. How many wives do you know who would permit their husbands to do all the extracurricular activity that he does, and not only permit it but get involved and enjoy it? That is his secret to success—his wife. She has been a huge part of his success. They have two great sons and they worship the ground their dad walks on. He couldn't be a success without his family. Glenn is so dedicated to his music, and his singers are so dedicated to him. He knows how to get a team and he knows how to get out of that team what he needs. It is just unreal to watch.

I don't care if it is twenty degrees outside or five below zero, when he gets through directing music, he is perspiring all over. I go a lot of times and just watch him; I listen to the music, but I watch him. He is the most optimistic person I believe I have ever seen. I don't think there is a negative bone in his body. He will not take no for an answer, he will find a way to get around an objection better than anybody I have ever seen in my life. When he makes up his mind where he is going and he goes, there is no stopping him.

James H. Cooley Jr.

When I look at Glenn and his life, and look at what he has meant to me and then countless others, first I see that total, total commitment to Christ. Then I think everything else feeds off of that commitment. Glenn is so committed in his faith; he is committed to his wife; he is committed to the ministries and the mission fields that he touches. Through his seventy-three or seventy-four years, he has probably ticked off a few people because he doesn't know the word "no." I have watched this guy in so many different settings and in terms of being true to who he is, what you see with Glenn Draper is what you get. I know that is an overworked and overused phrase, but here is a guy who has led choirs for presidents in the White House, and yet, Glenn is basically going to be the same person in the White House that he is at his house around the dinner table. That is just who he is. With that sense of genuineness, you always know what you are going to get with Glenn. You get an incredibly motivated and passionate man who is so driven to the final mark, whatever that goal may be.

I was fortunate enough for two years to be able to serve as president of the UTC Choir, and that gave me an opportunity to see the man up close and to see the way he works. No matter what the odds are, this is a can-do guy. We would go into various venues and look at the places and think, *How are we going to be able to get forty people lined up here to sing? How is this going to happen?* With Glenn, it's going to happen. As we started moving stuff around in a very respectful way, you could see them wondering what was happening to their sanctuary. By the time the night was over and the concert had been sung, they would say, "Wow, we have never heard anything like that in our lives!" Glenn is where he is because God energized him and gave him the drive and purpose.

Jean D. Hanlin

I think he is so enormously talented and manages to get a response from people in the choir. You don't just stand up there and sing mamby-pamby for him, he is not going to have it. Everybody I know loves success, and I think that Glenn has been successful because he is able to elicit from people a response that would have been beyond them in the hands of a different conductor. I also think he and Lounelle are so caring and so interested in you, and you, and you . . . and I think that is why the students just adore him. He is their friend, they know him, and they love him for what he helps them see as their objective, and when they follow through on that they are proud of themselves! That is so important. It doesn't seem to matter, Glenn blooms wherever he is planted. He goes to Junaluska and everybody thinks he is wonderful. He goes to the church and everybody thinks he is wonderful. You would think after a while he would get tired of producing a triple A rating every time, but I don't think he ever will. Every performance is a new day.

Lee S. Anderson

I can sum him up. He does with amateurs what Fred Waring and Robert Shaw did with professionals.

Stacie Caraway Coder

I think Glenn has an anointing from the Lord. I think the Lord has placed a gift in him. I have sung all over the world, with Glenn and without Glenn, and have never seen an anointing like that. I think that is what drives him. I have been in situations with him where there were five people in the audience and where there were fifty thousand, and he gives the same amount of energy and enthusiasm for every concert. You can discern whether somebody is in it for the glory or for the Lord. It's when they give the same 100 percent, no matter if it's just the Lord listening or if it's fifty thousand people at a Billy Graham Crusade in Moscow.

Lenette Glass
Member First Presbyterian Church; longtime choir supporter

Glenn's choirs have a unique sound that is different from other choirs. I think about when Glenn Miller was looking for a sound—a distinct sound—he kept rearranging his instruments until he captured that sound, and it was different from any other band at that time. When he heard it, he knew it. To me, that is similar to Glenn Draper's method. He knows the sound he wants, and how he balances that sound is different from other choirs. It is unique and wonderful. I can hear a musical program on the radio with a variety of artists, and when they play something from one of Glenn's choral groups without announcing who it is, I know. I can tell the sound. It may be mixed up with other things, but I can tell, it is amazing.

Jennifer Odom

It's definitely a divine gift, a blessing. Glenn has this way of just pulling things off that is just unbelievable. He is so successful because he knows how to make things fit together. His medleys that we all joke about are brilliant with the key structure. Another major reason for his success is that he knows how to choose the musicians with whom he works. For example, Kim Cargile, his accompanist for fourteen years, is amazing. Glenn knows how to make things fit together. He has been doing it for so long, and has developed such a craft and a talent for picking personalities for the groups. Glenn has this sixth sense of choosing the people who are going to be in the groups. That helps make the group.

Dr. Reginald Mallett

What is it that makes this man so effective? I think first of all it is the special spark which God put in his heart. He has a gift, a talent, that he has carefully and conscientiously offered back in committed service. Secondly, there is his phenomenal energy. In a quite amazing way he has been able to do several things superbly, keeping several balls in the air at once—directing three groups of singers as well as being the music director of the First Presbyterian Church, Chattanooga, and serving as professor of music at the university. As if this were not enough, he adds to his workload by organising choral tours across the world. What phenomenal energy he has!

Perhaps Glenn's greatest source of strength other than his deep Christian faith is the loving support of his wonderful wife Lounelle. In her lovely, gracious way, she supports and encourages him. I believe she is his best counselor and truest friend. I am sure Glenn would be the first to say that he would not have accomplished anything like he has had it not been for that remarkable and dedicated lady.

Martin W. Hamby Jr.

Glenn has the ability to take music off of the printed page and, through the medium of singing, communicate that piece to the listener. He does that better than anybody I have ever seen. He is very logical, and I am not sure how he does it. I think there are several facets that I have seen him employ that help. A lot of it is just Glenn and his passion for life and his passion for communicating messages through music to audiences. He is just good at that.

One thing I think he does, and Glenn will chuckle when he reads this and may not be aware of, is to have his group just maybe 96 to 98 percent prepared. He keeps them just under 100 percent so that they are dependent on him. He likes to have their attention. If you know something backward and forward really well, you are prone to wander and look off now and then and see what the people in the audience are doing. If you are not sure what the next word is, you will make sure you are going to get it right and all your senses are into what you are doing. I think he does this, and it's very shrewd.

Glenn motivates people out of a desire to want to participate. He doesn't do it out of obligation or anything like that. You want to get in on what he is doing because you are afraid you are going to miss something. He makes it a great experience. I can't imagine there being a dull moment around Glenn Draper. Life is exciting for him. Like I said, he leaves that room for change. He always says he doesn't want the audience to get through before he does.

Dee Dee Brogan
Lake Junaluska Singers; Glenn Draper Singers; choir director

Glenn pushes himself. He puts great demands of perfection on himself, and his expectations for himself are unbelievably high! That carries down through his singers. What you learn under his direction, spoken or unspoken, is very powerful, and I don't think words can express it. Music is such an abstract experience that you can't necessarily put it into words. However, he is able to understand and feel the music, and communicate it to his audiences, and communicate it through his body to his singers of what he physically wants vocally. He can do this better than any person I have ever worked with, whether in college with Roger Wagner as a premier soloist or with other directors or whether it is operatically or in a pop group. What he wants musically, words can't describe. He feels his music so passionately, so spiritually, if you will, that he teaches us that we have to demand the best of ourselves, both chorally and even through our solo life, even after we are away from Glenn.

You can never get that same kind of music unless you are with a group of people that he has trained to understand it. I think that Glenn is a man of God, and that God has genuinely given him a gift and has blessed it and has given him opportunities that other people would die to have. His gift is different. We laugh and say there are angels all over Glenn, there have to be the way he drives! He has always been taken care of and the only way to describe that, if you are talking about financial success and so forth, is to say that it is totally a God thing. I think his music is a gift from God, and he has found his niche and what he does he does better than anybody else out there. Nobody can compare to Glenn Draper. If I was someone who was musical but had never trained under him, music would never have the same meaning to me, compared with what it has now. What he has taught [me] and what he has written on my spirit, as far as music goes, is so imprinted that no one can ever take that away and nobody can ever touch that.

Dr. Melton E. Harbin

Glenn is a musical technician. He knows his craft and he will not allow a singer to do less than his best. He requires a very strict performance and adherence to quality. He is able to inspire the singers to be their best and to bring out the potential that is in them. As good as any man I have ever seen in any field, he is able to do that with the singers. Glenn leads by example. He is not only a good technician, but he is also a very loving person, and that is a necessary quality with the close relationship that he has with his small group of singers. I guess in many ways, Glenn Draper is one of the richest people in the world because of the friends he has made through the singers, and all that they have shared with one another. Lounelle is a great contributor to all of this in her lovely way of supporting Glenn and everything he does.

Sara Smith Youngblood

Glenn is so personable, and though he can't know everybody's name, he reaches everybody as though they are somebody he has known all his life and he calls them Friend and puts his arm around them. Everyone feels so hugged up to Glenn, it doesn't matter if he knows who you are. If he doesn't know you, he just has that, "I'm going to like you" approach. He said to me, "If I don't know their names, I just call them 'Friend,' because I know they are." He is so focused, maybe to a fault because sometimes it is hard for him to make an adjustment, but he just has high expectations and focus. When he is choosing singers in auditions, he is careful and he is listening for somebody he thinks can be flexible.

His success as a person is because he sees everybody as a friend, and his success as a showman is because he knows everything there is to know about music. He has been there, and his remarkable memory means that he can reach back and grab a piece of music that he knows will just suit the situation. And he loves music. I don't know if you have ever heard him describe the time he heard the Russian Male Chorus sing, but he uses that as the defining moment when he knew that he wanted to direct choral music. It just overwhelmed him. Quickly into each year, all of us have that kind of experience, we hear the sound that we are capable of and then suddenly we are there. He turns us into a group.

Maimunah Natasha
Indonesian member, World Methodist Council;
president, Toastmasters International, Far East
[English is not her first language.]

Glenn is successful, I believe, number one [because of] his love of music. To me, music is Glenn's life. He lives with it, he devotes all his life to music, and he doesn't ask anything of his life—he just gives everything to music. He focuses only on music, nothing else in the world. He is a people person, with all of his passion and his caring. The way he speaks, the way he acts, he is just so close with his singers.

I also believe that Glenn is successful because he works very hard. He is not only a fine person, but he is very idealistic, he wants everything to be perfect. He is also very sensitive. Music works a lot with emotion. Because of his sensitiveness, he can really conduct the music in such a way that the music is alive. It seems that they are not only singing, but they are enjoying it and being very creative, not only in voice, but also in actions and movement. He has great communication skills. He is performing there, but it's just as if he is performing for you alone. I also believe in his talent. He was born with that. Nobody else can duplicate it. He can use the voice of each singer to perform uniquely according to their own talent.

Roger and Nancy Geyer
Long-time summer visitors, now full-time Lake Junaluska residents;
retired Methodist minister

Every concert he gives, no matter that he uses the same music, it is his arrangement and his excitement that just keeps you on your toes. I think Glenn is so successful because of his commitment to Jesus Christ. I know that when he interviews the (Junaluska) Singers, he wants to know something about them. He wants to know more than their voices, because they can have a beautiful voice but if they don't have the spirit and the commitment and the spirituality, I don't think he would take them. That is very important to him. We also know that he encourages the group to have prayer every day. I think that is why it is always so exciting and he is so successful. He makes the group one, rather than sixteen individual singers! They are all close to each other and feel like one with each other. The music is so perfect because of that.

Merlin E. Johnson

Glenn is successful because he wants to succeed, he wants to be approved, he wants to do the best, and he wants to guarantee people that when they come they will want to come back. Glenn has never had to force himself to slow down, because he doesn't know there is any other gear. Just a while ago he said, "My vision was tunneled, I was seeing the goal." The goal is having excellent performances, which had to have excellent rehearsals, which had to have talented people, or people who were willing to develop their talents and it just goes on back. It is just like "Back of the seed is the snowy flour, back of the flour is the mill, back of the mill is the wheat, and the shower and the sun and the Father's will"— it is all that. To be successful, you have to have the spirit that God only can show you and interpret within you, and you have to be open to that. You also have to be stubborn, but you know what? That is a good trait in certain situations. You do not sacrifice or settle for anything except what God expects, and that is your best. If you are not quite there, you had better keep practicing.

Bob B. Davis

When people want to excel in something, first of all, they have to have a burning desire to do so. They have to really have a burn in their stomach to do it. Glenn Draper, while qualified to do marketing, corporate sales, even door-to-door, could have done any and all of that and become very successful at it, but that was not his desire to focus in that direction. He has focused on that one thing, choral conducting, period. All of that equals great choirs, male choruses, mixed choirs, and then he also through the years has done the contemporary type music with the rhythm section, the drum, bass, etc. Glenn is very well rounded, and is also very much a traditionalist. He has a concept and an intuitive way of knowing what is going to work and what isn't going to work.

Charles Middleton

I think Glenn is successful because he has a vision. He can see where some-thing can be and he has a way of getting to it. I think he realizes that something does not work, but something else does, so he tries it. He has a saying, "I am going to give the bat to the person that can hit the home run." The home run may not occur, but at least he knows who to give the bat to. He gives you that idea and you go with that, with the new thing in your mind and then it begins to blossom on the way and you grow out of that, and then when you get there it is so unfurled that you can't recognize where you started from. I don't mean to say that he is Superman, but he allows you to see his vision and to create an image, and then he smiles, oh man . . . he is so happy.

I know we don't use all of our brain, in our vision and in what we are able and capable of doing. I think capable and able are two different things. I divide those two, because capable means the ability to be, and able is sort of abstract, like your vision. I think I am not capable of doing this because I know my arms only stretch to here! Then you begin to find ways to get there by moving yourself into a certain position. That is what Glenn does, he takes you to it and on the way you begin to know how to do it yourself. It is like a fire, one spark goes over here and you don't see that again, you just know that it is flaming. I think it is people he knows and he knows how to envision what they can be, rather than what they can't be, as in, "I can't do that."

I remember my second summer at the lake I had one pair of black shoes, and the sole of one came loose and the bottom part of it was flapping. I went to Glenn and said, "I can't sing this morning, I need to get my shoes fixed." Oh boy, that was the wrong thing to say. He just said, "When did you find that out?" I said, "Yesterday." He turned and went to his office and came back with two rubber bands. I laugh about that now. He said, "Here, now you can sing." Anybody who was listening to that would wonder how those rubber bands were going to help me sing. I put them on my shoe and went out on the stage and sang and then got my shoes repaired that afternoon. I didn't want to go out looking bad. It really had nothing at all to do with how you look, it is what you are committed to do. Although how you look has a lot to do with the perception that the listener has, you can go beyond that so that they don't even see that rubber band on your shoe! It became unimportant, insignificant, and I didn't even remember the rubber band was there after I walked out on the stage. That is Glenn's success. He knows how to deal with people. He knows how to get out of people what he wants.

Glenn would say, "Remember in 1967, I said, 'sink or swim'? Well, let's go brother." His legacy to me is how to deal with and respect people. He respected my opinion of things. This man is Mr. Music extraordinare and he asked my opinion, "How do you think this is going to sound?" One Sunday night, he said, "We are going to sing this piece and this one too, but I wish we had something else." I told him in school we did "Oh Happy Day" by Evan Hawkins, and Glenn asked how it sounded. "That is great, hum a little more of that for me." He said, "I think I have that," and he found the music. We all started singing and did it that night for the service. Not everyone knew the piece, but the audience loved it. I thought that (the white) people wouldn't like it, but they embraced that piece. That was an opening for Glenn to do other types of music that he may not have done, but he did do because of "Oh Happy Day" and the fact that audiences accepted it everywhere we went! It was almost like a theme, and we did an album with "Oh Happy Day." He has a feel and has his finger on the pulse of the listener, even before we would sing.

Glenn Wright Draper II

I have always heard it said that if someone can do what they are gifted in and have a passion for it, then that's the formula for success. Early on, as Dad grew up, he was always forming quartets or a choir and he knew that he had that unique ability to be with a group and to lead them. He knew he was so gifted there. I am reminded of 1 Peter 4:10, "as each one of you has received a special gift," meaning every believer is a hodgepodge of certain gifts. He has an incredible ear and at the same time the leadership ability to know what it takes to have success, and a determination like I have never seen. He dreams something that he sees, and in his mind he puts together what it is going to take to get there, and then he will sweat and do whatever it takes to get there.

Someone has said that courage is the transfusion of enthusiasm, and so because he believed in what he was going to do and where he was going, it would be natural for those who were his peers or those he was around to want to follow him. He always has been a leader and is always thinking and dreaming and planning. There is not any idle time for him, he is always networking wherever he goes.

It is the power of God on display in his life, it is like John the Baptist said, "I must decrease, but He must increase." My dad understood early on that God had called him to do what he was doing and he understood that God would give him the desire and the power to accomplish incredible things for His glory. It is exciting when you see the results.

I think Dad was nine years old when he had his conversion experience, and as he grew and matured he realized and understood what he was called to do. It was to glorify God with music. He had a belief system and when you have that you are not going to be diverted, no matter how much adversity comes. You are going to rise above that because you realize your calling. My brother and I were fortunate enough to see him, with his strong belief system, tackle big challenges and to persevere through them. If I had to say a word that describes him it would be "belief." He also had perseverance if he thought this was something he was supposed to do. He also surrounds himself with good people who have quality and character. Any good coach will hire assistants who are better.

The favorite introduction that I ever heard someone give for my dad was from Lee Anderson who is an elder at First Presbyterian, when my dad won the Chattanooga Award in 1989. Lee Anderson said, "All these years ya'll that have been listening to Glenn's choirs have been sitting in the cheap seats, because he is doing it for the Lord." That would be my hope and prayer always, that it is for God's glory first and that is the One we have to please. He has a passion and going back to a rehearsal, his diligence to get it right. And even as a father, it was a great lesson for my brother and me that if you are digging a ditch or whatever you are doing, you should be excellent at it.

Julius Walthall

I think he has great honesty, truthfulness, and I think that has an impact on success. I remember growing up with Glenn, he would not tell a lie, he would get awfully close to it as kids will do in order to get along and do whatever it is you wanted to do, but he wouldn't tell a lie. Glenn is persistent, and I don't mean this derogatorily at all, he is a little selfish in that he will focus on what he wants to do with his objective. I have never known him to intentionally hurt anybody or even be discourteous, he is just not that kind of guy.

He has a long-range objective and he focuses on that. I remember a lot of times in high school he would be doing something and I would find that I was waiting for him. I thought, *Why am I always waiting* . . . well, I waited because we were good friends, but that was kind of a lack of concern for my particular situation at the time because he wanted to do whatever he was doing to get to where he was going. That is what it takes, persistence and a focus on what you want to do.

Dr. John Stokes

Wherever Glenn has been, he has been most successful. He's so dedicated and so committed to achieving the best sound out of any of his choruses. It's just who he truly is. If imaginable, he did improve himself when he married Lounelle. It must have been his smooth approach that carried the day. There's one other thing, Glenn and Lounelle have remained committed to their faith. It shows in their relationships with any singing groups I have been associated with. A big turning point in my life also occurred at Junaluska when I went to Glenn for help to get me pointed in the right direction. He had the faith, and I wanted some of it.

Lisa A. Haywood
Lake Junaluska Singers; Glenn Draper Singers

I think Glenn is so successful because he truly loves what he does, this isn't just a job for him like he will tell you, over and over again. He will never retire because he has never had to work a day in his life. He loves this with a passion and he loves the people too. A lot of people either love what they do in their jobs consistently or love the people they work with consistently, but rarely do you find people who love what they are doing plus love the people equally (and the group changes every year or so). This has been going on for almost fifty years, and he still loves it. It is just wild to meet somebody doing the same thing for fifty years who still has the same stamina, energy, drive, love, and passion now that he had when he started. Music is probably third in his life. First God, then his family, and then Junaluska or other groups, but particularly I think the Junaluska Singers.

I think another reason that he is so successful is that he is one of the best darn salesmen I have ever met in my entire life. He could sell you a rock from here on Lake Junaluska for a million dollars if he could sit down with you. It wouldn't take him long—we always hear all the stories about the little things he has gotten people to do over the years—whether it is people in the group, or airlines giving him flights for basically nothing to different places. Choral activities are not as welcome and prominent now. Somehow he still manages to make (choirs) appealing to people because it is very rare to find a choir that people are just falling over themselves to come see.

Jay Lifford

Chiefly, I think he has determination like I have never seen in my life. He is one of the best salesmen I have ever seen. He has always said that he is selling the best product in the world, the gospel. He won't take no for an answer. He has met his match in Maimunah Natasha because she is a strong person, just like him. I remember being in Singapore and we were supposed to fly from Singapore to Jakarta, and then have a layover in Jakarta and fly back to Singapore and then fly from Singapore to Paris. Air France had told us that if we didn't get on the plane at Jakarta, we couldn't get on the plane if it stopped in Singapore. We had to be at our original starting point. Maimunah went to the counter and argued with them until they were like, "Okay, fine." She did that and then when Jonathan lost his passport, they were not going to give him a new passport at the U.S. Embassy in Jakarta. Maimunah flew from Bali to Jakarta, went to the embassy, and Jonathan said that all he remembers is that Maimunah kept talking and fussing in Indonesian, so finally the guy, with a frustrated look, just stamped his passport and said, "Here!" It just reminds me so much of Glenn, because he will stay with you until he gets what he wants.

YOU HAVE TO SELL IT

AT THE END of my sophomore year at Marion College, I received a scholarship to attend Indiana University and also a scholarship to attend the University of Alabama, who had the Million Dollar Band. I had been down there to audition and was praying about which direction I should go. The more I prayed about it, the more I felt that I should go to Indiana. That summer I was trying to make money any way I could to go to school. On a Saturday morning, probably in July, I received in the mail several sample boxes of Christmas cards. My brothers and I were at the breakfast table, and they said, "Glenn, what are you going to do this afternoon?" I said, "I think I am going to take these Christmas cards and go out and see if I can sell them and make some money for school." They said, "Why don't you go with us? Some girls have invited all of us to come over for a swimming party." I said, "That sounds fantastic, but I still think I better try to sell these cards." My brothers laughed at me for doing that, but I set sail around noon. I saw people in their yards milling around, cutting their grass, swimming in their pools, just relaxing like people do on a warm summer afternoon. I was laughed at by everybody, and most of them said, "Come back and see us in November, we don't even want to think about Christmas cards until later on."

As the afternoon went on, I hadn't sold anybody any Christmas cards, but I still kept going, as if I was going to set the world on fire. Along about six o'clock I got back to within a block of my house and thought what it would be like to walk in my home and my brothers would be home from swimming and ask how many cards I sold. Well, I would have to tell them I didn't sell any! I could imagine them laughing at me, so I thought, *If I have to stay out here all night, I am going to sell these cards to somebody! I will not go home and face them.* They were big teases and they would have never, ever let me forget it.

Anyway, I walked right across the street from where I was to a nice brick house, and as I came up on the front porch, the door was open, except for the screen. I knocked on the screen door and could hear people inside laughing and talking, and it sounded like they were eating and, sure enough, they were. They called out, "Who's there?" I said, "Glenn Draper," and they replied, "We know your mother and dad. How are you doing?" I walked in and walked around the table and I said, "I am selling Christmas cards," and they all laughed. They told me they never thought about Christmas cards until December. I said, "I know who you are, you are the man who owns the Gulf station down the street. I buy gasoline from you. Did you ever think about sending Christmas cards to your customers?" He said, "No, I never thought about that." I said, "Why don't you give that a thought," and he said, "Pick out a card." I made forty dollars on the deal. Back then, around 1949 or 1950, as a sophomore in college, that was a lot of money. I was so inspired that I went in another direction and started knocking on other doors. A lady in her sixties finally answered my knock and said, "I am selling Christmas cards myself." I said, "I bet your cards are beautiful. I would love for us to compare cards, and see what my competition is." She said, "Sure, come on in, Glenn Draper, I know your mom and dad." So we started comparing cards, and she said, "Your cards are better looking than mine." I said, "Yes, they are really nice looking." So she bought two boxes of my cards even though she was also selling Christmas cards.

I have never forgotten that lesson. Don't let anything derail you or change your mind from doing what you are doing. I learned a lot of lessons that summer, far more than just selling Christmas cards. I think one of the hardest things to take in life is rejection. You have to take rejection and yet keep on going. It's like a cat landing on its feet. "No" doesn't mean "no," you just leave there and you go some place else and start again. I have sold a lot of Christmas cards since then, and a lot of other products. One of them was Stanley Products.

I directed a church choir my first year at Indiana University, and I met a lot of wonderful people. I remember meeting this family from the church that had us guys from the choir over to eat many times. I noticed that she was selling Stanley Products. She said, "Glenn, you ought to get interested in this, I think you could make some money doing it." I said, "Maybe this summer I could do that." So the end of my junior year, I sold Stanley Products in Roanoke. I bought an old 1930 model Chevrolet that had a rumble seat in it where I put mops, brooms, liniments, and some other things that I had no idea in the world what people used them for. I had my first Stanley Products party one morning at somebody's house. I didn't know a lot about these products, but I went to this lady's home and she had about eight or ten ladies who came over to hear my speech about the products. Stanley used lamps, which I had to pay for, to give away as gifts. I said to these ladies, "Whoever can sell the most of this liniment or give me the best reason why you should buy it, I will give you a lamp." That is how I learned about those products! Stanley did tell me what they were good for and I passed that on to other people.

That summer I won first place in Roanoke for total sales and for the total number of parties booked. I was going to a staff meeting one morning in Roanoke on the other side of town and the old Chevrolet would only get up about three quarters of the way of a long hill, so I turned it around and backed the rest of the way up the hill. The reverse in the car was better than the first gear! You have to find a way to get there. If one thing doesn't work, you try another. That is what bothers me about a lot of people today, they give up before they ever start because they say, "This car won't make it." "How do you know it won't make it, did you ever try driving backwards?" They say, "Well, I never thought about that." I say, "You need to think about that."

I finally arrived at the meeting, and a man from upstate Maryland was there. He was the area coordinator of Stanley Products, and he had on a nice gray sport coat with a tie, and a handkerchief in his pocket. There must have been about twenty people in a big room. We were all sitting around in a circle and he went around to everyone and asked them how much money they were going to make the next week. One said, "I would like to make one hundred dollars." He said, "You aren't going to do it." The next person said, "I would like to make one hundred dollars," and he said, "You won't make it either." He came to a little lady who had on tattered clothes, and she said, "I have to make one hundred dollars in order to pay my bills," and he said, "You will." He came to me and I said, "I am going to make two hundred dollars." He said, "You will make two hundred dollars, if you really want to do that." By the end of the summer, he offered me a job as the area manager of the upper part of Virginia and lower Maryland. I said, "No, I can't do that, I am in school." He asked me what I was majoring in and I said, "Music." He said, "Music? How are you going to make a living in music?" I replied, "I don't know, but I have to try!" He said, "What are you going to do when you get old and ugly and nobody will come out to hear you?" I told him, "I have to take my chances." So I have spent my life taking my chances, by dreaming and following what I thought was God's plan for my life.

One summer I worked for a man we called Old Man Henry. He was a farmer and he had a produce place down on the market where people would come and buy his vegetables of all kinds. In the wintertime on Saturdays, we had a group of singers called the Young Roanoke Sings, and we did a broadcast on radio every weekend. I was elected president of the choir and student director, and from that group all us guys organized a group called the Vulture Club. (I had no idea how we got that name.) In the summer we rented a cabin outside of Roanoke and all of us would stay there for a whole week. On Friday nights, our parents would come out to the place and we would have dates. So the parents were, more or less, the chaperones. We would frog gig, turn over boats, and everything you could think of. Anyway, sometimes in the afternoon, I worked for Old Man Henry, and those six guys would come down to where I was and we would stand around and sing. All these crowds of people would gather to hear us, and I suppose it took business away from Mr. Henry's market. After about three or four days of doing that, my friends left, and he said, "Brother Glenn, we like you very much, but we are going to need to get somebody to work with us who doesn't sing and is more interested in selling our produce than just singing songs. These people who come to hear you sing, don't come here to buy." I mean it just crushed me. How was I going to explain this to my mother and father? I had disgraced my family. I had been taught to be dependable and honorable, and to do my job and do more than was expected of me.

When I left that afternoon I was sobbing as I walked up the street, and as I looked across the street there was People's Drug Store. I brushed my tears away, went in, and said, "I would like to see your manager. I am Glenn Draper, I live between here and Salem, and I would like to get a job." They called the manager and he told me to come in. I told him I had to have a job. He said, "I don't know whether we have an opening or not," but he got on the telephone and called his assistant and he said, "Yeah, we can use probably one more person behind the counter at the fountain." He asked me if I could be there the next morning at seven to start work. The next day I was the most determined guy you have ever seen in your life! I went after business, I grabbed mops, I grabbed everything, just to be busy doing something. I waited on customers everywhere. That evening about 5:30, the manager said he wanted to see me. That scared me and I thought, *I haven't done a good job, I will be so embarrassed, because I have really tried.* I went into his office and he asked me how long I wanted to live in this world. I asked, "What do you mean?" He replied, "Son, if you keep going at that pace, you are going to kill yourself. I have never seen anybody work that fast in my life. Our business has improved about 30 percent today." I said, "That is great! Do I get to stay?" He said, "Not only that, but I am going to give you a raise." I was thrilled to death, and I had all the confidence in the world. I worked for him for the rest of the summer and that was a good experience for me because I was constantly being put in front of people to meet them. Treating people right is important. You can't learn how to meet and greet people out of a book.

On Saturday mornings when my dad would go to work at the office, I would go with him. I would take a whole fistful of *Look* and *Life* magazines and sell them for a quarter each, with a nickel profit. I would sell those magazines all over and many times people would say, "Oh, I am not interested," and I would have to smile and say, "Thank you," and turn and walk off. I might go two blocks without selling anybody a magazine, but you know what, somebody down the road would buy two, and before long, I would go three in a row and they would buy magazines. So I learned the art of what I called people business by selling, and I have been selling all my life. I think I sell the greatest product in the world, and that is Christianity through music. Not only does it make you feel better, but it changes your whole life, and it prepares you for life after death. Utilizing music to do that for me is a great thing. But I learned a lot of that by selling those magazines, and selling green beans down on the market, and selling ice cream cones behind the fountain at People's Drug Store. Since then, I have sold many things.

REHEARSALS

Dr. Robert K. Dean

We all knew that Glenn had a very deep Christian faith, but he never preached to us. His example was his sermon. He never swore or said anything off-color. He never even really lost his cool. He was just like our parents; a decent and caring teacher. He always talked about what the text of a piece of music meant to him, sacred or secular. He never expected everyone to agree with him in a religious sense. We could interpret it however we wanted to, but we had to sing it like we believed it!

Glenn had the nicest way of expressing his displeasure with us. His reprimands were never harsh, but they were demanding. He would turn to a section during rehearsal and say, "Don't do that!" Then, as if embarrassed at his own intensity, he would immediately smile and tell us how good we could be, how he loved us, and how he wanted only the very best for us. He would always say, "I never want to be associated with a second-rate choir." He could smile and look at you with that warm face of his and you would forgive him for anything.

Musically, I also learned many, many things from Glenn; almost too many to enumerate. He was a perfectionist, and he had great rehearsal skills. One thing that sticks out in my mind was the way he could get the text to jump off the page. He was the first conductor I sang with who would have us singing a line of music with just the vowels and then carefully adding in the consonants; or drilling the pronunciation of diphthongs and triphthongs. Shaw did a lot of this too, but my first experience was with Glenn, so I always thought that he invented these things.

His best work, I always felt, was with the male voices. He just knows how to get either the edgy tone that it sometimes needs or the silky smooth tone for other passages. His sense of timing is superior, and he has a marvelous sense of how the music should go.

His rehearsal pace was almost frenetic. You couldn't keep up with him. He would rehearse the same way every day, whether he was sick or tired or whatever. Patience was definitely not his strong suit. As he has always said, he knows only one speed—full throttle.

A few points about Glenn's rehearsal management. He had the ability to hear a mistake or a tone he didn't like in rehearsals and knew exactly what to do to correct the problem. Most importantly, he did it immediately, whereas a lot of conductors will wait until the end of the phrase, or the end of the piece and waste everyone's time going back to explain what was wrong. Glenn would stop and correct the problem right when the problem occurred, which to me is the mark of a great rehearsal manager and teacher.

Another very successful technique of Glenn's was to introduce the ending of a piece to the choir first, or even after one run-through. Rehearsing the ending until it sounded good gave the choir a great sense of where the music was headed. It also gave you the sense that you had already "finished" the piece, which was a psychological boost. I've used this one a lot over the years.

John A. Murphy
Multi-talented compiler of recordings
and pictures of the Lake Junaluska Singers

He is a perfectionist with the drive to get something as good as possible and then figure out how to make it even better. Glenn will go over things in rehearsals, time after time, to make sure they get the cut off just right and the correct annunciation. If you don't have the right note, he'll go back and make sure you have it. The details are what's important to him. It is the difference. He will say, "No, no, you can't do it like that friends. Let's do it this way, think about what you are singing about, think about the words, think about those lyrics, think about the passion of this music." He gets the people to understand where his thoughts were coming from and what he is trying to get out of them. He is always able to do that. In 1963, I think it was, we had an all-county choir clinic in Palm Beach County, when he was at the University of Miami, and he came up to be our clinician as the director. We did "How Lovely Is Thy Dwelling Place" from Brahm's *Requiem*. We rehearsed in the morning, took a lunch break, rehearsed again in the afternoon, and then did the concert at night. What he was able to get out of those five hundred young people in such a short time was phenomenal and very beautiful.

Dr. Alan W. Miller

I'm not sure I've ever met anyone with so much energy! At Junaluska, most of the singers would drag themselves out of bed just in time to barely get to the rehearsal at 8:30. At the onset of the rehearsal, Glenn would have us jumping up and down, exercising, vocalizing, rubbing each other's back. Anything to get us awake! Then, for the next three hours of rehearsal, he would have us doing more of the same! Amazing! Scooter (Nancye Formo) used to say, "He's gonna have a heart attack if keeps up this pace." We now know that it is because of this fast pace that Glenn stays young.

─────────────────────

Rev. Daniel H. Taylor Jr.

I think the thing that makes Glenn so successful is the fact that he wants a performance to be an experience that you will enjoy and that you will like what you hear. That's why he does a lot of variety in his music. I have enjoyed the fact that singing for him as long as I have has exposed me to such a variety of music. I have become very eclectic and I can sit and listen to a lot of different things, and actually listen to them for the beauty of what they are, as opposed to saying I don't like classical music, or I don't like this or that.

There are a lot of things about Glenn that I think drive singers crazy. However, if you stick with him, you can take out in the world what you learn from him. Caring about my craft and being able to learn quickly has helped me a lot in being able to absorb things very fast and move on and use them.

You know that when he hands you "what's going to be on the concert tonight," it's a "lie." That concert is going to change for sure. You might get the first song in, but that's not even guaranteed. I have seen him go out there and change the first song, which speaks to the accompanist and the singers about their abilities to go with the flow. I was in a concert and he told me that my solo, "Old Man River," was going to come after so and so. We got in the concert and he went right past "Old Man River," and I didn't think anything about it. I figured we weren't going to do it that night, not a problem. We got to the last point in the concert and he said, "Dan Taylor to sing 'Old Man River,'" and I could have killed him! But that's okay, and he is right. Sometimes he writes the program thinking it will be great, but then he gets into the concert and perhaps the crowd is totally different and looking for something else, so he changes the program.

─────────────────────

Richard Lockery
First Presbyterian Church choir member for many years
and current president of the choir

Being in a rehearsal with Glenn is a work out! When he is working with a paid, or professional group, he drills harder and longer. Even with a volunteer church choir, he doesn't stop until he gets the sound that he wants.

Sometimes, he will focus on just one word or one phrase to get the sound he wants and the enunciation so that there is a feeling coming through in that particular song.

He doesn't like the wobble, the vibrato. I directed a small church choir for eighteen years, and I knew even then that there was something wrong when all you could hear was "woowoowoo." When I got to First Presbyterian Church and started singing with Glenn, one of the first things he said he wanted was a smooth tone with either no vibrato or very little vibrato. It just clears up so much and makes it so much easier to listen to. I knew then that I had been right all those years when I was trying to get those ladies, particularly, to smooth out the wobble. Glenn says, "Get your iron. Iron it out. Hold your hand out and wobble it like this, and then gradually stop." You are singing all the time, and the idea is that once you get your hand steady, your voice is steady too.

Glenn just has a way of bringing people together and bringing the best out of those of us who are singing. He can drive you nuts sometimes, because he is so driven and so focused on what he is doing that he forgets time. I have been president of the church choir for almost four years. Sometimes I just have to say, "Glenn, we have got to quit," and he will quit. But he gets focused on what he is doing and he is listening for the sound that he knows is going to communicate to the audience. One of the many things that I like about singing with Glenn is that we don't sing the same kind of music all the time. He has such a wide variety of things that we do all the way from classical, the *Messiah*, to contemporary things with spirituals thrown in somewhere in the middle.

It is refreshing to change styles, and his idea is that you have many different people in the audience and they don't all like the same thing. If you don't like it this Sunday, wait until next Sunday or the next time you hear us sing and it will be different. It is true, I enjoy singing more because I know that we are going to sing different types of songs. I have my own particular favorite style, but I have almost adopted his philosophy. When someone asks what my favorite song is, I say, "Whatever I'm singing! Whatever I'm directing!" He really approaches the songs that way, whatever piece we are singing is his favorite at the time, until he can get it over to us what he wants.

James P. Wilson
Pianist and accompanist for First Presbyterian Church choir,
on overseas tours, and Glenn Draper Singers

The thing that I noticed almost immediately about Glenn was when I would hear groups sing that he was conducting, I would think, *This guy gets more out of less in a shorter period of time than anybody I have ever known!* He can take a group and he molds them into what he is after. It is incredible. I bet when he gets a book he reads the last chapter first. I'm just kidding about that, but the way he approaches rehearsals is interesting. He will often go to the end of a piece of music and work out the ending. It may be a piece of music no one has ever seen in his group, and they are just learning it for the first time. He will work right from the outset on the sound that he wants, the blend that he wants, and he gets that going before they ever look at the first part of the music. It is really amazing, and I have never seen anybody do it quite like that. It's that finesse and sound that he is after that he begins with. He doesn't wait.

Most conductors say, "This is a new piece of music. Let's read through it and work on it until we get familiar with the music, and then we will go to the finer points." Glenn starts with the finer points. But he does get them very quickly to the sound that he wants. I have worked with several conductors through the years in various capacities, and the technique and the art of conducting is not a real concern to Glenn. He has his unique style of conducting, and it is not as much conducting as it is coaxing the people to do the shading and the emotions and the meaning and the text. The whole thing of the music. He is something else to work with as an accompanist.

Stacie Caraway Coder

If Glenn says something during rehearsals and you quote back one of those sayings to him, he doesn't remember saying it. He will say, "That was me?" That goes for anger, if he or you lashed out or said something back, he won't remember afterwards. Most directors will come up and confront you again, and say, "Don't ever talk back to me in a rehearsal again." He honestly has no idea that he said that, did that, or you did it either. He has no recollection, whether it is funny, sad, or whatever. Sometimes that is good and sometimes it is not. You might say, "Glenn, why did you say that?" And he will say, "Say what?" "You just told them that I couldn't sing." "No, I didn't." "Yes, you did." It is really crazy! But again, he has that anointing, that kind of vision where he doesn't even recall anything except how the music should sound. To other incidental things he is oblivious.

Sara Smith Youngblood

When we get into a rehearsal with Glenn Draper, it is nonstop unless he is certain that we are not getting the picture. Then he stops and says, "You are not paying attention to what I'm trying to do here." Once in a while, if he felt that we were wearing out, he would stop and tell us a funny story. He is a very spiritual man and deeply feels how music can contribute to helping people understand the love of Christ, that if he is not getting it out, then he will point it out. "This is not going to happen, are you listening to what you are saying?" He didn't waste time. He would race through pieces and we were expected to circle our mistakes and fix them later, unless it was just horrible and then he would correct the problem.

Any unsuspecting pastor who comes backstage before a service while we are rehearsing is thrown in the middle. That is Glenn's favorite place to put somebody! This is after he has called him "Friend," and hugged him, and patted him on the back.

Rehearsals can often be exhausting and he would expect performance quality from the moment you started reading a piece of music. You didn't soft-pedal at all. You were expected to go all out, even though you were in the process of sight-reading. You were expected to see the dynamics and to sing like you were performing.

GLENNISMS

The 22 Theses: An Epistle for His Choirs

1. "In all thy ways acknowledge Him and He will direct your paths." (Prov. 3:6)
2. Coming together is a beginning.
3. Keeping together is progress.
4. Working with right notes and rhythms is success. Even God loves it!
5. Being late or leaving early is a no-no.
6. Focus, intelligence, laughter, love, and appreciation are essential.
7. Love and respect for each other is very important.
8. Thank God each day for your accompanists if they are good. If they are not good, pray for them.
9. Catching the first elevator is a good start.
10. Call your family and friends each day to encourage them. Tell them how much you love them.
11. Say "thank you," no matter what.
12. One mistake is an accident. Two mistakes is a habit. Three mistakes is, "Where can I get another job?"
13. Love God, your fellow man, and yourself with all your heart. You will understand heaven better.
14. Be sharp, be natural, and never B flat.
15. Beware of little ladies who sit low in the seat when they are driving and beware of drivers of red pickup trucks.

16. Watch your weight or others will.
17. Attitude is very important. It is more important than your aptitude, and it will determine your altitude.
18. Do not follow where a path may lead. Go, instead, where there is no path and leave a trail.
19. "Never let formal education get in the way of your learning." —Mark Twain
20. The true measure of a man is how he treats someone who can do him absolutely no good at all.
21. To make music and have joy, you must share it. Happiness and joy are twins.
22. Love the Lord thy God with all thy heart, mind, and soul. He first loved us.

Glenn's Creed

AN UNCOMPROMISING LIFE is characterized by an unashamed boldness that calls one to an uncommon standard. Never compromise, but allow God to do with your life as He pleases to broaden your influence and glorify Him.

_____

Jennifer Odom

One of his famous sayings is, "For it." (For example) "Lounelle is going to bring us the clothes here later, *for it*." Or, "We are going to have the country medley and then we are going to have this, and then we are going to have a mike check, and then after that we are going to have a pizza, *for it*." It is very hard to hear. It took me a long while, but if you just tune into things that he says, "for it," is just a little phrase that he uses. In my opinion that is his most famous Glennism.

_____

Kim Cargile

Some of the Glennisms don't seem to make sense, yet we understand them because we know the context it is in. For example, "Church choirs can't do it, Mozart can't do it, but we can do it because we are all the same people!" What he was trying to say is that we are not pigeonholed, church choirs can't do what we do, Mozart couldn't do what we do because he did Mozart, but we do everything. I understand the Glennisms because I just know him so well.

_____

Martin W. Hamby Jr.

He is one of the wisest men I have ever known, and he has such a good way of illustrating a point by using stories. I could never remember them, but when he is motivating his choir in rehearsals, the stories come out about when he was a young man and the lessons he learned in life. He has a way of telling them, and he speaks briefly, and I don't remember details but I remember the lesson and that is the goal—to impart that lesson to the choir.

HE ". . . GATHERED STICKS, KINDLED A FIRE AND LEFT IT BURNING"

The Ed Brothers

Adapted from the **Ed Brothers** *brochure*

The "brotherhood" began during the summer of 1980, while Fred Ed (Ron B. Whittemore), Asheville, North Carolina; Ed Ed (Dr. Alan W. Miller), Peoria, Illinois; and Jed Ed (Bill Dixon), Quincy, Florida; were singing with the Junaluska Singers at the World Methodist Conference grounds, Lake Junaluska, North Carolina. They originally began to perform a simple sing-a-long song during a summer concert. The improvised group was so well received that they became a regular part of all major concerts during the next four summers. In 1987, the "Eds" added a fourth member to their ranks, Cuz'n Red, (Jeff Stith of Gadsden, Alabama) and the quartet continues to perform professionally. They have recorded one excellent CD thus far. "They're country hicks . . . and they're city slicks!"

Dr. Alan W. Miller

Rarely would anyone view Glenn Draper exhibiting a less then zealous lifestyle! Glenn is frequently in the fast lane and, for the most part, "pulling people along." I can hear him now, "C'mon, ya'll." None of us could ever understand how he could have so much energy. We all swore that Lounelle would feed him pure pancake syrup for breakfast! He is always on a high. However, I now realize that it is a "lifestyle high." He simply doesn't want to waste time and wants to get the most out of life while he's here.

Unlike many famous choral directors, Glenn has the proper zeal for life. His zeal is evident in his choice of music and lifestyle example. Glenn could have been many things in his life, yet he chose to serve the Lord with his music. Why? Because he knows it is eternal and, therefore, because of God's amazing grace, Glenn will be eternal. For all we know, Glenn will probably be battling with St. Peter over tempo in heaven.

Glenn is gifted from God with the ability to communicate to the audience. I have known many professional choral directors who might "take a poke" at him, regarding his interpretation of a specific genre, however, none can equal his ability to "pack a house." Glenn's music communicates. That's the gist of it. In a paraphrase of Glenn's words, "What good is it if it doesn't get off the printed page and communicate its message?" Glenn has the uncanny ability to "get the music off the page" and communicate to the listener. It is a God-given gift, and Glenn has developed that gift.

I count it a blessing to have been mentored by Glenn Draper. It all comes down to how one extracts blessings from life. We can choose to focus on the negative or benefit from the people and situations that God brings our way. Glenn has been both a mentor and friend.

As we mature in life, God places people in our path to challenge us spiritually and professionally. We can choose to benefit from those challenges or ignore them and sacrifice the benefit God intended. I praise God that He chose to allow me to benefit from Glenn's life. Glenn always demanded our best, both musically and spiritually.

Jeff Stith
Lake Junaluska Singers; Glenn Draper Singers;
minister of music, Gadsden, Alabama

As I think back, I have great and fond memories about (my time) with Glenn. Most of them because Glenn always brought people together with a common experience. We all worked hard at something great, and when it was done there was a bond that would last a lifetime. I remember the first time I met Glenn was at his home in Chattanooga. A friend who was already singing with Glenn at the lake, Steve Rhodes, talked me into going up for an audition. While I was there, we took the "walk through history tour"—at least that's what I call it. Glenn has an office in his home with pictures on every wall, or should I say every inch of every wall of all of the things and groups and places and people he has ever been, done, or met. I was not quite sure what I was in for after that first meeting, but it has changed my life. Through Glenn and singing with him, I have come to know many of the musician friends that I hold dear today. It is certainly true that I have a world of tremendous experiences that I never would have been a part of if it were not for Glenn Draper.

Ron B. Whittemore
Lake Junaluska Singers for ten years;
church minister of music; Glenn Draper Singers

Here is a guy who has heart, he has soul, he has visions, he has energy, he has the expertise, certainly has the drive, and he has the support in a loving wife and kids. He dreams big and only maybe 10 percent of that dream might become a reality, but that 10 percent is very big. When I look back, I see what I have done under his direction. I have traveled the world, recorded many albums and CDs, and met some of the dearest friends I have in the world. Friendships that we still value to this day. It has been nothing but a pleasure (working with) the experience and the success of the man.

I thank God, probably on a daily basis, for Glenn Draper, because of what he taught me. In my church work, when people are in my face about the way I am trying to do something, I think, *What would Glenn do, and what would happen if he were here?* Man, then all of a sudden you get a reward, maybe it is a pat on the back, or someone compliments you, and then to God be the Glory for that. I always thank God for Glenn Draper, because he taught us the better way. He has so many young shoots that he has planted and now they are growing off on their own.

The Ed Fest

Charlie Flatt

Every year at my farm in Rising Fawn, Georgia, I have an Ed Fest, named after the Ed Brothers. The Ed Brothers, however, are not brothers and their real names are not Ed. They are all in Christian education and music directors in different churches. One in Peoria, Illinois, at Grace Presbyterian Church; another in a Presbyterian church in Asheville, North Carolina; another at First Baptist Church in Quincy, Florida; and another at a Baptist church in Gadsden, Alabama. They have been coming to my farm for sixteen years. They started by coming to sing at a little Bible study that I had in my home, and the people didn't want them to quit. They would rather hear them sing than hear me teach. The "Brothers" said, "We will come back in the fall and have a regular Ed Fest," and they asked me to pick the time. I said, "I'm going to let the Lord pick the time. He colors the mountains the third weekend in October, so let's have it then and we will have a crowd. If the people don't like singing, and don't like good food, and don't like to travel, and don't like crowds, they might still want to see what the Lord is going to do to the side of that mountain!"

That was seventeen years ago, and I tell you this simply to emphasize that 95 percent of the approximately two thousand singers and friends who were here (in 2000, from nine states and guests from twenty-two states) came out of loyalty to Glenn Draper. Every one of the Ed Brothers sang with him, at Lake Junaluska, and none of them have been Lake Junaluska Singers in more than twenty years. They will sing with him from time to time, and they are considered some of the Glenn Draper Singers. Anyway, it got started with the four of them, then people they sang with sixteen years ago heard about it and so what it has become is a great reunion for Glenn Draper's singers. People ask what it costs. It doesn't cost anything. I do make a request of everybody and that is to bring a non-Christian friend. I want non-Christians to see how much fun we have. I want them to want what we have. Glenn is usually there and he just goes from one to another, meeting former singers who sang with him fifteen or twenty years ago, up to the current singers who have come to join in the festivities. He is not only a great friend to them, but he just has people all over who love him. I don't know a man more loved than Glenn Draper.

The Singing Men of America

Tommy Holmes and Jerry Thomas

When we got to Pfeiffer College there was a closeness between the men there that started something in me that I never got over. In fact that is why I started the Singing Men of America and someday we hope to have chapters all over the country, because of the seeds that were planted by Glenn Draper in my heart.

The Singing Men of America is part of a ministry called Musical Ministries Inc., a nonprofit organization that Tom Holmes and I started in the 1970s. After Pfeiffer College, I always wanted to start a male chorus in Charlotte, but just didn't have time. I was a full-time minister of music in churches and raising a family. However, ten years ago I really got down to business and had a vision about singing men and we started our first chapter here in Charlotte, which is going great. Tom helped me to start the Singing Men and it is still going, and our plans are to start chapters all over the country. It is a men's ministry and it works kind of like a civic club. Men pay dues and they pay their own expenses here and on trips, buy their own music, and buy their own outfits. Our wives really back us up and we have some great concerts, at least one concert a month. It is something that is really close to our hearts and for ten years the vision has not dwindled and faded like so many things, but has become stronger and stronger. We are getting ready to make our second album. We really don't know how to go about starting chapters all over the country, but that is the vision that we have and we are working toward it. That is all you can do. Glenn is interested in what we are trying to do. The seeds were planted by him and those men at Pfeiffer.

CHORAL DIRECTORS

Todd Gaither

I have been a full-time church music director at Covenant Presbyterian Church for about eleven years, and we have a choir and ensembles. We have recorded an album and I probably decided to do that as a result of working with Glenn and doing recordings with him. I do solo concerts, so I would say that I have learned most of what I do with a choir from Glenn, by observing and watching and hearing a line first sung and hearing it after it has been worked, and noting how we got there. I apply what I learn with my own choir and groups. There will always be those of us who have worked with Glenn and have studied with him to some degree, who will continue to do things because we learned them from him. I hope for my life that I will also impact people so that when I die they will continue to live out those things that I taught them or shared with them long after I am dead, and they will share it with someone and carry it on down.

If I am struggling, trying to get a sound, we will get everybody in a circle. You have somebody's voice right across from you and the sound is very good. That is a great tool for me because you are in the center of all that sound. One of the things that I have admired about Glenn but that I have not done and I don't know if I could do, is conduct a concert for two to two and one-half hours. His concerts do not have a lot of pauses, you go from one song right to another, but they are usually related in some sense, with the key or the theme. When we do those concerts, and I am unsure about our next song, he knows the song that is coming up next, and it is amazing.

Ron B. Whittemore

[Glenn has] a technique that I have taken into our church with the small ensembles very effectively. I think to produce his sound, he is looking for a very open throat, a half yawn with a lifting of the soft palette. It doesn't have a tremendous amount of an edge to it. It is vibrant; but it is not an operatic sound, because he breaks a lot of that down from your voice. He loves the operatic bass and baritone and operatic soprano sound, but not in the choral music sound. We did everything from Bach to Broadway, and he continues to do that, and he expected us to adapt slightly to that. A lot of directors don't necessarily do that, they find one thing [and stick with it].

I remember him telling stories about other directors coming up and asking, "How did you do that?" He would say, "How did I do what?" They would say, "How did you begin that concert with Brahms or Bach and end with Broadway show stuff?" He said, "Because the people demand it." Everybody is a little different. It is not a perfect musical theater voice that we tried to do when we were out on stage, (even though) he certainly had enough talent. I think technique wise, his blend is really made by learning how to break the voice down a little, from everything you have ever learned in a voice studio and taking it to the choral setting. He would say, "This is how you blend by a nice open throat," and he talks about hushed tones and colors. He is like a master chef, a little more energy here, a little more open on that vowel.

David Fowler

Some of the other things that I guess I remember about Glenn was that he would wear his velour shirts at practices and sweat like crazy. He was the most energetic man I had ever seen who wasn't playing a sport—he was directing. I eventually directed church choirs myself while I was going through school, and a lot of Glenn's personality I guess I picked up in the way I direct, in the way I move and bounce. If you made me a little taller and a little wider and stuck a velour shirt on me and looked from the back, you might say, "What's Glenn doing up there directing," because he had such a strong influence on me.

As I directed music in churches later on, I wasn't professional by any means, I was going to law school and practicing law and directing on the side. I tried to understand and appreciate that there is a wide variety of music and to be willing to be diverse to reach a broader audience so that everybody hears something that they like. I learned that from Glenn.

Nancye "Scooter" Formo
Lake Junaluska Singer for ten years;
longtime music teacher and children's choir director

I have a handbell choir, a children's choir, and I sing with a small symphony in Winston. I am a retired music teacher, with thirty years in public education and now have a home school course at my house and also teach guitar and piano. A lot that I learned from my college and Glenn is how to make a phrase, you don't just crescendo, you are not just soft and then loud. There is something that happens to get there. I feel like I have had two master conductors. What I have learned from both of them is that you can do a whole lot more than what is on that printed page. It is the aesthetics that you get from their personality, how they interpret the music, and then you think, *Okay, what would really sound better there and how do I get it?* I know I am thinking it because they planted the seed, first of all, to do that. A lot of choirs do exactly what is on the music, they never think how it can be changed, or that it can be done any differently. Probably, they were taught that way and you just kind of reiterate what you were taught. I am very grateful to both of them for that, for teaching me to love diversity. Glenn, more than anybody else I had, planted that seed with me.

Dee Dee Brogan

His music reaches you because it is so imprinted on your heart and it makes you who you are. When I find myself working with children, I find myself saying things or doing things that are straight from Glenn Draper. My husband has had the privilege of directing some groups and some ensembles that are based around the same philosophy of Glenn's, with his sound. Even the way he directs and illustrates makes you think that either Glenn said that or he would have. When you listen to a piece of music you always question, *How would he make this song better?* Once we stop doing that, music never goes anywhere. Once we stop questioning that, we don't grow anymore. I think Glenn has never stopped growing. He is always looking for an exciting and a new way to present the gospel and to present Jesus Christ and to present it through music. Always. It is his passion. Not very many people can go through life and say, "I don't want to retire, I don't want to quit, all I want to do is what I do best." He has truly found something where he does not feel like he is working. He feels like he is doing exactly what he is put on this earth to do.

Charles Middleton

In 1976, I started at George Hills Presbyterian Church as the assistant director of music, and I have been doing that now for twenty-six years. I would never have gone into music or directed a choir [without Glenn]. When I do direct, I think of Glenn and it is like a light in the back of my head that says, *Well, what would Glenn do? How would he interpret this?* It gives me a point of starting.

I liken it to a spark and a forest fire. That one little spark [from him], and look at all that has come out of it. He became a mentor for me and my life is patterned after his morals and the things that he holds dear and his family.

Jerry Thomas

If you know Glenn, you love him. He has never met a stranger and he always remembers you and he will always take time with you. Like Tom [Holmes] said, "It was natural." It was born into Glenn Draper, and it is a God-given talent. To me, he has a unique combination that very few people have. To me, he is one of the finest choir directors in the world, there is none any better anywhere. I was fortunate to be able to be under him and be his student assistant director for the four years that I was with him. He has the ability to get things done. A lot of choir directors have the ability, but they don't have the ability to get things done. You know what he wants when you are standing in front of him and he is directing. Everybody knows what he wants. He taught me a lot of that, of course, I am nothing like he is. But the greatest compliment I ever get is when people say, "You direct like Glenn Draper." He taught me a lot and I tried to learn everything that I could. I was like a sponge when I was under him. I got just everything I could from him and I have used it for all these years.

Laurie Harper Evans

Throughout those years at the lake, I closely observed Glenn's gifts of music and have incorporated so much of what I learned from him into my own work as a music director. For example, everything from the warm ups to the choice of music selections relates back to Glenn. There are such various needs in a church congregation and in order to meet those needs, it is vital for a choir to provide musical selections of various styles (Inspirational, Southern Gospel, Spirituals, Contemporary Christian, Classical, Hymns). This is one of the most influential things I learned from Glenn. Music is healing, and when one sings from the heart for the glory of God, it can bring joy and comfort to all who listen.

Lynne Swafford
Lake Junaluska Singers; professional voice and piano teacher

Young singers under him today do not understand what they are experiencing and won't know what fabulous training they are receiving in the art of putting together a show until years have passed. His ability to run sixty-five songs in one show and make it fit both in flow of rhythm, key, and context is phenomenal, and I thank God that I had the privilege of working with him. It has aided me in my own show production, both in churches in Dallas and at the Dallas Summer Musicals School of Musical Theater where I teach.

10

Glenn Draper's
Recommendations
for Choral Directors

What would I retire from? I never worked a day in my life.

~Glenn Draper

ADVICE

If you want to direct a choir and you have none, go out and organize one. You will have to develop a following of people in some way.

Get someone (for example, a business) to sponsor your singing group—the IBM Singers, the Coca-Cola Chorale, the Rotary Club Showoffs, Newlyweds or Nearly Deads, Young Chattanooga Sings . . .

The sky is the limit! Don't wait for them to come to you—that may never happen! Almost every position I've had, I've had to organize the choir myself: sixth grade quartet; high school quartet; Young Roanoke Sings quartet; Air Force choirs, orchestra; Dallas Male Chorus; Lake Junaluska Singers; Pfeiffer College male chorus and choral union; five choirs at the University of Miami; UTC choirs, Chattanooga; First Presbyterian Church, Chattanooga, Tenn.; Glenn Draper Singers; and the Chattanooga Festival Singers and Orchestra.

My dad always said they never build monuments to critics . . . I'll be the first one to tell you, I have not always been accepted by everyone—God loves them anyway!

TO MUSIC DIRECTORS

DR. WILFORD BAIN, former dean of the Indiana University School of Music, once said:

> In order to be successful in music, you have to have two main qualities:
> 1. Talent—know yourself . . . practice . . . God loves right notes!
> 2. Sell it and yourself.

QUALITIES YOU MAY NEED:
1. A God-given talent—stretch your three talents to four, study piano or play in a band if at all possible.
2. Education—Study to show thyself approved unto God, a choir director that needeth not be ashamed, rightly dividing eighth and quarter notes. Go to school where you can get the best training to match your talent. Talk to people everywhere who can help you learn.
3. Faith—Have faith in Almighty God . . . Seek ye first the kingdom of God and all His righteousness, and He will direct your paths. Accept Him as your personal Savior.
4. Love—music and people.
5. Personality.
6. Salesmanship.
7. The king's English.
8. Health.
9. Historian.
10. Love yourself—you are the only you God ever made!
11. Good Health—exercise each day. Eat right, sleep right, and think right.

KEEP LEARNING. Sharpen your pencil and your mind, and when you know it all—quit.

New music: remember that it's hard to just preach last week's sermon. Find new stories, new illustrations, and new experiences.

Be a true friend to your singers and accompanist. Share their joys and hurts. Arrange tours, socials, etc. *Pray for each other.* Give a lot of "atta boy" or "atta girl" compliments. Call them on special occassions and their birthdays, they will love you for that.

THAT CERTAIN SOUND

YOU EITHER LIKE the sound or you don't. The sound needs to match the style of the music you are singing. What makes the chimes on a clock sound the way they do? The size of the clock, and the size of the bell determines that. What causes a trombone to sound like a trombone is the way it is built. It cannot sound like anything but a trombone. But the human voice is different, you can make the human voice sound many ways. In addition to being loud or soft, you can make it sound corny, blatant, strident, flute-like, harsh, nasal, covered, round, falsetto, hushed. The human voice is an incredible instrument when used in a choir, and not every choir director utilizes that because of their own preconceived ideas. The sound of the voice should reflect the word[s].

I think choir directors have to be able to cry with both eyes. If you have a little bit of hurt would you sing differently than if you had a big hurt? My conviction is that you absolutely would. If you have on a tuxedo, would you sing differently? You sure would. Many times I will say to the choir, "I want that tuxedo sound," and they know I mean a "dressed up" sound. I have tried to study choir directors, and I asked many questions after I decided that choral directing was what I wanted to do. I would go to a rehearsal when I did not know the choir director at all and I would say, "I want to pick your brain. Why did you do what you did? Why did you put an 'n' on this word where you did, and why did you tell them you want a covered tone? What do you mean by covered tone?"

To go back to my earlier years, I was a trombone player and I loved it, but I always liked other instruments including the trumpet, clarinet, violin, or strings. Sometimes I want my choir to sound like strings, for example, the Schubert "G Major Mass." I have even played that for singers and said, "I want you to sound like these strings. Very warm and gentle, if you can imagine violins playing that as opposed to tubas playing it or trumpets." But too many of us never get into that. I think you have to have an image of the kind of sound you want, and you have to be able to illustrate [the sound] to the choir members that are doing it, otherwise how are they going to know how [to get the sound you want]? How loud is loud? How soft is soft? If I say I want it 20 percent louder, or 30 percent louder, would there be a difference? Yes. Sometimes, if you repeat a phrase or word four times, I will say I want the first one really loud and the second softer, for example, 100, 75, 50, and 25, so they know the parallel relationships.

Dynamics are so important. The loudest point is not always the attack. You have to sing through the syllable. You are either arriving, going through, or leaving—one note does not always sound like the next one.

Nancye "Scooter" Formo

If I say anything about his talent, it would be the sound. He knows the sound he wants and he knows how to get it and how he gets it is with the blend of light soprano and tenor voices, and with lyric, heavy alto and heavy bass. That is how he gets the sound. Also, what he does that drives the singer crazy is straightening out vibratos, you can't have a really wobbly sound. Basses and altos with big, thick voices, will have a slow vibrato. They have to make those a little faster and then sopranos and tenors like mine, we have to slow ours down a little bit. The secret is to get it matched, and that is where his sound comes from. That takes time.

A LOVE SONG has joy in it and usually also has sorrow in it. Sometimes I will go to each person in a choir and ask, "Have you ever been hurt by your girlfriend or by your boyfriend?" Invariably every one of them says yes. I want that hurt sound. You have to cry. You have to feel it. "Black is the color of my true love's hair" or "Winter is past and the leaves now are green." How can you make that sound so the people think, *Wow, I understand that.* Last summer a girl said, "I just broke up with my boyfriend," and I said, "Maybe that is bad, but now you know how to sing a hurt song, you have been there." She said that she never thought of it like that. I said, "That is exactly how it is."

Someone asked Frank Sinatra why he was so successful and he said, "Because I had been to both places." He had had the lowest despair and he had been "King of the Road." I am not saying choral directors have to go through those kinds of events, it's life. That is why I think that at my age I am a better choral director than I have ever been, because of all the experiences I have had through the years. You know what? The more you learn, the more you find that you didn't know. That is frightening. But, if I didn't have confidence in myself I would never have tried to be a choir director. I have had the privilege of directing bands and orchestras, but I have never been so thrilled as when I have directed both or choral music alone. You have words to go with the music—that's an advantage.

What caused Fred Waring, or Robert Shaw, or Norman Luboff to have a certain kind of sound? Usually people give a downbeat and the choir sings. The ones who "fix it" are the ones who determine how it is going to sound. I used to ask my band director, Mr. Christiansen, what was different about Fred Waring and Robert Shaw compared to other directors? He would always point to the ear. What they hear and what they don't hear and what they fix. I have never forgotten that "and what they fix." We are all different. I fix something that some other director wouldn't fix, and wouldn't even think about fixing. But in the collegiate ranks, where I taught many years, when I met choir directors they all followed a pattern of what everybody else was doing. This college choir sounds like that college choir, and they all do basically the same kind of music.

GET YOUR ACT TOGETHER

I TRY TO memorize the music before I go to rehearsals so I can listen better during rehearsals. In the Air Force, I had a stack of music under my bunk-bed, and when everybody went to sleep, I slipped out about midnight and went over to the chapel and memorized music till 3:00 or 4:00 A.M. Then I came back and put that music back under my bed, because I knew that some day I would be using it. So when I got the male chorus started, I didn't have to go back and study scores that much, I had already been through much of the music.

You lead by example. The better you listen, the better your choirs will be. Study all the parts and know how one part relates to another. Sing high major thirds and major sevenths. You may have to study and restudy each part.

***

Shawn Clark
UTC choirs; current president, Glenn Draper Singers; UTC band member

I never met someone who knows the music as well as he does. Most every-thing that we sing is in his head. He knows it, he dissects it, and he knows where all the problem parts are going to be so when we start a rehearsal, most of the time we start somewhere in the middle or at the end. If we can do the stuff at the end first and get it to sound right, then we can go back and get the other parts easier. We memorize most of the music that we do, especially on tours. That helps us out a lot, because we don't have to sit there and look down. We can concentrate on the words and on watching Glenn, because a lot of times he has us spread out so we have to look at him or listen to the pianist. He really knows his music and the pitches. If you sing something wrong, he will turn around and say, "Okay, somebody over here sang it wrong and this is how it goes." He will go over it again and again and again until you get it right. That is what makes it work.

***

A REHEARSAL NEEDS TO BE AS EXCITING AS THE PERFORMANCE

Kim Cargile

He doesn't let you get away with being less enthusiastic in rehearsal than you would be on stage. He makes you sing it in rehearsal just like you would during a performance.

THE WAY YOU rehearse it is going to be the way you sing it. We are creatures of habit, if you slop through it in the rehearsal, all the prayers in the world aren't going to help you when you come to the performance—you are going to do it exactly like you did in a rehearsal. Some say, "Glenn, we are just practicing!" I say, "I know it, but you are going to practice it right. Don't practice your mistakes. I want it to be like you just scored a touchdown in football and you have been there before. I don't want you to act like it is a world-shaking event and you have never done it before. I want you to recognize it if you get it right. I don't want that to happen on a stage, I want you to say that we have been here before and we have proved that we can do this." We are all victims of habit. If you get in the habit of doing it right, that's how you are going to do it on stage. A mistake is when you miss it. A habit is when you miss it twice. The third time is a tragedy.

I love to rehearse in a circle. It makes it easy to hear all the parts equally well. Balance, blend, and articulation are so important. Your togetherness creates a mood.

Nancye "Scooter" Formo

You really have to pace yourself, and don't let him know that you are not giving it all, which is hard because you are singing in a circle and he is right in the center and that's how he hears.

There were a couple of other things that he did that were kind of unique, I thought, and I don't know where he got these ideas, maybe he just thought of them. He would put soprano, alto, tenor, bass; soprano, alto, tenor, bass; he would line you up in quartets which would really mean you are not near anybody singing your part, to see how well you knew your part. It almost had a stereo quality sound, and was just a wonderful sound. Some singers can't do it. They are just so used to singing soprano with soprano and alto with alto. He didn't do it a lot. It really works better in sacred music, like requiems. I thought it was a neat idea. You must have very good musicians to make it work. Even if they are reading music, you still have to know what you are doing.

TWO SUMMERS AGO at Lake Junaluska, one of the tenors had left some music from his prior college school year in my office. One of them was a difficult madrigal piece. I don't remember the name of it, but it was old English and the lyrics didn't really make sense in today's world, and it was difficult. He had every kind of marking you can think of, "sharpen this, flat this, put an '*n*' right here, make sure cutoffs are . . ." all the way through it, there must have been eighteen pages. I got to the next to last page and saw that he had written, "I hate this piece." How many who hear that song will think the same thing? You can do a theory piece in a class, but too many times our rehearsals are like theory classes, they are meaningless. They are mainly for demonstrating technical parts of music, but have no life in it. If a car didn't have gasoline in it, would it run? Only downhill.

Dr. Robert K. Dean

The most significant thing, musically, was the sense of excitement in singing a piece of music. He knew just how to create the mood and sound for a piece, and was unequaled in getting that out of us. I remember once he ran over to the light switch and flipped the lights off to get the mood of a sixteenth century cathedral for a rehearsal of a Victorian piece. It was a terrific idea and it brought us right down to the place where we needed to be for that music.

DO MUSIC THAT YOUR AUDIENCE WILL LIKE

I THINK YOU have to know who it is you want to please and what kind of personality they have, in order to know how to sing it. Most people want things that are honest, not fake, not a put-on, that has a beautiful sound, and is easy to listen to. The last people who can be a fake are choir directors and preachers. We cannot be fake because if we are, you don't like anything that we do. I don't care how beautiful it might sound, you size us up and we can only make one first impression. Sincerely love people, but sing some people music. You have to sound good and make sure the audience understands your words. If it is a happy song, looking happy doesn't hurt.

Dr. Robert K. Dean

One of Glenn's biggest strengths was that he knew who his audience was, and he knew how to please them. People who would typically never go to a classical concert would come to our concerts and discover that they loved hearing choral music. (My parents were a perfect example.) He was able to mix in music that the non-musician would appreciate better than anybody I know. That, of course, caused some of the purists in the department to sometimes cringe a bit, but Glenn's choirs have never sung to empty seats—a fact that the purists also didn't fail to notice. He was, also in that same vein, a wonderful showman. His concerts and tours were carefully choreographed and they flowed effortlessly. He had (and has) the most natural and easy way of speaking to audiences. I remember thinking that the English audiences, especially, were totally charmed by Glenn. They weren't used to an energetic, kick-up-your-heels group of college singers, and they loved it. I think they also loved his unbridled enthusiasm (more typically American than British).

On our 1972 tour to England, the first of many for Glenn, we mostly sang for churches and stayed in the homes of members overnight. It was a wonderful experience that I will never forget. Glenn put together a medley of Protestant hymns that flowed from one to the other and built to a tremendous climax on "O God Our Help in Ages Past." They were very simply done, almost straight out of the hymnal, but the way that he arranged them was pure Glenn Draper. I enjoyed seeing the reactions of the English people whom we sang for. They would practically be in tears when we finished the hymns.

═══════════════════════════════════

I WAS IN COLORADO one time for an American Choral Directors convention, and there were about six or seven directors sitting around a table near a fireplace waiting for a bus to come to take them to a concert. I just sat down with them, while each one was telling what their choirs had done during the past year. I think they all were trying to impress each other. The last guy, from Colorado, said, "I think the thing that we had the most success with last year was probably 'Greensleeves' and 'The Battle Hymn of the Republic.'" Everybody laughed. We were all trying to impress each other, but who cared—here was the only honest guy in the crowd. I sided with him. That was my kind of guy because he did music for the public. What good is a choir if nobody comes to hear it? What is an orchestra good for if it doesn't have an audience? So I must sing "people music" in order to get people to come.

═══════════════════════════════════

Martin W. Hamby Jr.

Glenn is good at reading an audience and determining what they want to hear. He may have five or six songs in his back pocket and not know what he is going to do until he gets out there. He just takes the "temperature of the land," and then he chooses this one and maybe a song and dance; he is very good at that.

═══════════════════════════════════

I THINK WE cannot always sound like choirs have sounded in the past, nor can we make it on last month's, or last year's, or the last century's music.

Some of the most beautiful choral pieces in the world are Italian, English, German, or Latin, but you can't use those today like you could fifty years ago. I went to a concert last spring to audition some singers for Junaluska. This choir was from a wonderful school with a great reputation, and they had maybe 100 to 110 people there at the concert. You know why? They sang the music long-faced, dull, and with no expression—they went through the motions. They had been on tour for a week, and had sung the same music every night. I could tell. That is what we call leftovers. Not everybody likes leftovers in music. It must be a refreshing thing every time you sing it. A new creation. That is why I mix up the program, so that the singers won't get bored. I could do the same program for the audience, because they weren't there the night before, but the singers were. If the singers don't have that agility and light, you are going to know it. They will sing just straight, with no enthusiasm, and no inspiration.

Also, you have to be up-to-date and current in your thinking. Even if you hate sports you still have to read about sports, because somebody in your choir loves sports. If you don't like movies, you have to at least be aware of what is going on around you. It wouldn't hurt every now and then to see a movie, because somebody in your choir rehearsal will say to you, "Glenn, did you see . . ." and you can say, "Yeah, I saw that. Wasn't that a great show?" You have to have something to talk about so you can identify with each other. You become friends like that, so you need to be well-versed in things that are going on around you in your world. Don't be so focused that you obliterate everything else. Be up-to-date. Communication is so important and liking each other helps.

TO MOTIVATE PEOPLE YOU MUST MOVE THEM OUT OF THEIR COMFORT ZONE

IN YOUR REHEARSALS you have to light a fire under people. You have to be a motivator, but many people don't like to be motivated. If you could talk to trees in a forest and say, "I'm going to dig all of you up and move you to another forest with some huge dump trucks," all those trees would say, "Don't come near me, I'm too comfortable. I like it here, and my roots are deep." People are just like that, "Don't move me. Don't push me to do anything else." But, I think a choir director is a person who takes a group of people and forces them to do things they do not want to do, don't feel led to do, and will dislike you for forcing them to do the things that you want them to do in order to become who they would like to be. They would like to be on the stage with people yelling for more. Thunderous applause is a beautiful sound, they would like that, but they don't want to pay the price. You have to somehow sell them on that idea. That is hard, isn't it? We have to move them out of their comfort zone.

Dr. Alan W. Miller

While there are many who confuse his enthusiasm with "perfection for perfection's sake," I now realize his zeal for life is centered on excellence. Among a lazy generation, Glenn has been a front runner of pushing people well beyond their expectations. Frankly, he demands excellence and I think it is refreshing as I look back on my time with him. Those of us who followed in his footsteps would love to get the response that he has and still does. When we push people beyond their comfort zone, wonderful things happen. It is here, where learning and discovery takes place. Glenn is a master of creating excellence and striving for an initiative in people to fulfill dreams they never thought possible. I am an example of that process.

YOU MUST TRY new or different ideas or music to keep your singers motivated. Rehearse in a circle or in quartets. Be sure to get new music regularly. Rehearse in a hall with good acoustics. Have other people come into your rehearsals and sometimes put them in the middle of the circle while rehearsing. Have get-togethers, outings, tours, sing at different functions. Variety is the spice of life.

Charles Middleton

Glenn is successful because he knows people; he knows what you can do, and he knows your limitations. He knows how to push you beyond that and you think, *I didn't believe I could do that,* and that gives you motivation to go beyond. It is not in trying to be good or great, but to be better than what you think is good. He let's you know that there are limits that you set on yourself. That is what he knows—that people are limitless.

WHO'S THE BOSS?

I HAVE HAD the privilege of working with some of the finest ministers in the world. I am indebted and grateful to Ben Haden for first inviting me and my family to serve for thirty-four years at the large First

Presbyterian Church in Chattanooga, Tennessee. Ben is a businessman, lawyer, ex-CIA, and minister of the gospel of Jesus Christ. I have also been his music director for his nationally televised programs for over thirty years. His talk (message) is as on-target with people as anyone I have ever seen. He is a genius and definitely called of God to proclaim His gospel.

Ben preached the Bible message in everyday language, and the choir sang people music. I often said to him, "Ben, I have found ths wonderful music for you," and he would ask me, "Would the dogs like it?" He told me the story of the famous dog food convention held out west.

The leader got up and said, "Who has the greatest product in the world?" They would answer back, "We have!"

"Who's got the greatest salesmen in all the world?" They would answer, "We have!"

He said, "Gentlemen, how come we are not selling more dog food?" Finally, a man stands in the back and says, "The dogs don't like it!"

The minister is the boss and has the last word, but—being that none of us knows everything—he also needs to seek out advice on certain musical questions. When he needs musical advice, the minister needs to listen. It's best not to show your ignorance by opening your mouth and, therefore, removing all doubt.

I have worked with all kinds—one minister called church music "elevator" music. I do think in some cases that the choir can become too popular. They can become very jealous. Remember the mirror on the wall story . . . Who's the fairest of them all? The Bible says not to be unequally yoked—that means ministers and choir directors.

Sara Smith Youngblood

[At Junaluska in the summer] the preacher spoke and Glenn never competed with the sermon. He always had just the right way to finish. Sometimes some of the visiting ministers would be concerned about his music, but he always charmed them by putting them in the middle of the circle [during rehearsal]. He would say, "Sit here, you have to hear this." They would leave completely won over.

I LEARNED a whole lot from Ben [Haden]. We saw eye to eye on a lot of things. He never got into my business, and we never had a meeting on what I was going to sing on Sunday morning. I never asked him about his sermon topics because, if he had told me, I guarantee you he wouldn't have preached it. Sometimes Ben changed his mind coming down the steps from his office to the sanctuary.

WHAT ARE YOU WORTH?

WHAT YOU DO is what you'll be known for—you help establish your own reputation. A minister asked me one day to define the difference between a full-time director and a part-time director. I jokingly said, "It's determined by the length of his coffee breaks!" I didn't take coffee breaks, and I gave whatever time it took to get the job done. It takes a lot of time calling and recruiting people. New people, new music, and new ways to worship are worth a lot. Research compensation at similar positions. Remember, if you start too low, your worth may never be appreciated for many years. Don't be timid about your abilities and your value to the congregation or school. A $25,000-a-year choir director will always be known as a $25,000-a-year choir director.

SOME FINAL THOUGHTS

MAJOR IN PEOPLE, their needs, and their friends, as well as music. Congratulate them on any and everything when they do a good job. Even a dog gets a cookie when he does a good deed. Be interested in what your choir members do. Go with them to ball games, concerts, hospitals. Cry and laugh with them—they need your love and encouragement. Love and respect them and pray with and for them. Expose them to music occasionally that is over their heads, that is how they learn.

===

Kim Cargile

Previously, Glenn was totally focused on the product and the music—everything had to be just so. In the past few years, however, I have noticed one thing that is completely different about Glenn. He is investing so much more of himself into the lives of the individuals. It may be because the older we get we start to realize what is really important. Many times, with people who aren't great singers and who might not be asked to return [to sing] since they are not as strong [vocally] as singers as they have been in the past, Glenn invests [time] in them and it seems to change their whole lives. He has always done this, but Glenn has recently become very good about taking kids "under his wing."

===

WHAT IS PERSONAL to people is special to them. One thing that is really special to them is their name. Don't ever misspell their name and don't ever mispronounce it. I don't really remember when I started calling people on their birthdays, because I did this when I was in college to people back home or a girlfriend. That is a little thing for me to know and to do. But it is a big thing to them.

Kim Cargile

Glenn is so positive all of the time. I can rarely count the times that I have heard negative words come out of his mouth. He believes that whatever you expect from people, they will fulfill that.

IT SEEMS so obvious to say, but we can always learn. It is importat that you study other respected choral directors and look for something different that they are doing, that you can use. Remember, change sometimes brings out the very worst in people, so you must be willing to overlook that response in your choir members and attempt to sell them on your contemplated changes.

Kathy Tugman

He is such a loving, loving person and he promotes that love within the groups he is in, the groups he puts together, the choirs, and the singers. Love has a lot to do with his success.

APPENDIX A

GLENN DRAPER'S LEGACIES

Compilation of former singers of Glenn Draper who have taught, arranged, directed, or performed in a musical career field; or used their musical talents in some other way.

1. UNITED STATES AIR FORCE

N. C. Armstrong, Dr. Euel Belcher, Bob B. Davis, Herbert Eckhoff, Harry Evers, Lt. Col. Roger Hinkley, Jennifer Lyons, Eldon Moen, Adam Ortez, James Oxley, Rev. Charles Poole, Deborah Lee Reardon, and Bob Tibault.

2. LAKE JUNALUSKA

K. C. Armstrong, Euel Belcher, Michael Best, Dr. Vic Bilanchone, George Bitzas, Dee Dee Brogan, Jim Brogan, Kim Cargile, Jay Craig, Marty Hamby, Bill Dixon, John Dominick, Julie Dout, Lynn Duke, Laurie Harper Evans, Gerald Floyd, Nancye Formo, Tim Fudge, Melodie Gallaway, Wes Guilliland, Lisa Harper, Paul Hickfang, Michael Johnson, Doris Knisley, Heather Kormeyer, James Markey, Charles Middleton, Dr. Alan W. Miller, Jennifer Odom, Chris O'Rear, Gloria Parvin, Ann Peacock, Rita Potter, Debra Lee Reardon, Allison Redmon, Karen Shafer, Chris Stigall, Jeff Stith, Bryan Stratton, Gerald Strickland, Lynn M. Swafford, Rob Swafford, Mark Tilley, Jennifer Trent, Jean Upmeyer, Margaret Vaughn, Pat Vaughn, Ron Whittemore, Courtney Williams, Misty Williamson, Gene Wilson, and Sara Smith Youngblood.

3. PFEIFFER UNIVERSITY

Milton Barden, Dot Chance, Martha Dawkins, Jimmy Griffith, Tommy Holmes, Jimmy Irby, Bobbie Leonard, Tony Philmon, Al Rose, Roger Saunders, Dr. John Stokes, Jerry Thomas, and Sammy White.

4. UNIVERSITY OF MIAMI

Barry Babst, Linda Powers Bilanchone, Vic Bilanchone, Meri Lee Bitzs, Betty Brett, Bill Brett, Bill Brown, Glenda Cupp, Douglas Daubenspeck, Jerry DeGennaro, Michael Eaton, Judy Idema, Pat Kirby, Jack Long, Joseph Lowe, Paul Marino, Julie Rohr McHugh, Joy McGrew, Jack McNamara, Lydia Metlika, and Al Yudakufski.

5. UNIVERSITY OF TENNESSEE, CHATTANOOGA

Kim Cargile, Dr. Joseph Chapman, Stacie Caraway Coder, Rebecca Cook, Jimmy Cooley, Denise Craig, Jay Craig, Andy Culley, Dr. Robert K. Dean, Dr. Gail Dooley, Dr. Kevin Ford, David Fowler, Todd Gaither, Lucy Campbell, Marty Hamby, Sherri Henderson, Wesley Jackson, Michael Johnson, Pat Kennedy, Carlene Kidwell, Doris Knisley Moreland, Mike Lees, Steven Markum, Susan Martin, Michael Mays, Dr. Alan Miller, Pat Mulligan, Ty Parker, Marty Parks, Lori Beth Perry, Rebecca Randolph, Allison Redmon, Gaye S. Slaten, Gretchen Striebeck, Daniel H. Taylor Jr., Tommy Taylor, Kim Thompson, Joe Troxel, Kathy Tugman, Daniel Varnell, Robert J. A. Waller, Aaron Webb, Misty Williamson, and Jim Wilson.

DEGREES, HONORS, AWARDS,
AND PROFESSIONAL AFFILIATIONS

DEGREES

Indiana University, bachelor of music.
Southern Methodist University, master of music, conducting.
High Point University, honorary doctorate.

HONORS, AWARDS

First Place honors in National Military Male Chorus competition, Keesler USAF Base, Keesler Male Chorus, 1954 and 1955.
Show Biz Award, NBC (WDSU).
Department of Defense, Certificate of Esteem.
U.S. Air Force, Outstanding Service Award.
Oscar from Entertainment Center, Seoul, South Korea.
University of Miami, Omicron Delta Kappa, Certificate of Meritorious Service.
University of Miami, Iron Arrow.
University of Miami, Inter-Fraternity and Student Government Council, Special Merit Award.
Who's Who in Music Around the World Award.
Men of Achievement Around the World.
Personalities of the South.
First Place for Best Locally Produced T.V. Show in America, UTC Singers.
Phi Mu Alpha, Orpheus Award, UTC.
Phi Mu Alpha, Outstanding Teacher Award, UTC.

Dorothy Patten Love of Chattanooga Award, 1989.
Chattanooga Optimist Club, Distinguished Service Award, 1992.
Indiana Wesleyan Univ.(Formerly Marion College), Fine Arts Outstanding Achievement Award, 1993.
State of Tennessee, Chattanooga, Tenn., Distinguished Citizen Award.
UTC, Golden Key Honor Society, 1995.
Andrew Lewis High School, Salem, Virginia, Hall of Fame Award, 1996.
State of Tennessee Senate, Honored for World Wide Success, Music Education/Choral Music, 1998.
UTC, Mortar Board Award, Most Influential Teacher, 2001.
UTC, Glenn W. Draper Endowment Fund, Vocal Music, established by the UTC Foundation, 2002.
Glenn W. and Lounelle Draper Endowment for Music Ministry, Southeastern Jurisdiction of the Methodist Church at Lake Junaluska Assembly, North Carolina, 2003.

PROFESSIONAL AFFILIATIONS

American Choral Directors Association.
Music Educators National Conference.
National Association of Teachers of Singing.
East Tennessee Vocal Association.
Phi Mu Alpha Sinfonia Fraternity.
Rotary Club.

TOURS

KEESLER AIR FORCE BASE MALE CHORUS

1953, 1954, 1955: Tours all over America each year in the contiguous United States.

PFEIFFER COLLEGE

1956: Washington, D.C., and Virginia
1957, 1958, 1959, 1960: New York, Florida, Georgia, South Carolina, North Carolina, and Virginia each year.

UNIVERSITY OF MIAMI

1961: New Orleans; Eight-week tour to Europe sponsored by U.S. Defense Department.
1962: Washington, D.C.
1963: Six-week tour of Greenland, Newfoundland, Iceland, Defense Department. Performed at Radio City Music Hall Fortieth Anniversary Celebration.
1964: Dallas, Texas; Third Army tour; Louisiana, Mississippi, Georgia, and South Carolina.
1965: Eight-week tour to Europe, sponsored by Defense Department.
1966: Eight-week tour to Japan, Korea, Philippines, Okinawa, Iwo Jima. Defense Department sponsored.
1967, 1968: Washington, D.C., Virginia, North Carolina, South Carolina, Georgia, and Florida.

UNIVERSITY OF TENNESSEE, CHATTANOOGA
All are University of Tennessee, Chattanooga singers tours unless designated otherwise; (LJS) Lake Junaluska Singers; (GDS) Glenn Draper Singers.
1969: Alabama tour.
1970: Ten-day tour to Washington, D.C., Tennessee, North Carolina, Virginia; tour to Florida, (LJS).
1971: Eleven-day tour to Texas, Arkansas, Mississippi, Louisiana, Alabama. Nine-week Defense Dept. tour of Europe; tours to Florida and Colorado, (LJS).
1972: Ten-day Florida, Georgia tour; Two-week tour of England—Sang at Royal Albert Hall, London.
1973: Ten-day Florida tour; Mobile, Alabama for Jr. Miss National Pageant. Two-week tour of England (LJS).

1974: Washington, D.C., New Jersey, Delaware, Virginia ten-day tour; Two-week tour, England, Wales; tours to Tennessee and North Carolina, (LJS).

1975: St. Louis, Louisville, Indiana, and Tennessee, ten days.

1976: Tennessee ten days; Russia and Germany, fourteen days.

1977: Washington, D.C., Virginia, Tennessee, New York, ten-day tour.

1978: Ten-day Florida tour; Chattanooga Singers tour to England; Fourteen-day tour to England, (LJS).

1979: Ten-day tour of Texas, Arkansas, Louisiana, Mississippi, Alabama, Tennessee.

1980: Washington, D.C., Delaware, Virginia, Tennessee, ten-day tour.

1981: Ten-day tour of St. Louis, Indiana, Kentucky, Tennessee.

1982: Seventeen-day tour of England; island tours (LJS).

1983: Eleven-day tour of Texas, Arkansas, Mississippi, Alabama, Tennessee. Panama tour (LJS).

1984: Ten-day tour, Tennessee, Georgia, Florida; Twenty-one-day tour of California, Australia, New Zealand. Tour of the Holy Land (LJS).

1985: Seventeen-day tour of England and Wales.

1986: Crystal Cathedral on TV en route to three weeks in Australia (Melbourne Town Hall) and New Zealand. Four days at Carnegie Hall and St. Bartholomew concerts in New York.

1987: Seventeen-day tour to England.

1988: Three weeks to California, Australia, New Zealand, Crystal Cathedral on TV en route. Sydney Opera House performance and performance at World's Fair, Australia. National Prayer Breakfast, the White House, Washington, D.C., (GDS).

1989: Sixteen-day tour of England; White House concert, Washington, D.C., (GDS).

1990: Eleven-day tour of Washington, D.C., Virginia, North Carolina, Tennessee.

1991: Twenty-one-day tour. Sang at Crystal Cathedral in California, en route to New Zealand and Australia. Performed at Sydney Opera House.

1992: Seventeen-day tour of England.

1993: Ten-day tour of Florida, Georgia, Alabama; Christmas concert at White House.

1994: Tour of England for ten days (GDS); Crystal Cathedral en route to three-week tour, Australia, New Zealand.

1995: Ten-day tour of Texas, Oklahoma, Alabama, Louisiana, Mississippi.

1996: Georgia, Florida, Alabama for ten days; Performance at the 1996 Olympics, Atlanta (GDS); Sang at World Methodist Conference, Rio de Janeiro, Brazil, (LJS).

1997: England for two weeks, March (GDS); one week to England at Christmas with 115 singers from UTC and First Presbyterian Church.

1998: Crystal Cathedral en route to three weeks in Australia (GDS).

1999: Ten-day tour of England (GDS).

2000: Three weeks to Korea, Indonesia, Bali, Hawaii (GDS). Sang at Crystal Cathedral en route. Three-day tour of Virginia (GDS).

2001: Washington, D.C., Presidential Prayer Breakfast, January 31–February 2; two-week tour of England (GDS); one-week tour of Georgia, Alabama, Mississippi, Tennessee (LJS); one-week White House Christmas concert tour (GDS).

2002: Three-weeks, Indonesia, Singapore (GDS). White House Christmas concert (GDS).

2003: England, March; Estonia, September; England, December.

RECORDINGS OF LPs, CASSETTES, AND CDs

PFEIFFER COLLEGE

1. PFEIFFER COLLEGE CONCERT CHOIR
   No record co. or number. LP 1960

   "All People That On Earth Do Dwell"
   "Let All The Nations Praise The Lord"
   "Voix Celestus"
   "The Last Words Of David"
   "Jesu, Friend Of Sinners," soloist: Tony Philmon
   "O Thou In Whose Presence"
   God's Trombones, Becky Johnson, Prayer Leader; Joe Parker, Preacher Man
   Introduction
   Opening: A Prayer
   "The Creation"
   "Go Down Death"
   "The Judgement Day"
   Closing: A Prayer
   "Deep River," soloist: Tony Philmon
   "The Lord Bless You And Keep You"
   Accompanist: Martha Dawkins

THE LAKE JUNALUSKA SINGERS

2. HALLELUJAH, AMEN
   Century 25114 LP 1966

   Mary Neill Rogers, organist
   The Lake Junaluska Quartet: Terry Schreckengost, mezzo-soprano; Julie Rohr, soprano;
       George Bizas, tenor; Darrell Alsip, baritone
   "Hallelujah, Amen," The Lake Junaluska Singers
   "O Make Our Hearts to Blossom," The Lake Junaluska Singers
   "When Thou Comest," The Lake Junaluska Singers; Terry Schreckengost, soprano
   "Every Time I Feel The Spirit," The Lake Junaluska Singers; Darrell Alsip, baritone
   "When I Survey The Wondrous Cross," Men's Chorus
   "God of Grace and God Of Glory," The Lake Junaluska Singers
   "Now God Be Praised In Heaven Above," The Lake Junaluska Singers
   "Come, Come Ye Saints," Men's Chorus; George Bitzas, tenor
   "Praise To The Lord, The Almighty," The Lake Junaluska Singers
   "Deep River," The Junaluska Singers; Darrell Alsip, baritone

"*Jesus, The Name High All Over,*" The Lake Junaluska Singers
"*Abide With Me, 'Tis Eventide,*" The Lake Junaluska Singers; George Bitzas, tenor
"*The Lord's Prayer,*" Lake Junaluska Congregation
Bob Davis, recording engineer; Ray Rouser, photographer; Barry Rogers, producer

3. KUM BA YA
Century 28976   LP   1967

Mary Neill Rogers, organist
"*Kum Ba Ya,*" arr. Rackley; soloist: Eddie Rackley, baritone
"*Oh For A Thousand Tongues To Sing,*" Wesley
"*How Great Thou Art,*" Hine; soloist: Clint Nichols, tenor
"*Let Us Break Bread Together,*" arr. Lynn; soloist: Joan Storr, soprano
"*Deep River,*" arr. Shaw; soloist: Darrell Alsip, baritone
"*Lord, Guard And Guide The Men Who Fly,*" Hamilton
"*Eternal Father,*" Whiting; soloist: Darrell Alsip, baritone
"*Battle Hymn of The Republic,*" Howe
"*Holy, Holy, Holy,*" Heber; soloist: Jarvis Nichols, soprano
"*Christian Dost Thou See Them,*" Pfautsch
"*Rock Of Ages,*" Toplady
"*Unto Thee O Lord,*" Auback; soloist: Terry Schrekengost, soprano
"*O Love Divine,*" Wesley; soloist: Clint Nichols, tenor
"*Silent Night,*" Gruber; soloist: Jarvis Nichols, soprano
"*Mary Had A Baby,*" (Folk Song); duet: Anne Peacock, soprano; Genie Peacock, alto
"*Now The Day Is Over,*" Barnby; soloist: Darrell Alsip, baritone
Bob Davis, recording engineer; Jack Bowers, photographer; Barry Rogers, producer

4. SING UNTO GOD
Century 35873   LP   1968

Rick Holley, organist
"*Sing Unto God,*" G. F. Handel
"*How Lovely Is Thy Dwelling Place,*" Johannes Brahams (*Requiem*)
"*Bless The Lord,*" Ippolitoff-Ivanoff
"*Santus,*" Charles Gounod; Douglas Robinson, tenor
"*Canticle Of Praise,*" Theodore Beck
"*Awake The Harp,*" F. J. Haydn (*Creation*)
"*Laudate Dominum,*" W. A. Mozart; Claudia Higgins, soprano
"*The Heavens Are Telling,*" F. J. Haydn (*Creation*)
"*I See His Blood Upon The Rose,*" Roberton
"*Didn't My Lord Deliver Daniel,*" arr. Miller
"*Old Time Religion & Amen,*" arr. Draper
"*Shenandoah,*" arr. Muller; Daryl Alsip, baritone
"*Kentucky Babe,*" arr. Muller
"*Gossip, Gossip,*" Hairston; Frank Calhoun, bass
"*I Will Arise,*" arr. Shaw
"*Who Will Answer,*" arr. Miller; Marty Miller, baritone
"*Edelweiss,*" Rogers-Hammerstein; Nancye Formo, soprano
"*There is a Ship,*" arr. Rackley; Eddie Rackley, baritone
"*Island in the Sun,*" arr. Draper
"*Goin' Away for to Leave You,*" arr. Eaton
Bob Davis, recording engineer; Jack Bowers, photographer; Barry Rogers, producer

5. I'M GOIN' TO SING
    Century 38837   LP   1970

    "I'm Goin' to Sing," arr. Shaw
    "Were You There," American Folk Hymn; Charles Middleton, tenor
    "Ain't That Good News," arr. Dawson
    "Sometimes I Feel Like a Motherless Child," arr. Wagner; Anne Peacock, alto
    "Go Tell It on the Mountain," arr. Work; Nancye Formo, soprano; Charles
        Middleton, tenor
    "Balm in Gilead," arr. Smith; Charles Middleton, tenor
    "Didn't My Lord Deliver Daniel," arr. Miller
    "Old Time Religion & Amen," arr. Draper
    "Shenandoah," arr. Muller; Daryl Alsip, baritone
    "Kentucky Babe," arr. Muller
    "Gossip, Gossip," Hairston; Frankl Calhoun, bass
    "I Will Arise," arr. Shaw
    "Who Will Answer," arr. Miller; Marty Miller, baritone
    "Edelweiss," Rogers-Hammerstein; Nancye Formo, soprano
    "There is a Ship," arr. Rackley; Eddie Rackley, baritone
    "Island in the Sun," arr. Draper
    "Goin' Away for to Leave You," arr. Eaton
    Bob Davis, recording engineer; Jack Bowers, photographer; Barry Rogers,
        producer

6. OH HAPPY DAY
    United Sound USR-3241   LP   1971

    William Christmas, accompanist
    "Oh Happy Day," arr. Hawkins; Charles Middleton, tenor
    "You Can Touch Him," Carmichael
    "He's Everything To Me," Carmichael
    "Mary Had A Baby," arr. Shaw; Nancye Formo, soprano
    "The Lord's My Shepherd"
    "I Will Sing of My Redeemer," Bliss
    "Lonely Voices," Hanks
    "The Savior Is Waiting," arr. Ross
    "Jean," arr. Gannon
    "What the World Needs Now," arr. Gannon
    "Joy is Like the Rain," arr. Formo; Nancye Formo, Susan Martin
    "Jordan River," (Traditional)
    "You Can Tell the World," (Traditional)
    "We Are One in the Spirit," arr. Draper
    "Redeemed," arr. Eaton: Frank Calhoun, bass
    "O The Games People Play," arr. Gannon
    "Let The Sunshine In," arr. Metis
    "One of These Days," Carmichael
    Earl Justice, recording engineer; Jack Bowers, cover photo; Waylon Cooke, producer

7. TEACH THE WORLD TO SING
    Century 40972   LP   1972

    William Christmas, accompanist
    "Teach the World to Sing," arr. Draper

"What the World Needs Now," arr. Cannon
"We Need More Love," Skillings
"Put Your Hand in the Hand," arr. Draper; Nancye Formo, soprano
"Don't Be Afraid to Love," Carpenter; Nancye Formo, Susan Martin, Carlene Kessel
"I Wish you Love," arr. Jenkins
"There's a New World Comin'," arr. Eaton
"Ain't Gonna Study War No More," arr. Lubboff; Susan Martin, soprano
"Personality Medley," arr. Draper
"Come, Let us Sing of His Glory," Young
"Come Thou Fount of Every Blessing," arr. Pfautsch
"Is There Something Missing?" Carmichael
"Living Circle," Carmichael
"He Touched Me," arr. Draper; Victor Bilanchone, baritone
"I Don't Know How to Love Him," arr. Slater; Nancye Formo, soprano
"I Looked for Love," Carmichael
"Pass It On," arr. Draper
Singers: Brenda Arthur, Victor Bilanchone, Frank Calhoun, Jim Chitwood, Lounelle
    Draper, Gerald Floyd, Nancye Formo, Johnny Fowler, Linda Havens, Carlene Kessel,
    Susan Martin, Charles Middleton, Betty Lou Stroud
William Christmas, accompanist; Sam Allison, electric bass; Robert Allison, drums
Earl Justice, recording engineer; Ray Rouser, photographer; Waylon Cooke, producer

8. HYMNS
   Century 41920   LP   1973

   William Christmas, organist
   "God of Grace and God of Glory"
   "This is My Father's World"
   "Come Ye That Love the Lord"
   "Abide With Me"
   "Praise, My Soul, The King of Heaven"
   "How Can A Sinner Know"
   "Come, Thou Almighty King"
   "Fairest Lord Jesus"
   "Majestic Sweetness Sits Enthroned"
   "'Tis Midnight, And On Olive's Brow"
   "Battle Hymn of the Republic"
   "Rise Up, O Men of God"
   "When I Survey The Wondrous Cross"
   "He's Got The Whole World In His Hands"
   "Were You There"
   "At The Cross"
   "Turn Your Eyes Upon Jesus"
   "Fare You Well"

9. MERRY CHRISTMAS FROM THE LAKE JUNALUSKA SINGERS
    Davis Sound RSR-64 LP 1974

    William Christmas, accompanist
    "Good Christian Men Rejoice"
    "Silent Night, Holy Night"
    "Pat-a-pan"
    "O Come All Ye Faithful"

"O Sanctissima"
"Joy To The World"
"Come, Thou Long Expected Jesus"
"Angels We Have Heard on High"
"Hark, The Herald Angels Sing"
"Winter Wonderland"
"The Christmas Song"
"Carol of the Bells"
"Fum Fum Fum"
"March of the Kings"
"The Drummer Boy"
"Coventry Carol"
"What Child is This," soloist: Nancye Formo
"He Came Here For Me"
"In the Bleak Midwinter"
"Glory To God in the Highest"

Singers: Lounelle Draper, Nancye Formo, Linda Havens, Brenda Lundy, Barbara Crowder, Margaret Leatherman, Lynne McNeill, Betty Lou Stroud, Gerald Floyd, Charles Middleton, Ted Smith, Daryl Alsip, Frank Calhoun, Stan DeJarnette, Melvin Foster

Stan DeJarnette, guitar, trumpet; Betty Carol Zinavage, flute, bells; Nancye Formo, guitar

Earl Justice, recording engineer; Frank Arnette, photographer

10. GET ALL EXCITED
Davis Sound RSR-64   LP   1975

William E. Christmas, organ, piano, bass synthesizer
"Let's Just Praise the Lord"
"This Little Light of Mine"
"Reach Out and Touch"
"Day By Day"
"People to People"
"Something Beautiful"
"Let's Just Praise the Lord"
"Get All Excited," soloist: Ted Smith
"Lord We Praise Thee"
"Alleluia"
"Because He Lives"
"King of Kings"
"Sweet, Sweet Spirit"
"I'd Rather Have Jesus"
"In Remembrance"
"And Can It Be"
"Song of Mary"
"Come, Come Ye Saints"

Singers: Vic Bilanchone, Melvin Foster, Al Jeter, Gerald Floyd, Charles Middleton, Ted Smith, Jan Ahlstrum, Nancye Formo, Clare Nesmith, Margaret Leatherman, Lynne McNeill, Mindy Snyder

George Shaw, acoustic guitar, bass synthesizer; John Wilhelm, drums; Reginald Cooke, guitar; Clare Nesmith, flute

Earl Justice, recording engineer; Bob Davis, remixing and dubbing at Davis Sound Studios; Michael Jones, photographer

11. HYMNS, SONGS, AND ANTHEMS OF OUR GREAT COUNTRY
    Davis Sound   LP   1976

    William Christmas, organist/pianist
    "America the Beautiful"
    "Strawberry Patch"
    "Shenandoah"
    Medley: "Time in a Bottle"
    "Lady, Sweet Lady"
    "Do Not I Love Thee"
    "When I Can Read My Title Clear"
    "O Happy Day"
    "Lift Your Voice"
    "Come Together"
    "Amazing Grace"
    "Freely, Freely"
    "Hallelujah His Blood"
    "The Beatitudes"
    "God Be With You"
    Singers: Margaret Butler, Gerald Floyd, Al Jeter, Nancye Formo, Karen
        King, Clare Nesmith, Phyllis Mayo,Charles Middleton, Sara Smith,
        Craig Wahlgren, Ron Whittemore, Tom Wilcox
    Stan Jacques, acoustic guitar; Mike McDow, drums; Jamie Hoover,
        bass guitar
    John Murphy, cover picture;   Mark Williams, Bob Davis, sound
        engineers; Dr. Edgar H. Nease Jr., executive producer

12. CHRIST TRIUMPHANT
    Davis Sound RSR-683 LP, 8-Tk Cass. 1977

    William Christmas, organist/pianist; Kathy McNeil, organist
    "Christ The Lord Is Risen Today," soloist: Cindy Morris
    Praise The Lord Medley
    "Jesus Loves Me," soloist: Nancye Formo
    "Come Holy Spirit"
    "It Is Finished"
    "Victory In Jesus"
    "Greater Is He," duet: Doris Knisley, Ron Whittemore
    "Jesus, We Just Want To Thank You"
    "Come Ye Sinners Poor And Needy"
    "Joy In The Morning"
    "If My People"
    "It Is Well With My Soul"
    "A Parting Blessing"
    Singers: Jeff Clark, Gerald Floyd, Nancye Formo, Al Jeter, Karen
        King, Doris Knisley, Cindy Morris, Clare Nesmith, Sara Smith,
        Ted Smith, Ron Whittemore
    Earl Justice, recording engineer; John A. Murphy, cover and back montage photographer

13. THE UNCLOUDED DAY
    Performing Arts KM-5068   LP, Cassette   1979

    "A Closer Walk With Thee," soloist: Cindy Morris
    "Precious Lord, Take My Hand," soloist: Doris Moreland

Medley of Spirituals: Lisa Harper, Laurie Harper, Al Miller, Tim Wilds, Randy
  Johnson
"I Am Bound For The Promised Land"
"I Will Arise and Go To Jesus"
"The Unclouded Day," soloist: Sara Smith
"Alas and Did My Savior Bleed"
"Spirit of the Living God"
"O God Our Help in Ages Past"
"What A Friend We Have in Jesus"
"Savior Like A Shepherd Lead Us"
"Amazing Grace," soloist: Sara Smith
"I Need Thee Every Hour"
"There is a Balm in Gilead," soloist: Charles Middleton
"Praise God From Whom All Blessings Flow"
Singers: Laurie Harper, Carol Mitchem, Sara Smith, Lisa Harper, Doris Moreland,
  Cindy Morris, Craig Collins, Randy Johnson, Al Miller, Tim Wilds, Ron
  Whittemore, Randy Walker
Guest Singers: Nancye Formo, Jeff Price, David Baker
Marty Hamby, piano; Dr. Albin Whitworth, organ; Perky Gunter, drums; Kenny
  Corn, bass; Kent Holmes, guitar
Earl Justice, sound engineer; Dr. Mel Harbin, producer

14. AMERICA IS
(No Co. or #) LP, Cassette   1981

"Southern Hospitality," Lisa Harper, Laurie Harper, Al Miller, Tim Wilds
"America Is"
"All The Gold," Bucky Grant
"Ole Man River," Bill Dixon
"When I Fall In Love," Laura Lonas
"This Land Is Your Land," Wesley Gilliland, Davis Chappell, Kay Holder
"Celebrate America," Ron Whittemore
*"Alive To Be His Witnesses," Recorded at Memorial Chapel, Lake Junaluska
*"I Live," Ron Whittemore, Recorded at Memorial Chapel, Lake Junaluska
"O How He Loves You And Me," Ron Whittemore
"On Yonder Cross"
"Surely The Presence Of The Lord Is In This Place"
"He's Got The Whole World In His Hand," Sara Smith, Ron Whittemore, Cheryl Harris,
  Tim Wilds, Al Miller
"American Hymns: When We All Get To Heaven"
"Bye And Bye"
"Revive Us Again"
"Rise Up O Men Of God"
"All Hail The Power Of Jesus Name"
Loonis McGlohon, Michael Johnson, piano; Doug Burns, drums; Bill Stowe,
  percussion
Steve Hagler, sound engineer; Dr. Mel Harbin, Loonis McGlohon, producers
Singers: Laurie Harper, Lisa Harper, Laura Lonas, Cheryl Harris, Sara Smith, Kay
  Holder, Davis Chappell, Bill Dixon, Wesley Gilliland, Ron Whittemore, Bucky
  Grant, Tim Wilds, Al Miller
William Christmas, accompanist; Sam Allison, electric bass; Robert Allison, drums
Earl Justice, recording engineer; Ray Rouser, photographer; Waylon Cooke,
  producer

15. PRECIOUS LORD
    Martin Productions (No #)   Cassette   1984

    "Holy Lord God"
    "Precious Lord"
    "Here's One"
    "This Is My Father's World"
    "Treasures In Heaven"
    "It Is Well With My Soul"
    "Alleluia Sing To Jesus"
    "You Are There"
    "Kum Ba Ya"
    "Jesus Loves Me"
    "All My Trials"
    "Soon And Very Soon"
    "Fare You Well"
    J. Alton Murphy, photographer; Mel Harbin, producer

16. CHRISTMAS WITH THE LAKE JUNALUSKA SINGERS
    Martin Productions (No #) Cassette   1984

    "The Heavens Sing Hallelujah"
    "This Little Child"
    "Coventry Carol"
    "He Came Here For Me"
    "In The Bleak Midwinter"
    "Silent Night"
    "We Are The Reason"
    "Joy To The World"
    "Hallelujah"
    "Jingle Bells"
    "Winter Wonderland"
    "The Christmas Song"
    "Pat-A-Pan"
    "The Little Drummer Boy"
    "Carol Of The Bells"
    "Santa Claus Is Coming To Town"
    "O Come All Ye Faithful"
    "The First Noel"
    "It Came Upon The Midnight Clear"
    "While Shepherds Watched Their Flocks"
    "Hark The Heralds Angels Sing"
    "Joy To The World"
    J. Alton Murphy, photographer; Mel Harbin, producer

17. BECAUSE OF EASTER
    Martin Productions MPCS-1006 Cassette   1985

    "Come Praise The Lord With Me"
    "At The Cross"
    "Were You There"
    "There's Life In Jesus' Name," soloist: Tim Fudge
    "Christ The Lord Is Risen Today," soloist: Gloria Parvin

"I Live"
"Hosanna," soloists: Camilla Shelton, Wade Rogers, Beth Borders, Wesley Gilliand
"O Love Divine," soloist: Beth Borders
"Jesu, Word Of God Incarnate"
"'Tis Midnight, And On Olive's Brow"
"Majestic Sweetness Sits Enthroned," soloist: Michael Adair
"We Are The Reason," duet: Laurie Harper, Lisa Harper
"We Shall Behold Him," soloist: Jennifer Trent
J. Alton Murphy, photographer; Mel Harbin, producer

18. GREAT IS THY FAITHFULNESS
Martin Productions MPCS-1009 Cassette 1986

"O Magnify the Lord"
"The Majesty and Glory of Thy Name"
"The Vesper Hymn"
"To Thy Heavenly Banquet"
"Ubi Caritas"
"Great Is Thy Faithfulness," soloist: Tim Fudge
"He Is The King"
"Count Me In," soloist: Ron Whittemore
"Everything's All Right," soloists: Michael Adair, Lisa Harper, Tim Fudge
"We Shall See Him As He Is," soloist: Jennifer Morrell
"More Than Wonderful," soloists: Gloria Parvin, Tim Fudge
"My Jesus I Love Thee," soloist: Gloria Parvin
Singers: Jennifer Morrell, Camilla Shelton, Laurie Harper, Lisa Harper, Gloria Parvin,
    Joy Williams, Tim Fudge, Wade Rogers, Wes Gilliland, Ron Whittemore, Michael
    Adair, Bill Dixon.
Brad Gee, accompanist; Buddy Chatten, Matt Huesman, percussion

19. GLENN AND THE MEN OF THE LAKE JUNALUSKA SINGERS
MasterSound MS-1707 Cassette 1986

Marty Hamby, keyboards
"Ghost Riders In The Sky"
"Colorado Trail"
"Amici"
"Brothers, Sing On"
"Down In The Valley"
"The Old Ark's A Movin'"
"O Love Divine"
"O Bone Jesu"
"Precious Lord"
"We Shall Walk Through The Valley In Peace"
"The Twenty-Third Psalm"
"Light At The End Of The Darkness"
Singers: tenor: Tim Fudge, Wes Gilliland, Wade Rogers, Greg Shockley, Jeff Stith; bass:
    Michael Adair, Bill Dixon, Alan Miller, Steve Roads, Ron Whittemore

20. THE MORNING TRUMPET
MasterSound MS-1711 Cassette 1987

"Bless The Lord"
"Look Down O Lord"

"Ubi Caritas"
"Christ We Do All Adore Thee"
"Glory To God In The Highest"
"Salvation Belongeth To Our God"
"Slumber Now, Beloved Child"
"Let All The Nations"
"Have Ye Not Known—Ye Shall Have A Song"
"The Morning Trumpet," soloist: Mark Tilley
"Come Ye That Love The Lord/Shout On"
"When I Can Read My Title Clear"
"Do Not I Love Thee"
"Beautiful River," soloist: Brian Stratton,
Medley of Spirituals
Singers: soprano: Molly Bennett, Joy Gayler, Jennifer Trent, Kaye Walton; alto: Tamula Browning, Becca McLemore, Gloria Parvin, Julie White; tenor: Andre Ashley, Alan Miller, Greg Shockley, Bryan Stratton; bass: Bill Dixon, Tony Offerle, Steven Roads, Chris Stegall
Jim Deal, recording engineer
℗1987 by Glenn Draper & The Junaluska Singers, P.O. Box 67, Lake Junaluska, NC

21. THE SOUND OF MUSIC
MasterSound MS-1712   Cassette   1987

Marty Hamby, keyboards & sequencer programming
"When I Fall In Love," soloist: Molly Bennett
"Sleep Baby Sleep"
"O Danny Boy," soloist: Brian Stratton
"Halls Of Ivy"
"Lil' Liz I Love You"
"Climb Every Mountain"
"Ole Man River," soloist: Bill Dixon
"God Bless The USA"
"National Anthem"
"I Go To The Rock," soloist: Jeff Stith
"Shine Down"
"No Other Name," soloist: Al Miller
"In The Name Of The Lord," soloist: Jennifer Trent
"O For A Thousand Tongues"
"In The Shadow Of Your Wings," soloist: Gloria Parvin
"The Majesty And Glory Of Thy Name"
Singers: soprano: Molly Bennett, Joy Gayler, Jennifer Trent, Kaye Walton; alto: Tamula Browning, Becca McLemore, Gloria Parvin, Julie White; tenor: Andre Ashley, Alan Miller, Greg Shockley, Brian Stratton; bass: Bill Dixon, Tony Offerle, Steven Roads, Chris Stegall
Jim Deal, engineer; Ron Whittemore, production assistance
Recorded by Mastersound, Inc.
℗ 1987 by Glenn Draper & The Junaluska Singers

22. GLORIOUS IS THY NAME
MasterSound MS-1722   Cassette   1990

Accompanists: Marty Hamby, keyboards; Brad Gee, organ
"Glorious Is Thy Name," W. A. Mozart

"The Eyes Of All," Berger
"Holy Radiant Light," Grechaniwov
"Ubi Caritas," Duruflé
"O Bone Jesu," Palestrina
"Look Down O Lord," Byrd
"Twenty-third Psalm," Newman
"O Man Thy Grief And Sin," Williams
"Hallelujah from Mt. of Olives," Beethoven
"Witness," (Traditional)
"De Animals a-Comin'," (Traditional)
"Every Time I Feel The Spirit," (Traditional); soloist: Bill Dixon
"Rock-a-My Soul," (Traditional); soloists: Jeff Stith, Andre Ashley
"Sweet, Sweet Spirit," Akers
"Make Me An Instrument," Medema
"Fairest Lord Jesus," (Traditional); soloist: Mark Tilley
"My Jesus I Love Thee," Featherstone/Gordon; soloist: Mark Tilley
"Nearer My God To Thee," Adams/Mason
"When I Survey," Watts/Mason; acc. by Brad Gee, organ
Jim Deal, recording engineer; Bill Spake, photographer; Jerry DeCeglio, art direction
®© 1990 by Lake Junaluska Assembly

23. MERRY CHRISTMAS
MasterSound MS-1723   Cassette   1990

"In The Bleak Midwinter"
"Lo, How A Rose E'er Blooming"
"And The Glory Of The Lord"
"Heavenly Light"
"Candlelight Carol"
"Slumber Now"
"Ave Maria"
"For Unto Us A Child Is Born," Handel (*Messiah*)
"Hallelujah," Handel (*Messiah*)
"O Tannenbaum"
"Carol Of The Bells"
Winter Medley
"Mary's Boy Child"
Medley
"I Sing Of A Maiden"
"Coventry Carol"
"Silent Night"
Jim Deal, recording engineer; Bill Spake, photographer; Jerry DeCeglio, graphics
®© 1990 by Lake Junaluska Assembly

24. JOY IN THE MORNING
MasterSound MS-1735   Cassette   1992

"Then Will The Very Rocks Cry Out"
"Great Is Thy Faithfulness"
Medley: "Old Rugged Cross," soloist: Laura Scott, soprano
"Jesus Died On Calvary's Mountain," soloist: Tim Little, baritone
"Via Dolorosa," soloist: Kim Roads, soprano
Medley: *"Les Miserables"* soloists: Kim Roads, soprano; Chrissy Floyd, alto; Jay Craig,

tenor; Chris O'Rear, bass; Melody Kvalvik, soprano; Dee Dee Hook, soprano; Jim
Brogan, tenor; Tim Little, baritone; Kelly Luther, alto; Julie Povall, alto; Sissy
Mallard, alto
"Joy In The Morning"
"Battle Hymn Of The Republic"
®© 1992 by Lake Junaluska Assembly

25. UPON THIS ROCK
MasterSound-1743CD   CD, Cassette   1994

Kim Cargile, Sandra Robbins, keyboards
"A Mighty Fortress/Upon This Rock," arr. by John Ness Beck; © 1967 by G. Schirmer, Inc.
"Majesty/He Is Lord/Great Is The Lord," by Jack Hayford; arr. Bill George. ©1981,1982
   Rocksmith Music. +Trad., arr. David Clydesdale. ©1987 Royal Tapestry
   Music/ASCAP. by Michael W. Smith and Deborah D. Smith, ©1982 Meadowgreen
   Music Co.
"I Can See," by Gloria Gaither and David Meece, arr: Gary Rhodes.©1985 Gaither Music
   Co./ASCAP & Meece Music (Admin. by WORD Music).
"In This Very Room," by Ron and Carol Harris. © 1979 Ron Hams Music. ASCAP.
"Freely, Freely," by Carol Owens. ©1972 Communique Music, c/o Spectra Copyright
   Mgmt., Inc.
"He Has The Power," from The Mass of St. Augustine by Leon Roberts. © G.I.A.
   Publications, Inc.
"I Bowed On My Knees And Cried Holy," arr: Larry Goss ©1990 WORD, Inc.; soloist: Jay Craig
"Lord, Listen To Your Children Praying," by Ken Medema; arr: Jack Schrader. ©1973 &
   1983 by Hope Publishing Co.; soloist: Stacie Caraway
"Almighty Medley," arr. John E. Coates, © 1990 Material Music/ASCAP and Word Music.
   Almighty by Wayne Watson; Immortal, Invisible arr. ©1991 by John T. Benson Pub.
   Co./ASCAP. Holy, Holy, Holy arr. © 1991 by John T. Benson Pub. Co.
"I Will Call Upon The Lord," by Michael O'Shields, arr: Gary Rhodes. ©1981 & arr.
   ©1991 Sound III, Inc.
"Glorify Thy Name/I Love You Lord+/Holy, Holy, Holy"* (Sanctus) *by Donna Adkins.
   ©1986 by Maranatha! Music. by Laurie Klein, arr. by Eugene Thomas. ©1978,
   1980 by House of Mercy, by Franz Schubert.
"Jesus Paid It All," by E. Hall and J. Grape, arr. Robert Sterling ASCAP. © 1985 Harold
   Flammer Music, Div. of Shawnee Press, Inc.
"At The Cross," by Watts/Hudson, arr. Ronn Huff. ©1972 by Dimension Music.
"Just As I Am," arr. Lee Holdridge, ©1981 Birdwing Music/Cherry Lane Music Co.
"Joyful, Joyful We Adore Thee," by Beethoven, arr. David Clydesdale. © 1990 Royal
   Tapestry Music/ASCAP; Div. of Diadem, Inc.
Jim Deal, recording engineer; Bill Spake, photographer; special thanks to Mr. Dan
   Miller, organist on "Jesus Paid It All" and "Upon This Rock." Organ recorded at
   Calvary Church, Charlotte, N.C.
A Production of Lake Junaluska Assembly. Produced & Copyright 1994. All Rights
   Reserved.

26. WE BELIEVE
MasterSound 1752CD   CD, Cassette   1996

Kim Cargile, keyboards
"God So Loved The World," Stainer
"I'm Goin' Up," McDonald; soloists: John Dominick, Allison Redmon
"Spirit Of The Living God," (Traditional)

"Grace," arr. Hayes

"Lord Make Me An Instrument," arr. Hayes

"O Happy Day," Hawkins; soloist: Charles Middleton

"I Believe," arr. Ades; soloists: Allison Redmon, Tim Little

"We Believe," arr. Hayes

"Amazing Grace," (Traditional); soloist: Rachel Heer

"O Divine Redeemer," Gounod; arr. Cain

"My Eternal King," Marshall; Dan Miller, organist

"Mary, Did You Know?" arr. Fettke; soloist: Allison Redmon

"As Lately We Watched," arr. Black; soloist: Karen Byrd Sweett

"Sweet Little Jesus Boy," (Spiritual); soloist: Chrissi Floyd

"Go Tell It On The Mountain," arr. Rutter; soloists: John Dominick, Tim Little, Courtney
  Williams, Dee Dee Brogan, Jim Brogan, Karen Byrd Sweett, Michael Smith

Singers: soprano: Rachel Heer, Kim Sanders, Dee Dee Brogan, Kimberly Sweet; alto:
  Karen Byrd Sweett, Chriscynthia Floyd, Allison Redmon, Cammie Rowe; tenor: Jay
  Craig, Jim Brogan, Jerod Kirby, Chris Riggins; bass: Tim Little, John Dominick,
  Michael Smith, Courtney Williams

Jim Deal, recording engineer; Bill Spake, photographer

Produced and Copyright 1996, Lake Junaluska Assembly

27. SHINE ON US
SoundResources CD-SR-001   CD, Cassette   1998

Kim Cargile, keyboards

"The First Noel," arr. Kirkland

"No Eye Had Seen," arr. Krogstad

"I Have Seen the Light," Sterling; trio: Jim Brogan, Jay Craig, Michael Mays

Medley: *"In the Bleak Mid-Winter,"* arr. Rouse

"All Is Well," arr. Huff, soloist: Rachel Heer

"Hark, the Herald Angels Sing," adapted by Hamby; soloist: Michael Mays

"And Can It Be?" arr. Linn; soloist: Mark Tilley

"O For A Thousand Tongues to Sing," arr. Coates

"How Great Thou Art," Hine; soloist: Gretchen Striebeck

"Shine on Us," Glenn & the Men

"Spirit Song," arr. Wimmer; soloists: Misty Williamson, Mark Tilley

"Light at the End of the Darkness," arr. Dixon; soloist: K. C. Armstrong

"Ole Man River," Kern, soloist: John Dominick

Jim Deal, recording; Steve Babb, Fred Schendel, engineers

Charles Ellsworth, Michael Roach, Dot Carter, jacket design and production

© 1998 Glenn Draper. All rights reserved.

28. THROUGH THE YEARS WITH THE JUNALUSKA SINGERS
Jon-A-Lou Records #2063   CD   2001

Kim Cargile, Marty Hamby, Bill Christmas, keyboards

"Come To The Water"*

"Oh, For A Thousand Tongues To Sing"

"Oh, Happy Day," soloist: Charles Middleton

"Greater Is He," soloists: Doris Knisley, Ron Whittemore

"In the Shadow of Your Wings," soloist: Gloria Parvin

"I Bowed On My Knees and Cried Holy," soloist: Jay Craig

"All Rise," soloist: Al Miller

"In the Name of the Lord," soloist: Jennifer Trent

"I Have Seen the Light," trio: Jim Brogan, Jay Craig, Michael Mays
"The Morning Trumpet," soloist: Mark Tilley
"We Shall Walk Through the Valley in Peace"
"The Twenty-Third Psalm"
"Beautiful River," soloist: Bryan Stratton
"My Eternal King"
"The Majesty and Glory of Your Name"
"Precious Lord"
"And Can It Be," soloist: Mark Tilley
J. Alton Murphy; cover photo; Bill Spake, other photos
Bob Davis, Jim Deal, Junaluska Singers recording engineers
J. Alton Murphy, audio restorations
A Production of Lake Junaluska Assembly, Compiled and Copyright © 2001
*The Glenn Draper Singers—Recorded By Sound Resources

29. THE HILLS ARE ALIVE
    Jon-A-Lou Records #2064   CD   2002

    Marty Hamby, Brad Gee, Kim Cargile, keyboards
    "The Sound Of Music"
    "Then Will The Very Rocks Cry Out"
    "Glorious Is Thy Name," W. A. Mozart
    "Come To The Water" *
    "Surely The Presence Of The Lord Is In This Place"
    "Salvation Belongeth To Our God"
    "O Bone Jesu," Palestrina
    "Slumber Now, Beloved Child"
    "We Are The Reason," duet: Laurie Harper, Lisa Harper
    "The Eyes Of All," Berger
    "Rock-A-My Soul," soloists: Jeff Stith, Andre Ashley
    "Every Time I Feel The Spirit," soloist: Bill Dixon
    "I Go To The Rock," soloist: Jeff Stith
    "God Bless The USA"
    "Battle Hymn Of The Republic"
    * Recorded Live in Performance at Stuart Auditorium, Lake Junaluska, N.C.
    Kim Cargile, musical assistant to the director
    Jim Deal, Bob Davis, Steve Babb, recording engineers
    J. Alton Murphy, cover photo and audio restorations
    A Production of Lake Junaluska Assembly, Compiled and Copyright © 2002
    A Re-Release of Archived Junaluska Singers Recordings in First CD Publication

THE GLENN DRAPER SINGERS

30. JESUS, OUR SAVIOR
    Sound Resources (No #)   CD

    Kim Cargile, accompanist
    "Holy Truth, Truth Divine," arr. Flemming
    "What A Friend We Have in Jesus," (Traditional); soloists: Jim Brogan, Rachel Heer, Dan
       Fogle
    "How Tedious And Tasteless The Hours," (Traditional); soloist: Jennifer Odom
    "Jesus, Lover Of My Soul," Wesley
    "Amazing Grace," Medley arr. Draper; soloist: Steven Abernathy

"How Great Thou Art," (Old Swedish Folk Melody); soloist: Gretchen Striebeck
"A Mighty Fortress Is Our God," Luther
"And Can It Be?" Wesley; soloist: Mark Tilley
"Ye Shall Have A Song," Thompson (*A Peaceable Kingdom*)
"O Make Our Hearts To Blossom," Clokey
"Once To Every Man And Nation," York
"Jesus Died On Calvary's Mountain," arr. Parker; soloist: Dan Fogle
"O Love Divine," Wesley
"'Tis Midnight, And On Olive's Brow," Bradbury, soloist: Mark Tilley
"We Will Overcome," Cymbala; soloists: Gretchen Striebeck, Jim Brogan
"The Lord Bless You And Keep You," Lurkin

Singers: soprano: Dee Dee Brogan, Rachel Heer, Jennifer Odom, Gretchen Striebeck,
    Jennifer Trent; alto: Chara Ashworth, Stacie Caraway Coder, Gloria Parvin, Kelly
    Luther Stultz, Misty Williamson; tenor: Steven Abernathy, Jim Brogan, Jay Craig,
    Thomas Hammett, Michael Mays; baritone: Dan Fogle, Mark Tilley; bass: K.C.
    Armstrong, Bill Dixon, John Dominick
Jim Deal, recording engineer; mixed and mastered by Steve Babb at Sound
    Resources; Sound Resources and Dot Carter, jacket production and design

31. HEAVENLY LIGHT
    MasterSound   MS-1725   CD   1990

"Glorious Is Thy Name"
"The Eyes of All"
"Heavenly Light"
"Song of Simeon"
"Lo, How a Rose E'er Blooming"
"Fairest Lord Jesus"
"The Lord's Prayer"
"Hallelujah Chorus"
"I Go to the Rock"
"Sweet, Sweet Spirit"
"Witness"
"Nearer My God to Thee"
"Now the Day Is Over"
"Navy Hymn"
"Battle Hymn"
"The Star Spangled Banner"

Singers: soprano: Kim Bramlett, Jennifer Trent, Laura Scott, Meth Malmede; alto:
    Karen Fairchild, Julie Kyker, Erline Spiller, Gloria Parvin, Becca McLemore; tenor:
    Jeff Stith, Tim Fudge, Todd Gaither, Al Miller, Brian Stratton; bass: Ron
    Whittemore, Mark Tilley, Jim Brogan, Bill Dixon, Steve Roads
Jim Deal, recording engineer; Jerry DeCeglio, art direction

32. GLENN AND THE MEN
    MasterSound   MS-1725(on CD)1726(on cover)   CD   1990

"Lone Prairie"
"Ghost Riders In The Sky"
"Whoopie Ti Yi Yo"
"Halls Of Ivy"
"De Animals A'Comin' "
"Come, Thou Holy Spirit"

"Salvation Belongeth To Our God"
"Divine Praise"
"My Jesus I Love Thee"
"Holy, Holy, Holy"
"The Navy Hymn"
"Rise Up, O Men Of God"
Singers: tenor: Jeff Stith, Tim Fudge, Todd Gaither, Al Miller, Bryan Stratton; baritone: Ron Whittemore, Mark Tilley, Jim Brogan; bass: Bill Dixon, Steve Roads
Recorded at the First Presbyterian Church, Chattanooga, Tenn.
Jim Deal, recording engineer; Jerry DeCeglio, art direction; Marty Hamby, co-producer

33. CHRISTMAS WITH THE GLENN DRAPER SINGERS
MasterSound C-1728   Cassette   1990

"Adeste Fideles"
"Wonderful Name"
"I Sing Of A Maiden"
"Ave Maria"
"For Unto Us A Child Is Born"
"Coventry Carol"
"What Child Is This"
"Silent Night"
"Hallelujah Chorus"
"White Christmas," Kim Bramlett, soprano
"Still, Still, Still"
"The Christmas Song"
"Ding Dong Merrily On High"
"Pat-A-Pan"
"Good King Wencesles"
"I Saw Three Ships"
"Deck The Halls"
"Carol Of The Bells"
"O Tannenbaum," Bryan Stratton, Andre Ashley, tenors
"Mary Had A Baby," Tim Fudge, tenor
"March Of The Kings"
"The Boars Head Carol"
"We Wish You A Merry Christmas"
Jim Deal, recording engineer; Jerry DeCeglio, art direction

34. THE GOSPEL TRUTH
Sound Resources SR-1759   CD

Kim Cargile, keyboard
"I Love You Lord," Medley arr. Draper, soloists: Jim Brogan, Dee Dee Brogan, Dan Fogle, Gloria Parvin
"Just A Closer Walk With Thee," arr. Kerr
"Step Into The Water," arr. Linn
"Down On My Knees," arr. Linn
"Peace In The Valley," arr. Hamby, soloist: Jay Craig
"Light At The End Of The Darkness," arr. Dixon, soloist: K.C. Armstrong
"Shine On Us," arr. Draper
"Spirit Song," Wimber, soloists: Mark Tilley, Misty Williamson

"My God Is Real," arr. Linn, soloist: Stacie Caraway Coder
"This Lonesome Valley," Besig
"Witness," arr. Halloran
Medley Of Spirituals, arr. Draper; soloists: Andre Ashley, Al Miller, Jennifer Trent, Bryan Stratton, Gloria Parvin
Singers: soprano: Dee Dee Brogan, Rachel Heer, Jennifer Odom, Gretchen Striebeck, Jennifer Trent; alto: Chara Ashworth, Stacie Caraway Coder, Kelly Luther, Sara Beth Nordmoe, Gloria Parvin, Allison Redmon; tenor: Steven Abernathy, Andre Ashley, Jim Brogan, Jay Craig, Thomas Hammett, Michael Mays, Al Miller, Bryan Stratton; bass: K.C. Armstrong, Bill Dixon, John Dominick, Dan Fogle, Michael Smith, Mark Tilley
Jim Deal, recording engineer; mixed and mastered by Steve Babb; Michael Roach, photographer; Dot Carter, Steve Babb, typesetting; Digital Express, graphics

35. HYMNS & MORE
MasterSound D-1739   CD   1993

"Come Thou Fount," arr. Winch; soloist: Kim Roads
"Precious Lord," arr. Severier
"O God Our Help In Ages Past," arr. Red
"Fairest Lord Jesus," arr. Mann; soloist: Mark Tilley
"Come, We That Love The Lord," (Traditional)
"In The Garden," (Traditional); soloist: Al Miller
Promised Land Medley, arr. Draper; soloists: Tim Little, Dee Dee Hook
    Daniel Shorb, keyboard
"The Morning Trumpet," arr. Richardson; soloist: Mark Tilley
"Jesus Paid It All," arr. Sterling; Kim Cargile, keyboard; Dan Miller, organist
"It Is Well," arr. Krogstad; soloist: Tim Little
"Joyful, Joyful, We Adore Thee," arr. Clydesdale
"Great Is Thy Faithfulness," arr. Sjolund
"O Thou In Whose Presence," arr. Cain
"I Will Praise Him," (Traditional)
"Father, We Love You / I Love You, Lord," (Traditional)
"Take My Hand," arr. Ringwald
"Motherless Child," arr. Wagner; soloist: Chrissi Floyd
"Abide With Me," arr. Draper; soloist: Al Miller
"Beautiful River," arr. Rutter; soloist: Kelly Luther; organist: Daniel Miller
"His Truth Is Marching On," arr. Krogstad
Jim Deal, recording engineer; Marty Schoocraft, Samuel "Pete" Hunter, Robert Faulkner, jacket production/design

36. THE CLASSICS
MasterSound D-1740   CD   1993

"The Heavens Are Telling," Hayden; Jennifer Lyons, soprano; Tim Fudge; William Dixon, bass
"He Watching Over Israel," Mendelssohn
"Alleluia," Thompson
"The Majesty And Glory Of Your Name," Fettke
"Ubi Caritas," Durufle'
"The Eyes Of All," Berger
"Look Down, O Lord," Byrd
"Hallelujah," Beethoven (*Mount of Olives*)

"Come Thou Holy Spirit," (The Men) Tschesnokoff
"Bless The Lord, O My Soul," Ippolitof-Ivanoff
"Heavenly Light," Kopylow
"Holy, Holy, Holy," Schubert *(Sanctus)*
"Wonderful Peace," Nordqvist
"Adoramus Te," Palestrina
"Christ, We Do All Adore Thee," arr. Farnsworth
"I Wonder As I Wander," (Traditional); soloist: Melodie Kvalvik
"O Man, Thy Grief and Sin Bemoan," Williams
"Fierce Was The Wild Billow," Noble
"Abide With Me," arr. Draper, soloist: Al Miller
"Gaelic Blessing," Rutter
Jim Deal, recording engineer; Marty Schoocraft, Samuel "Pete" Hunter, Robert
    Faulkner, jacket production/design

37. Give God the Glory
MasterSound D-1741   CD   1994

"I Will Call Upon The Lord"
"Give God The Glory," soloist: Jay Craig
"At The Name Of Jesus"
"More Than A Song"
"He's Been Faithful To Me," soloist: Stacie Caraway
"All Rise," soloist: Al Miller
"I Bowed On My Knees And Cried Holy," soloist: Jay Craig
"I Go To The Rock," soloist: Jeff Stith
Faith And Hope Medley, (*"I Know Whom I Have Believed," "My Faith Has Found A Resting
    Place," "The Solid Rock"*)
"Precious Lord"
"Just A Closer Walk With Thee," Marty Hamby, keyboard
"Peace In The Valley," soloist: Jay Craig; Marty Hamby, keyboard
"Are You Washed In The Blood?"
Jim Deal, recording engineer; Marty Schoocraft, Samuel "Pete" Hunter, Robert
    Faulkner, jacket production/design

38. Climb Every Mountain
MasterSound D-1742   CD   1994

"When I Fall In Love," soloist: Kim Bramnlett
"Come, Come Again," (The Men)
"Black Is The Color Of My True Love's Hair," soloist: Al Miller
"The Soldier Boy," soloist: Kelly Luther
"O, Danny Boy," soloist: Bryan Stratton
"The Sound Of Music"
"Climb Every Mountain," soloist: George Gray
"Down In The Valley," (The Men); Marty Hamby, keyboard
"Gossip, Gossip"
"Lil' Liz, I Love You," (The Men)
"Les Miserables" soloists: Stacie Caraway, LoriBeth Perry, Dan Taylor Jr., Melodie
    Kvalvik, Dee Dee Hook, Jim Brogan, Jay Craig, Kelly Luther, Tim Little, Denise
    Craig
"Ole Man River," soloist: Daniel H. Taylor Jr.
"Never, My Love"

"One Voice," soloist: Ron Whittemore
"God Bless The USA," soloists: Stacie Caraway, Jay Craig
"Let There Be Peace On Earth," soloist: George Gray; Marty Hamby, keyboard
Jim Deal, recording engineer; Marty Schoocraft, Samuel "Pete" Hunter, Robert
    Faulkner, jacket production/design

39. CLASSICS THROUGH THE YEARS
MasterSound C-1753   Cassette   1996

Keyboard: Kim Cargile
"All People That On Earth Do Dwell," arr. Jolley; Dan Miller, organ
"Come, Let Us Bow Down," (Traditional)
"Jesu, Word of God," Mozart
"Sheep May Safely Graze," Bach
"O Savior, Hear Me," Gluck; soloist: Kelly Luther Stultz
"Who Is At My Window, Who?," Russell
"Holy Lord Of Hosts," Posegate
"How Lovely Is Thy Dwelling Place," Brahms
"Mary, Did You Know?" arr. Fettke, soloist: Michael Smith
"How Shall I Fitly Meet Thee," Bach
"Carol Of The Birds," Shaw-Parker, soloist: Rachel Heer
"Ave Maria," Gounod, arr. Scott, soloist: Rachel Heer; Mark Reneau, violin
"I See His Blood Upon The Rose," Robertson
"O Ye People," Casals
"O Sacred Head Now Wounded," Bach
"Fair Lord Of Heaven," Brahms; arr. Cargile-Tugman
"The Twenty-Third Psalm," Newman
"The Doxology," (Traditional); Kim Cargile, keyboard
Jim Deal, recording engineer; Dot Carter, Gary Ashley, Samuel "Pete" Hunter, jacket
    production/design

40. TOWN-N-COUNTRY
MasterSound C-1755   Cassette   1996

Kim Cargile, keyboard
"Moonglow," arr. Hunter
"Night and Day," Kerns
"Evergreen," Streisand
"Georgia," arr. Muller, soloist: Allison Redmon
"Sleep, Baby Sleep," arr. Shaw
"That Lonesome Road," arr. Carrington
"He's Gone Away," Shaw-Parker, soloist: Rachel Heer
"Shenandoah," arr. Erb
"Amici," (College Tradition)
"Colorado Trail," arr. Luboff
"Lil' Liz, I Love You," arr. Draper
"Precious Memories," arr. Hacker-Draper
Country Medley, compiled by Draper (*"Jambalaya," "I Can't Stop Lovin' You," "Your
    Cheating Heart," "Sweet Baby's Arms," "Grandma's Feather Bed"*), soloists: Michael
    Smith, Chris Riggins, Tim Little
"All The Gold," Gatlin, soloist: Michael Smith
"I Believe," arr. Ades, soloists: Michael Smith, John Dominick
"The Ole Ark's a Moverin'," (Spiritual)

"Ain't Got No Time To Die," (Spiritual); soloist: Jay Craig
"Dry Bones," (Spiritual)
Jim Deal, recording engineer; Samuel "Pete" Hunter, Dot Carter, Gary Ashley, jacket
    production/design

41. MY FAMILY'S FAVORITES
MasterSound C-1756   Cassette   1996

Kim Cargile, keyboard; Dan Miller, organ
"All Hail The Power," arr. Hamby
"Spirit Of The Living God," (Traditional)
"Grace," arr. Hayes
"O Happy Day," Hawkins; soloist: Charles Middleton
"I'm Goin' Up," McDonald; soloists: John Dominick, Allison Redmon
Medley: *"Precious Lord,"* (Traditional); soloists: Al Miller, Charles Middleton, Bill Dixon
"I Want Jesus To Walk With Me," (Spiritual); arr. Draper; soloists: Charles Middleton,
    Bill Dixon
"Poor Wayfarin' Stranger," Spiritual, soloists: Jim Brogan, Charles Middleton
"I Will Arise," Shaw-Parker
"Lonely Voices," Hanks
"Just As I Am," Shaw-Parker; soloist: Al Miller; Jimmy Helman, guitarist
"Come, Come Ye Saints," (Hymn)
"Amazing Grace," Newton; soloist: Rachel Heer
"Guide Me, O Thou Great Jehovah," arr. Draper
"When I Survey The Wondrous Cross," arr. Martin
"O Love Divine," Wesley; soloist: Ron Whittemore
"Surely The Presence," arr. Marsh
"Precious Memories," arr. Hacker-Draper; soloist: Jim Brogan
"Do I Not Love Thee," (American Folk Hymn)
"We Believe," arr. Hayes
"O Happy Day," arr. Hayes; soloists: Andrea Perry, Mark Tilley, Chris Riggins
Jim Deal, recording engineer; Samuel "Pete" Hunter, Dot Carter, Gary Ashley, jacket
    production/design

42. CHRISTMAS-N-WINTER
MasterSound C-1757   CD, Cassette   1996

"Come, Thou Long Expected Jesus," Wesley
"In The Bleak Mid-Winter," arr. Woodgate; soloist: Al Miller
"Mary, Did You Know," arr. Fettke; soloist: Michael Smith
"Ave Maria," Gounod, arr. Scott; soloist: Rachel Heer; Kim Cargile, keyboard; Mark
    Reneau, violin
"Thou Didst Leave Thy Throne," arr. Red
"Slumber Now Beloved Child," arr. Nelson
"Lullaby," Keel
"O Come, Little Children," arr. Young
"Sweet Little Jesus Boy," (Traditional); soloist: Jennifer Trent
"Carol Of The Birds," arr. Shaw-Parker; soloist: Rachel Heer
"The Shepherd's Farewell To The Holy Family," Berloiz (*L'Enfance du Christ*)
"Silent Night," Gruber-Kerr
"O Holy Night," Adam-Krogstad; soloist: Mark Tilley
"Do You Hear What I Hear?" arr. Johnson
"God Rest You Merry Gentlemen," (Traditional)

"*The Drummer Boy,*" Davis
"*The Sleigh,*" arr. Johnson
"*Caroling, Caroling,*" Burt
"*Masters In This Hall,*" (Traditional)
"*Sing We Now Of Christmas,*" arr. Young
Jolly Ole St. Nick Medley, (Traditional)
"*O Happy Day,*" arr. Hayes; soloists: Andrea Perry, Chris Riggins, Mark Tilley
Jim Deal, recording engineer; Samuel "Pete" Hunter, Gary Ashley, Dot Carter, jacket
    production/design

43. GLENN AND THE MEN II
    MasterSound CD-1758   CD   1996

Kim Cargile, keyboard
"*O God, Our Help In Ages Past,*" arr. Red
"*This Is My Father's World,*" arr. Ringwald; soloist: Al Miller
"*In The Garden,*" (Traditional); soloist: Al Miller
"*Beautiful Savior,*" (Folk Tune); soloist: Mark Tilley
"*Great Is Thy Faithfulness,*" arr. Sjolund
"*Abide With Me, 'Tis Eventide,*" Millard; soloist: Ron Whittemore
"*Just As I Am,*" arr. Shaw-Parker; soloist: Al Miller; Jim Hellman, guitarist
"*Morning Trumpet,*" arr. Richardson; soloist: Mark Tilley
"*Let My People Go,*" arr. Scott; soloist: Bill Dixon
"*If I Got My Ticket, Can I Ride?*", arr. Shaw; soloist: Jeff Stith
"*The Ole Ark's A Moverin',*" (Spiritual)
"*O Tannenbaum,*" arr. Shaw; soloists: Bryan Stratton, Andre Ashley
"*In The Bleak Mid-Winter,*" arr. Woodgate; soloist: Al Miller
"*Carol Of The Drum,*" Davis
"*Thou Didst Leave Thy Throne,*" arr. Red
"*Adoramus Te,*" Palestrina
"*Fair Lord of Heaven,*" arr. Cargile-Tugman
"*Bless The Lord, O My Soul,*" Ippolitoff-Ivanoff
"*Pilgrim's Chorus,*" Wagner
"*We Shall Walk Through The Valley In Peace,*" arr. Appling
"*The Twenty-Third Psalm,*" Newman; Marty Hamby, keyboard
Jim Deal, recording engineer; Dot Carter, Gary Ashley, "Pete" Hunter, jacket
    production/design

44. A CHRISTMAS GIFT FROM THE GLENN DRAPER SINGERS
    MasterSound C-1759 Cassette 1997

Kim Cargile, keyboard
"*Hark, The Herald Angels Sing,*" ed. Marty Hamby; soloist Michael Mays
"*Little Drummer Boy,*" arr. Hamilton
"*This Child Is,*" arr. Greer; soloists: Andrea Perry, K.C. Armstrong, Stacie Caraway
    Coder, Mark Mays
"*All Is Well,*" arr. Huff; soloist: Gretchen Striebeck
"*Silent Night,*" arr. Purling
"*No Eye Had Seen,*" arr. Krogstad
"*Peace I Leave With You,*" Clausen
"*I Have Seen The Light,*" Sterling; soloists: Jay Craig, Jim Brogan, Michael Smith
"*In The Bleak Mid-Winter,*" Holst
"*Laudate Dominum,*" Mozart; soloist: Gretchen Striebeck, Mark Reneau, violin; Kim
    Cargile, keyboard

"Ave Maria," Biebl; soloists: Mark Tilley, Jim Brogan
"He Came Here For Me," Nelson; Kim Cargile, keyboard
"Alleluia," (Old German Melody)
"Joy To The World," Watts
"Noel," Kirkland
Singers: soprano: Rachel Heer, Jennifer Odom, Dee Dee Brogan, Gretchen Striebeck;
    alto: Chara Ashworth, Gloria Parvin, Kelly Luther, Misty Williamson; tenor: Jim
    Brogan, Thomas Hammett, Steven Abernathy, Michael Mays; bass: Mark Tilley,
    Dan Vogle, K.C. Armstrong, John Dominick
Jim Deal, recording engineer; Dot Carter, "Pete" Hunter, Gary Ashley, jacket
    production/design

45. CHRIST FOR THE WORLD
    MasterSound CD-1800   CD   1997

    Kim Cargile, accompanist, keyboard; Dan Miller, organ
    "The Lord Is My Light," arr. Young & Linn
    "Arise, Your Light Has Come," Danner
    "Shine On Us," Smith
    "This Child Is," Bruce Greer; soloists: Andrea Perry, K. C. Armstrong, Stacie Coder, Mark
        Tilley
    "The First Noel," arr. Kirkland
    "Ave Maria," Biebl; soloists: Mark Tilley, Jim Brogan
    "Crown Him With Many Crowns," Bridges
    "Christ The Lord Is Risen Today," arr. Danner; Dan Miller, organ
    "Step Into The Water," Talley
    "I Have Seen The Light," arr. Sterling; soloists: Michael Smith, Jay Craig, Jim Brogan
    "I Bowed On My Knees And Cried Holy," arr. Gross; soloist: Jay Craig
    "Peace In The Valley," arr. Hamby; soloist: Jay Craig
    "I Go To The Rock," Rambo; soloist: Jeff Stith
    "His Truth Is Marching On," arr. Krogstad
    Singers: soprano: Dee Dee Brogan, Rachel Heer, Sarah Beth Nordmoe, Gretchen
        Striebeck; alto: Stacie Caraway Coder, Andrea Perry, Misty Williamson; tenor: Jim
        Brogan, Jay Craig, Todd Gaither, Thomas Hammett; baritone: Michael Smith, Mark
        Tilley; bass: K.C. Armstrong, Bill Dixon
    Jim Deal, recording engineer; "Pete" Hunter, Dot Carter, Scott Wallace, Gary Ashley,
        jacket production/design

46. COME TO THE WATER
    Sound Resources DK-1079   CD

    Kim Cargile, accompanist, music assistant
    "Come To The Water," arr. Cargile-Draper
    Total Praise Medley, arr. Cargile-Draper; soloists: Michael Smith, Jay Craig, Stacie
        Caraway Coder
    "Be Still My Soul," arr. Cargile
    "Be Thou My Vision," arr. Rouse
    "I Wonder As I Wander," (Appalachian Carol); soloist: Stacie Caraway Coder
    "Winter," Vivaldi
    "In The Bleak Mid-Winter," (Traditional)
    "O Come, O Come Emanuel," arr. Greer; soloist: Dee Dee Brogan
    "Adeste Fideles," (Traditional)
    "Wise Men Still Seek Him," arr. Kingsmore; soloists: Jay Craig, Jim Brogan, Michael Smith

"Midnight Cry," Fettke; soloist: Mel Medaris
"'Tis Midnight And On Olive's Brow," arr. Draper; soloist: Mark Tilley
"On Yonder Cross," Peterson
"O Sacred Head Now Wounded," Bach
"Crown Him With Many Crowns," arr. Draper
"Christ The Lord Is Risen Today," Threlkeld
"Arise My Love," Clydesdale
Singers: soprano: Lisa Haywood, Kelly McClanahan, Dee Dee Brogan, Sarah Mentzer;
    alto: Kelly Stultz, Stacie Caraway Coder, Tracie Coats, Kathy Tugman; tenor: Jim
    Brogan, Jay Craig, Tom Hammett, Jay Lifford, Todd Gaither; bass: Chris O'Rear,
    Robert J.A. Waller, K.C. Armstrong, Courtney Williams, Michael Smith
Steve Babb, Fred Schendel, recording engineers; Dot Carter, typesetting

47. AMAZING GRACE
Sound Resources (No #)   CD, Cassette   2001

"Amazing Grace," arr. Shaw-Parker; soloist: Todd Gaither
"Der's No Hiding Place," arr. Shaw-Parker; soloist: Chris O'Rear
"Come To The Water," arr. Cargile-Draper
"O For A Thousand Tongues," arr. Draper
"My God Is A Rock," arr. Shaw-Parker; soloist: Chris O'Rear
"His Voice As A Sound," arr. Parker
"Do Not I Love Thee," arr. Gustafson
"Shout On, " arr. Shaw-Parker; soloist: Tony Offerly
"When I Can Read My Title Clear," arr. Shaw-Parker
"I Got Shoes," arr. Shaw-Parker
"Morning Trumpet," arr. Richardson; soloist: Mark Tilley
"Saints Bound For Heaven," arr. Shaw-Parker
"God Is Seen," arr. Parker
"Guide Me, O Thou Great Jehovah," arr. Draper
"Hark, I Hear The Harps Eternal," arr. Shaw-Parker
"How Tedious And Tasteless The Hours," arr. Draper; soloist: Jennifer Odom
"Be Thou My Vision," arr. Rouse
"Be Still My Soul," arr: Cargile
"My God Is A Rock Medley," soloists: Chris O'Rear, Jay Craig
Singers: soprano: Dee Dee Brogan, Lisa Haywood, Kelly McClanahan, Sarah Mentzer;
    alto: Tracie Coats, Stacie Caraway Coder, Kelly Stultz, Kathy Tugman; tenor: Jim
    Brogan, Jay Craig, Tom Hammett, Todd Gaither, Jay Lifford; bass: K.C. Armstrong,
    Chris O'Rear, Robert J.A. Waller, Courtney Williams, Michael Smith
Kim Cargile, accompanist and assistant to the director
Steve Babb/Fred Schendel, recording engineers; Dot Carter, typesetting

48. CAROLS BY CANDLELIGHT
Jon-A-Lou Records-2070   CD, Cassette   2002

"Adeste Fideles"
"Coventry Carol"
"What Child Is This"
"Pat-A-Pan"
"Silent Night," Gruber-Kerr
"Lo, How A Rose E'er Blooming"
"Slumber Now, Beloved Child," arr. Nelson
"Mary Had A Baby," soloist: Tim Fudge

"Sweet Little Jesus Boy," soloist: Chrissi Floyd, alto
"Ave Maria," Gounod, arr. Scott; soloist: Rachel Heer; Mark Reneau, violin; Kim Cargile,
  keyboard
"God Rest You Merry Gentlemen"
"Thou Didst Leave Thy Throne," arr. Red
"In The Bleak Midwinter," arr. Woodgate
"Joy To The World," Watts
"He Came Here For Me," Nelson; Kim Cargile, keyboard
"Hark The Herald Angels Sing," adapted by Marty Hamby; soloist: Michael Mays
"The First Noel," arr. Kirkland
Kim Cargile, musical assistant to the director
Kim Cargile, Marty Hamby, keyboards
Jim Deal MasterSound, Inc., recording engineer; J. Alton Murphy, cover graphics and
  layout

49. DREAMING OF A WHITE CHRISTMAS
Jon-A-Lou Records-2071 CD, Cassette 2002

"White Christmas," Berlin; soloist: Kim Bramlett
"The Christmas Song," Torme
"Carol Of The Bells"
"Ding Dong Merrily On High"
"Do You Hear What I Hear?" arr. Johnson
"The Drummer Boy," Davis
"The Boar's Head Carol," (Traditional)
"O Tannenbaum," soloists: Brian Stratton, Andre Ashley
"I Saw Three Ships"
"Deck The Halls"
"The Sleigh," arr. Johnson
"Still, Still, Still"
"This Child Is," arr. Greer; soloists: Andrea Perry, K. C. Armstrong, Stacie Coder, Mark
  Tilley
"We Wish You A Merry Christmas"
"O Happy Day," arr. Hayes; soloists: Andrea Perry, Chris Riggins, Mark Tilley
Kim Cargile, musical assistant to the director:
Kim Cargile, Marty Hamby, keyboards
Jim Deal, MasterSound, recording engineer; J. Alton Murphy, cover graphics and
  layout

THE SINGING HURRICANES OF THE UNIVERSITY OF MIAMI

50. THE SINGING HURRICANES . . . OFF CAMPUS
UMS-1001   LP   1966

"See The U.S.A."
"California, Here I Come"
"Oklahoma"
"Carolina In The Morning"
"Sioux City Sue"
"Georgia On My Mind"
"Shuffle Off To Buffalo"
"'Chicago,' That Toddling Town"
"Kansas City"

"Kentucky Babe"
"Back Home Again In Indiana"
"Moon Over Miami"
"The Eyes Of Texas"
"Alabamy Bound"
"The Yankee Doodle Boy"
"Are You From Dixie?"
"Swanee"
"This Is My Country"
"Shenandoah"
"Ain'-A That Good News"
"Give My Regards To Broadway"
"76 Trombones"
"Hallelujah!"
"The Sound Of Music"
"Climb Ev'ry Mountain"
"I Got Rhythm"
"I Can't Say No"
"There Is Nothin' Like A Dame"
"June Is Bustin' Out All Over"
Singers: sopranos: Vicki Berns, Margaret Bitz, Cheryl Claiborne, Julie Rohr, Lynn
    Schneider, Dorma Sisk; altos: Katherine Bentley, Francine Fabiani, Sue Holmberg,
    Pat Kirby, Dolores Lamanna; tenors: Bill Brown, Jerry DeGennaro, Nate Hayes, Jim
    Humphries, Lee Norbraten; basses: Doug Daubenspeck, Mike Eaton, Bryan Olson,
    Rick Whitney
Orchestra: saxophones: Bruce Bailey, Bill Gora, Mark Hurwitz, Paul Leviten, Don
    Muller; trumpets: Wally McMurray, Bob Wheatley; trombones: Bob Lampi, Mike
    Rausch; french horns: Regie Nicholson, Tony Tremblay; piano: Warren Broome;
    bass: Tom Janusz; percussion: Ben Green, Gregg Janusz, Bob Rogel
Don Muller, musical arrangements and orchestral direction; Sanford Schnier, album
    notes; Walter Cerny, cover art; Alfred Reed, production; Recorded at Dufoff
    Recording Studios, Miami, Fla., June 1966

THE CHATTANOOGA SINGERS, SINGING MOCS, AND CHAMBER SINGERS OF THE UNIVERSITY OF TENNESSEE, CHATTANOOGA

51. JUBILANT SONG
    (No #)   Davis Sound   LP Stereo   1968

Chattanooga Singers
"A Jubilant Song"
"Ave Verum Corpus"
"Awake The Harp"
"O Ye People"
"Zadok The Priest"
"Glorious Everlasting"
"God So Loved The World"
"When I Survey The Wondrous Cross"
"Song Of Simeon"
"All My Trials"
"Deep River"
"Fare You Well"
Jeff Lipham, piano; Don Smith, organ; Dan Taylor, photographer

52. I Believe
Majestic Sound Studios   GD-1001   LP

The Chattanooga Singers
"Gloria In Excelsis"
"Laudate Dominum," soloist: Gail Reneau
"Beautiful River"
"The Majesty and Glory Of Your Name"
Marty Hamby, piano; David Frieberg, organ
Steve Dyer, recording/re-mix engineer

The Singing Mocs
"Boy From New York City," soloist: Lori Battles
"Never My Love"
Broadway Medley; soloist: Lynn Powell; UTC Jazz Band; Tony D'Andrea, director
"I Believe"
Marty Hamby, piano; Preston Gonter, percussion; Gary Hicks, bass guitar

53. On Tour with the Chattanooga Singers
Davis Sound RSR-677 LP

"Psalm 150," Newbury
"Look Down, O Lord," Byrd
"Who Is At My Window, Who?" Russel
"Heilig," Mendelsohn
"The Best Of Rooms," Thompson
"Paternoster," Tchaikowsky
"Glory Be To God," Bach
"This Little Light of Mine," arr. Huff
"Do Not I Love Thee," arr. Gustafson
"Amazing Grace," (Traditional); soloists: Doris Knisley, Gail Dooley
"When I Can Read My Title Clear," arr. Shaw-Parker
"Sometimes I Feel Like A Motherless Child," arr. Terri; soloist: Claire Galbraith; Bonnie
     Baumgardner, oboe
"The Beatitudes," Evans; soloist: Robert Huitt
Joe Chapman, piano; Don Smith, organ

54. Chamber Singers and Singing Mocs of
    the University of Tennessee at Chattanooga
Century Records (No #) LP

"Sing Unto God," Handel
"Kyrie," Gabrieli
"Ave Maria," Devitoria
"Song Of Exaltation," Beck
"The Soldier Boy," arr. Shaw
"Polly-Wolly-Doodle," arr. Kubik
"Tobacco Is A Wasting Weed," (London, 1699)
"Shadrack," arr. Simon
"Lonely Voices," Hanks
"Aquarius-Spinning Wheel"
"Scarborough Fair"/"Canticle"

"It's Not Unusual"
"Dock Of The Bay"
"A Time For Us"
"Delilah"
"Jean"
"Oh, The Games People Play"
"Mc Arthur Park"
Above selections arranged by Tommy Gannon
"Rider," arr. Mike Eaton
Joseph Troxell, accompanist; Steve Haws, string bass; Henry Oxdale, drums
Gaye Sellers, Bob Dean, producers; Recorded by Bob Davis, Century Records

55. JOY IN THE MORNING
   Davis Sound (No #)   LP

   The Chattanooga Singers
   National Anthem
   "Joy In The Morning"
   "Slumber Now Beloved Child"
   "To Thy Heavenly Banquet"
   "To Thy Saving Health"
   "When I Survey The Wondrous Cross"
   "Doxology"
   "Brothers, Sing On"
   "Halls Of Ivy"
   "He's Gone Away," soloist: Laura Lonas
   Medley Of Spirituals; soloists: Pam Tallon, Doug Ward, Mike Rorex, David Fowler
   "Just A Closer Walk With Thee," soloist: Janey Danks
   "Precious Lord," soloist: Doris Knisley
   "Go Tell It On The Mountain," soloist: Janie Barnett
   Joe Chapman, accompanist; Doug Ward, bass; Zenda Snyder, drums
   Mark Williams, Davis Sound, recording engineer

56. A FAMILY CHRISTMAS FESTIVAL
   MasterSound MS-1727   CD, Cassette   1990

   Conducted by Glenn Draper
   Featuring:
   Southern College Symphony Orchestra; Dr. Orlo Gilbert, director
   Chattanooga Singers from UTC; Dr. Glenn W. Draper, director
   Southern Singers from Southern College; Dr. Marvin Robertson, director
   The Lee Singers from Lee College; Dr. Walt Maulding, director
   Weigle Concert Choir from Tennessee Temple; Dr. Paul Faulkner, director
   "Christmas Festival," Anderson
   "In The Bleak Midwinter," Rossetti
   "Lo, How A Rose," Praetorious
   "Let All Mortal Flesh," (Traditional)
   "O Come, O Come Emmanuel," (Traditional)
   "How Shall I Fitly Meet Thee," Bach
   "Break Forth, O Beauteous, Heavenly Light," Bach
   "Heavenly Light," Kopylow
   "Behold A Virgin"
   "O Thou That Tellest Good Tidings," Handel; soloist: Gloria Parvin